SpringerBriefs in Modern Perspectives on Disability Research

Series Editors

Gabriel Bennett, Independent Researcher
Klemzig, Australia

Emma Goodall, Healthy Possibilities
Seaford, Australia

AF794136

This book series on disability research is a comprehensive collection of research on disability and related issues. The series is designed to promote interdisciplinary collaboration and exchange, bringing together scholars and practitioners from different fields to share their perspectives and insights. Disability research is an interdisciplinary field that examines the social, cultural, historical, and political dimensions of disability. It encompasses a wide range of topics, including disability rights, accessibility, assistive technologies, healthcare, education, employment, and social welfare. Disability research scholars employ a range of theoretical and methodological approaches to understand the experiences of people with disabilities, as well as the ways in which disability intersects with other social identities such as race, gender, sexuality, and class.

The series seeks to advance knowledge and understanding of disability by publishing rigorous, innovative, and relevant research. It aims to promote disability rights and social justice by highlighting the ways in which people with disabilities are marginalized and discriminated against in society, and advocating for greater social inclusion and accessibility. The series also seeks to inform policy and practice by disseminating research findings that can help to shape policy decisions and contribute to positive social change.

Orhan Aydin

Optimal Performance Criteria in Autism Studies

Advancing Intervention Effectiveness

Springer

Orhan Aydin
Division of Autism Spectrum Disorder
Department of Special Education
Faculty of Educational Sciences
Ankara University
Ankara, Türkiye

ISSN 3004-9709 ISSN 3004-9717 (electronic)
SpringerBriefs in Modern Perspectives on Disability Research
ISBN 978-981-95-8541-0 ISBN 978-981-95-8542-7 (eBook)
https://doi.org/10.1007/978-981-95-8542-7

© The Editor(s) (if applicable) and The Author(s), under exclusive license to Springer Nature Singapore Pte Ltd. 2026, corrected publication 2026

This work is subject to copyright. All rights are solely and exclusively licensed by the Publisher, whether the whole or part of the material is concerned, specifically the rights of translation, reprinting, reuse of illustrations, recitation, broadcasting, reproduction on microfilms or in any other physical way, and transmission or information storage and retrieval, electronic adaptation, computer software, or by similar or dissimilar methodology now known or hereafter developed.
The use of general descriptive names, registered names, trademarks, service marks, etc. in this publication does not imply, even in the absence of a specific statement, that such names are exempt from the relevant protective laws and regulations and therefore free for general use.
The publisher, the authors and the editors are safe to assume that the advice and information in this book are believed to be true and accurate at the date of publication. Neither the publisher nor the authors or the editors give a warranty, expressed or implied, with respect to the material contained herein or for any errors or omissions that may have been made. The publisher remains neutral with regard to jurisdictional claims in published maps and institutional affiliations.

This Springer imprint is published by the registered company Springer Nature Singapore Pte Ltd.
The registered company address is: 152 Beach Road, #21-01/04 Gateway East, Singapore 189721, Singapore

If disposing of this product, please recycle the paper.

This book is based on previously published and secondary data analyses. No new data were collected from human participants. Therefore, formal ethics committee approval was not required.

To the memory of my sister, taken far too early, and to the memory of my grandmother, whose lifelong care continues to guide me.

Acknowledgments

In some parts of the text body, Grammarly Pro (primary option) and ChatGPT (secondary option) were used to make language edits. The two rubrics to set performance criteria in autism interventions proposed in Chap. 4 were finalized based on focus-group interviews and written feedback. The author sincerely thanks Dr. Üzeyir Emre Kiyak, Dr. Serap Dogan Aslan, Dr. Mahmut Serkan Yazici, Dr. Turgut Bahcali, Dr. Samet Burak Taylan, and Dr. Akin Gonen for their valuable contributions during the focus-group discussions. In addition, the author extends gratitude to Dr. Mehmet Donat Sulu and Dr. Muhammed Yasin Yassikaya for their constructive written feedback.

Competing Interests The author has no competing interests to declare that are relevant to the content of this manuscript.

About this Book

This book examines performance criteria as a core methodological component of autism intervention research and evidence-based practice. It focuses on how performance-criterion levels and frequencies determine whether behavioral change is meaningful, durable, and generalizable. The book is organized into four chapters that progress from conceptual foundations to empirical evidence and practical application. The first chapter introduces the structure and operationalization of performance criteria across behavioral, educational, and medical contexts. The second chapter reviews empirical findings on the impact of performance-criterion components on response maintenance and generalization, highlighting patterns supported by systematic and quantitative analyses. The third chapter synthesizes data from a large body of autism intervention studies to identify empirically supported performance-criterion thresholds and domain-specific patterns. The final chapter translates these findings into practice by presenting structured, evidence-informed rubrics for selecting optimal performance criteria for behaviors targeted for increase and reduction. Developed rubrics and interpretation tables are suggested to support transparent, data-informed decision-making and to bridge research, practice, and social validity in autism interventions.

Contents

About the Author

Orhan Aydın (In English, Orhan Aydin), PhD, is an Associate Professor in the Division of Autism Spectrum Disorder under the Department of Special Education at Ankara University, Türkiye. His research focuses on interventions for autism and other developmental disabilities, single-case experimental designs, performance criteria, and methodological rigor in applied behavior analysis. He has published many articles extensively in international peer-reviewed journals and is actively involved in teaching and supervising at the bachelor's and graduate levels.

Chapter 1
Introduction to Performance Criteria in Autism Studies

Abstract Autism spectrum disorder (ASD) is a neurodevelopmental disorder characterized by deficits in social communication and restricted or repetitive behaviors. Individuals with ASD often experience secondary difficulties in academic, daily living, and motor domains, further expanding the meaning of "spectrum." As the global prevalence of ASD continues to increase, selecting effective interventions has become a critical priority. In evidence-based autism research, performance criteria are considered a key element in determining intervention effectiveness and whether behavioral change is socially meaningful. Performance criteria are predetermined levels of behavioral change that define when an intervention has produced a meaningful outcome. They consist of two main components: the desired level of behavioral change and the frequency with which this level must be demonstrated. The level component reflects the magnitude of behavioral improvement (or decrease), while frequency represents the consistency of this change across sessions. This chapter explains how performance criteria are structured and operationalized through examples from behavioral, educational, and medical studies. By accurately defining performance criteria, researchers can more reliably determine whether an intervention produces socially meaningful behavioral changes. Consequently, careful consideration of performance criteria strengthens the methodological rigor of autism research and supports the development of truly evidence-based practices.

Keywords Performance criteria · Mastery criteria · Autism · Behavioral change · Evidence-based practices

© The Author(s), under exclusive license to Springer Nature Singapore Pte Ltd. 2026
O. Aydin, *Optimal Performance Criteria in Autism Studies*, SpringerBriefs in Modern Perspectives on Disability Research,
https://doi.org/10.1007/978-981-95-8542-7_1

1.1 Autistic Individuals and the Concept of Performance Criteria in Autism Studies

Autism represents a spectrum among neurodevelopmental disorders, which is characterized by two primary domains: (a) deficits in social communication and interaction and (b) restricted/repetitive behaviors and interests (APA, 2013). Furthermore, individuals with autism spectrum disorder (ASD) are also known to generally experience secondary difficulties in many areas, such as academic skills, for example, in math (Aydin & Tekin-İftar, 2020; Tonizzi & Usai, 2023), in reading (Brown et al., 2013; Randi et al., 2010), or in writing (Accardo et al., 2020; Delano, 2007; Finnegan & Accardo, 2018), daily living skills, for instance, in self-care skills (Aydin et al., 2025; Wertalik & Kubina Jr., 2017) or in leisure activities (Eversole et al., 2016; Kurt & Tekin-Iftar, 2008), and motor skills, i.e. fine motor and gross motor (Lloyd et al., 2013; Whyatt & Craig, 2012). In this context, the "spectrum" encompasses disruptions in much broader domains.

In addition to increasing support demands in different areas, the prevalence of ASD has also risen over time around the world. In the United States, the prevalence of ASD among children aged 4–8 years was 1 in 150 in the 2000s, 1 in 68 in the 2010s, 1 in 36 in 2020, and the latest data from 2022 was 1 in 31 (see the reports of the Centers for Disease Control and Prevention—CDC; https://www.cdc.gov/autism/data-research/index.html). On the other hand, across China, the prevalence of ASD among children aged 6–12 years was found to be 0.70 in 100 in the 2010s (Zhou et al., 2020), whereas in Beijing, the prevalence was found to be 1.05 in 100 in 2021 for only children aged 6 years old (Zhao et al., 2025). Across Europe, it was estimated to be 0.2 in 100 in the 1990s (Charman, 2002), 0.8 in 100 among 2-year-old Swedish children in 2010 (Nygren et al., 2012), and 1.4 in 100 among 5- to 18-year-olds across Europe in the 2020s (Sacco et al., 2022). According to the Global Burden of Disease study, the prevalence of ASD was 1 in 132 around the world in 2010 (Baxter et al., 2015). Recent data from the Global Burden of Disease Study 2021 showed it was 1 in 127 (Steinmetz et al., 2024).

Although a lesser increase is seen worldwide, data from developed countries clearly show that autism is becoming increasingly common. In order to minimize the burden of this population on society and support their independence in their lives, interventions that will alleviate their challenges in the primary and secondary areas they struggle with are of great importance. These interventions should be selected from evidence-based practices as emphasized by both government laws (e.g., Department for Education & Department of Health, 2015; IDEA, 2004) and many researchers (e.g., Anixt et al., 2024; Aydin et al., 2019; Cook et al., 2008; Ledford et al., 2021; Sulu et al., 2024). In addition, each individual should be evaluated individually when setting goals and structuring the instruction/treatment process, by taking into account their abilities/conditions and socially meaningful behavioral change contexts in terms of environmental conditions (Allport, 1961; Aydin, 2024; Baer et al., 1968; Coulter et al., 2015; Tan et al., 2025; Tetzlaff et al.,

2021; Wolf, 1978). These assessments should also apply to individuals with ASD, as each autistic person may have their own unique capabilities and environmental circumstances, even though they share a similar diagnosis (Frye, 2022; Lai et al., 2020; Lee et al., 2022; Love et al., 2024). The more accurately the assessments of autistic persons based on the abilities/conditions and environmental variables are raised, the more accurately it can be evaluated whether the results of evidence-based practices are positive and significant for individuals with ASD (Christopher & Lord, 2022; Hume et al., 2021; Yu et al., 2024).

In autism research, particularly in behavioral intervention studies, one of the core variables is the establishment of a performance criterion based on individual abilities, conditions, and environmental circumstances (Aydin & Tanious, 2022; Cordeiro et al., 2022; Fuller & Fienup, 2018; Pitts & Hoerger, 2021; Schneider et al., 2022). This perspective also aligns with Bloom's (1971) views on mastery learning. In these contexts, a performance criterion is a predetermined level of performance for the behavior being studied, indicating that the desired behavioral change has been achieved through treatment and that treatment can be terminated for that behavior (Fuller & Fienup, 2018; Richling et al., 2023). In educational and applied behavior analysis (ABA) research, performance criteria set in studies have often been referred to as mastery criteria (Bloom, 1971, 1968; Fienup & Brodsky, 2017; Johnston & O'Neill, 1973; Richling et al., 2023; Semb, 1974). Mastery criteria, on the other hand, generally imply that the direction of behavior change is always intended to accelerate upward and are more closely related to the acquisition process of the targeted behavior (Fuller & Fienup, 2018). In fact, the term mastery criterion (for plural format "mastery criteria") has more likely been derived from related terms such as success criteria, termination criteria, and acquisition criteria in behavioral and educational studies (Carlson & Minke, 1975; Johnston & O'Neill, 1973; Richling et al., 2023; Semb, 1974). However, we also know that many studies aim to decrease destructive behaviors in autism literature. These studies also seek to change the behavior level to a predetermined criterion. Generally, in such behavior--reduction studies, researchers use terms such as termination criterion, terminal goal, or reduction criteria (e.g., Briggs et al., 2019; Greer et al., 2023; Montes et al., 2021; Simmons et al., 2022). Since the term "performance criterion" can refer to both behavior acquisition and behavior reduction, researchers have recently preferred using it in behavioral intervention-related studies (e.g., Aydin, n.d.; Aydin & Tanious, 2022; Fienup & Carr, 2021; Richling et al., 2023; Wong et al., 2022; Wong & Fienup, 2022). In this book, we also prefer to use the term performance criteria to refer to predetermined criteria assigned in behavioral intervention studies for autistic individuals (to include both behavior acquisition and behavior reduction studies).

1.2 What Are Performance Criteria?

Performance criteria typically comprise two components: a quantitative specification, indicating the minimum required level of behavior change, and a frequency value denoting how often this level of change should be observed (Fuller & Fienup, 2018; Richling et al., 2019). For instance, from an educational perspective, suppose that a practitioner aims to improve the basic math skills of a child with ASD, including distinguishing between more and less, ordering by size, and counting rhythmically by ones up to five, through a teaching method. After conducting each intervention session, the practitioner gives the student five opportunities to demonstrate each skill (a total of 15 opportunities) and expects the child to independently perform four out of the five opportunities correctly per task. Furthermore, the practitioner aims for the child to demonstrate the correct answers on at least four out of five opportunities across two consecutive sessions. The practitioner continues instruction until these criteria are met. Once the targeted level and frequency are met, the teaching process is terminated.

For another perspective, suppose that a clinician aims to reduce disruptive behaviors, such as head-hitting, screaming, and non-contingent crying (identified separately for each child), in three children with ASD through a treatment. Over the duration of a play activity session, the clinician focuses on the frequency of occurrence of the head-hitting behavior of the child, whereas focusing on the duration of occurrence of the other two behaviors. In probe sessions after each treatment session, the clinician aims for head-hitting behavior to be reduced to zero in five consecutive probe sessions, whereas for the other two behaviors to be decreased in duration by 60% from baseline levels in three successive sessions. These criteria allow the clinician to evaluate the effectiveness of the intervention during the treatment process. Suppose the requirements for a behavior of one child are not met. In that case, the clinician can modify the intervention for the child's destructive behavior during the treatment process to ensure meeting the criteria (if there is enough time). While the intervention is discontinued for the other two behaviors, the process may take a bit longer for the more resistant behavior to meet the criteria; the treatment process is eventually terminated for that behavior as well.

From a medical perspective, a physician may aim to reduce irritability symptoms in a child with ASD through pharmacological treatment. In this case, irritability levels are systemically monitored on a daily, weekly, and monthly basis, and behavioral changes in response to medication are carefully documented. Once an acceptable level of irritability is achieved from the family's standpoint, the medication dosage is maintained at that level. Subsequently, the dosage is gradually tapered while providing additional behavioral or environmental support, with the goal of sustaining the child's behavior at an acceptable level throughout each dose reduction. The overarching clinical objective is to maintain the child's irritability at a tolerable level for the family over the long term. Although medical treatment is not entirely discontinued, the medication dosage is reduced as much as possible. In this context, the performance criteria for irritability symptoms are defined as achieving a tolerable level (based on the family's scaled assessment reports) and maintaining it long term (with follow-up extending for 1 year or more).

Combining the perspectives outlined above, and indeed, the treatment of performance criteria across many intervention studies, we actually need to focus on two primary components of the performance criteria. One is related to the desired level of behavioral change. And the other is related to the frequency with which the behavioral change remains at that level.

1.2.1 Desired Level of Behavioral Change

Baer et al. (1968) emphasized that the behavior under study should be socially important. Approximately a decade later, Wolf (1978) introduced the concept of "social validity" in behavioral studies. He suggested that behavioral studies should be evaluated in terms of three aspects: (a) the social significance of goals, (b) the social appropriateness of the treatment procedures, and (c) the social importance of the outcomes. In particular, the social importance of the outcomes is directly linked to determining the desired level of behavior change under study. In this aspect, Wolf questions, "Are consumers satisfied with the results? All the results, including any unpredicted ones?" Later, the concept of "clinical significance" came to the fore to emphasize its importance over statistical significance in empirical research (Fethney, 2010; LeFort, 1993; Page, 2014; Ranganathan et al., 2015). Clinical significance also emphasizes three aspects: (a) the magnitude of behavior change should be satisfactory, (b) its real-world impact on participants' lives should be at an acceptable level, and (c) the intervention process should be consumer-friendly, cost-effective, and practical. In this context, the behavioral change through a treatment should meet "consumer acceptability" so that both practitioner and participants and their environments can benefit at optimal levels (Aydin & Tanious, 2022). The first two aspects of clinical significance are also directly linked to determining the desired level of behavioral change.

Given that the desired level of behavioral change reflects clinical significance in experimental studies and social importance in behavioral training studies, focusing on the desired level of behavioral change in autism research may be vital for accurately determining evidence-based practices. If this is done properly, it would be much more feasible to speak of evidence-based practices in autism studies, even in all fields, not in name, but in essence. The purpose of this book is to accurately determine the desired level of behavioral change in autism research, and chapters 3 and 4 will focus on this point, but here, we elaborate on the component of the desired "level" of behavioral change.

The level of behavioral change can be dependent on frequency or count, fluency or speed, percentage or rate, score of behaviors according to a measurement tool, or initial level of behaviors. Level implies not only the tendency of values to increase but also their tendency to decrease. In addition, level can also reflect the measurement of any change in the body (e.g., sugar level in blood, changes in hormone functions). Moreover, level can also be related to the evaluation of more abstract concepts, such as measurements of changes in attitudes and perceptions. However, the level is more related to observable and measurable variables and denotes a quantitative value. To provide a more explicit operational definition of level, Table 1.1 summarizes the components of the desired level of behavioral change, extracted from representative autism research across various domains.

As shown in Table 1.1, seven studies from three domains (special education, behavioral sciences, and the medical field) were coded according to the performance criteria. Both skill-acquisition and behavior-reduction studies are shown in this table. In skill-acquisition studies, including those on academic, language, drawing, and daily living skills, the goal is generally to improve performance according to the steps of the task. These tasks are either assigned a point separately (e.g., Root et al., 2017) or rated based on the number of steps completed correctly, divided by the total number of steps (e.g., Yakubova & Chen, 2021). Then, considering 100 out of 100 when completing all steps in the task analysis correctly, the obtained values are generally converted to percentages. Hence, the level of performance criteria denotes a percentage value. For example, Akmanoğlu and Pektaş-Karabekir (2020) aimed to teach drawing a six-part person to three children with ASD. They used a task analysis with six steps to determine the performance level of children. They scored each step as 100/6 (= 16.66) and converted them into percentages. They used a 100% performance criterion for the targeting goal. This procedure can be conducted for discrete trials. For example, Geiger et al. (2012) instructed receptive language skills to three children with ASD. They asked the children three words three times. They then converted the responses from nine trials to percentages. That is, getting each trial correct out of nine was considered to be worth 100/9 = 11.11 points. Geiger et al. (2012) also set a 100% performance criterion for their customers. As a note, although the percentage format is not required, it is commonly preferred in the literature, due to allowing a straightforward interpretation of findings. However, it can also be used in a score format. For example, Root et al. (2017) preferred to use the level in a point format by obtaining scores from a nine-step task analysis, and set their performance criterion at least 24 points out of 30. Furthermore, the levels of performance criteria can also be used in count format (particularly for the number of accurately occurring behaviors) or in duration format (particularly for fluency and speed measurements) for behavioral enhancement studies.

In behavior reduction instances, as summarized in Table 1.1, including those targeting problem behaviors such as aggression, irritability behaviors, and toe--walking, the goal is typically to reduce their frequency below a specified percentage of the baseline level. These levels are generally determined either by counting the occurrences of problem behaviors using a time-sampling method or by scoring participants with standardized behavioral assessment tools. The measurements are then rated per minute, scored according to the tool, or converted to a percentage format. For example, Greer et al. (2023) used functional communication training to reduce problem behaviors of two children with ASD (they also included two other children without ASD). They recorded the frequency of each destructive behavior (e.g., aggression, self-injury, property destruction) in 10-s intervals during 1-min sessions

Table 1.1 Components of performance criteria in autism studies: A representative sample

Reference	Domain	Number of subjects with ASD	Independent variable(s)	Dependent variable	Performance criteria		
					Level	Frequency	Type of level
Akmanoğlu & Pektaş--Karabekir, 2020	Special education	3	Video-prompting	Drawing a six-part person	100%	Three consecutive sessions	Percentage (a task analysis with six steps)
Geiger et al., 2012	Behavioral sciences	2	Discrete trial teaching	Receptive language skills	100%	Three consecutive sessions	Percentage (count)
Greer et al., 2023	Behavioral sciences	2	Functional communication training	Aggression, property destruction, self-injurious behaviors	85% reduction from baseline	Two consecutive sessions	Rate per minute (count)
RUPP Autism Network, 2002	Medical field	49 (experiment) 52 (control)	Risperidone	Irritability behaviors	25% decrease from the irritability score of baseline	One measurement	Scores according to the aberrant behavior checklist
Root et al., 2017	Special education	3	Schema-based instruction with concrete and virtual manipulatives	Word problem-solving	At least 24 points in a session	Two consecutive days	Scores according to the task analysis
Wilder et al., 2020	Behavioral science	3	Auditory feedback and edible reinforcement	Toe-walking	10%	Three consecutive sessions	Percentage (count)
Yakubova & Chen, 2021	Special education	1	Parent-implemented video prompting	Daily living skills	100%	Two consecutive sessions	Percentage (three task analysis with 13 to 15 steps)

using continuous recording. The total number of responses was then converted to a rate measure (responses per minute) to represent the frequency of problem behavior during each session. They set the performance criterion at an 85% reduction from the baseline level. Similarly, Wilder et al. (2020) conducted an intervention incorporating auditory feedback and edible reinforcement to decrease toe-wolking behaviors of three children with ASD. They measured the frequency of the problem behaviors in 10-s intervals during 5-min sessions using partial interval recording. The total number of responses was first identified as a rate measure (i.e., the proportion of intervals containing toe-walking behavior per 5-min session) and then converted to a percentage to represent the frequency of problem behavior during each session. Wilder et al. (2020) assigned the performance criterion at 10% for behavior reduction rate across 5-min sessions.

In the medical field, the Research Units on Pediatric Psychopharmacology (RUPP) Autism Network (2002) conducted a study to determine the effects of risperidone on primary outcomes—namely, irritability behaviors such as tantrums, aggression, and self-injury—and secondary outcomes, including social withdrawal, stereotypy, hyperactivity, and inappropriate speech. For the primary outcomes, the researchers applied a criterion to accept risperidone's effectiveness. Specifically, caregivers completed a standardized checklist, the Irrability subscale of the Aberrant Behavior Checklist (ABC-I), which rates behaviors on a 4-point scale ranging from 0 (not at all a problem) to 3 (severe problem). The total subscale score (ranging from 0 to 45) represented the severity level of irritability for each participant. Although measurements were collected weekly for 8 weeks, treatment response was defined as a $\geq$ 25% reduction in ABC-I scores from pre-test to post-test at Week 8.

Overall, behavior reduction studies commonly use the level of change in rate or percentage formats. In addition, the level of behavior reduction can be presented as a score format, as in the RUPP Autism Network (2002) or as a frequency or count format. For example, Wilder et al. (2020) could have represented the level as a count format to indicate the frequency of problem behaviors across 5-min sessions. They could have determined the total count of problem behaviors during 30 observations using a 10-s partial-interval time-sampling method within a 5-min session. In this case, their targeted reduction level would have been 3 out of 30 intervals (i.e., 10% of the intervals in a 5-min session, see Table 1.1). Moreover, the level of behavior reduction can also be presented in a duration format. For instance, the out-of-seat behavior of a child with ASD can be measured as the total time spent out of the seat during a lesson, and a performance reduction criterion can be set based on this duration measure.

1.2.2 Frequency of the Desired Level of Behavioral Change

Another component of the performance criterion is the frequency of observations of the desired level of behavioral change during the treatment phase (Fienup & Carr, 2021; Fuller & Fienup, 2018; Richling et al., 2019). In general, if the number of observations at the targeted level of behavior under study meets the frequency criterion, then the treatment is wholly terminated. Sometimes, even though a frequency criterion accompanies the level in a study, the intervention can continue for additional sessions even after the level-frequency criterion is met (e.g., Belisle et al., 2020; Ferguson et al., 2020). Sometimes, the aftermath of meeting the level-frequency criterion can result in changing the intensity of the intervention (e.g., Gevarter et al., 2021; Tsami & Lerman, 2020), changing the intervention entirely or a component of it (e.g., Doherty et al., 2018). Sometimes, the treatment is terminated entirely, but observations of its impact on generalization and/or response maintenance of the intervened behavior can extend into separate phases (e.g., Burton et al., 2013; Naoi et al., 2007). And sometimes, the treatment is terminated once it meets the frequency-level criterion for the targeted behaviors, and the treatment can continue in another phase for novel targeted behaviors (e.g., Rajagopal et al., 2021). In the literature, a frequency value accompanied by the target level in these "sometimes" cases is usually assigned by the researchers.

Frequencies can be assigned on a session- or a trial-based basis in studies. For example, in Gerow et al. (2021), the frequency of performance criteria was session-based, defined as completing 100% (level) of task-analysis steps correctly for two consecutive sessions. This means the performance criteria were determined by overall performance across the entire session. In contrast, Rajagopal et al. (2021) used a trial-based frequency criterion, requiring at least 80% (level) correct responding across two consecutive trial blocks. Thus, the performance criterion was evaluated at the level of individual teaching trials rather than whole sessions, reflecting finer-grained performance measurement.

Frequencies can be set to mostly consecutive sessions or block trials, but rarely to nonconsecutive sessions or trials. For example, Akmanoğlu and Pektaş-Karabekir (2020) defined the frequency value of performance criteria as three consecutive sessions, meaning the participant had to demonstrate the target performance in back-to-back sessions to show stable learning. In contrast, McKeown et al. (2021) set the frequency value of performance criteria as five nonconsecutive sessions, requiring the participant to reach the level criterion in multiple sessions that were not necessarily sequential. The former emphasizes consistency and stability of the targeted level, the latter reflects a more flexible standard of performance criterion, showing that the desired behavioral change can be demonstrated reliably across time, even if not in immediately consecutive sessions.

Upon observing the targeted behavior across consecutive sessions, frequency can refer to consecutive sessions within a day, consecutive days within a week, or even consecutive weeks within a month. For instance, Root et al. (2017) set the frequency at two consecutive days, conducting intervention sessions daily during school days (as shown in Table 1.1). Conversely, Gerow et al. (2021) defined frequency as two consecutive sessions. In their study, therapists visited participants in their homes 1–3 days per week, with each visit consisting of four sessions. If a study were conducted with only one session per week, the sequential timeframe could be extended to weekly sessions over the course of the month. As another point, the frequency of the performance criterion is generally assigned in one to three consecutive sessions in the literature (Richling et al., 2019). Rarely, it can be assigned to more than three.

1.3 Concluding Remarks

The number of individuals with ASD has been increasing over time. In response, numerous studies have been conducted to enhance their skills or reduce their problem behaviors in various domains. And, many to come. Researchers have generally aimed to bring behaviors to desired levels, which are often associated with socially significant behavioral changes. In this context, the performance criteria set in intervention studies represent a key variable for accurately determining evidence-based practices for individuals with ASD, and indeed for all individuals. Performance criteria contain two components: levels and frequencies, which define thresholds at which behavior change is considered successful. The level component refers to the extent or magnitude of expected behavioral change, while frequency indicates how frequently the desired level must be observed to meet the criterion. These criteria can be assigned and measured in a variety of ways, depending on the nature of the intervention, the target behavior, and the characteristics of the participants. Therefore, accurately defining and applying performance criteria are vital not only for evaluating the effectiveness of specific interventions but also for properly establishing evidence-based practices. By doing so, researchers and practitioners can ensure that behavioral interventions are both meaningful and functional, ultimately supporting the long-term development and well-being of individuals with ASD.

References

Accardo, A. L., Finnegan, E. G., Kuder, S. J., & Bomgardner, E. M. (2020). Writing interventions for individuals with autism spectrum disorder: A research synthesis. *Journal of Autism and Developmental Disorders, 50*(6), 1988–2006. https://doi.org/10.1007/s10803-019-03955-9

Akmanoğlu, N., & Pektaş-Karabekir, E. (2020). The effectiveness of video prompting in teaching children with autism the skill of drawing a six-part person. *Journal of Developmental and Physical Disabilities, 32*(4), 617–631. https://doi.org/10.1007/s10882-019-09709-w

Allport, G. W. (1961). *Pattern and growth in personality*. Rinehart & Wilson.

American Psychiatric Association. (2013). *Diagnostic and statistical manual of mental disorders* (5th ed.). Author.

Anixt, J. S., Ehrhardt, J., & Duncan, A. (2024). Evidence-based interventions in autism. *Pediatric Clinics, 71*(2), 199–221. https://doi.org/10.1016/j.pcl.2023.12.004

Aydin, O. (2024). Rise of single-case experimental designs: A historical overview of the necessity of single-case methodology. *Neuropsychological Rehabilitation, 34*(3), 301–334. https://doi.org/10.1080/09602011.2023.2181191

Aydin, O. (n.d.). *Impact of performance criteria assignments on response maintenance and generalization: an investigation across study variables.*

Aydin, O., Sulu, M. D., & Ari-Arat, C. (2025). A meta-analysis of self-management interventions in teaching daily living skills to autistic individuals. *Journal of Autism and Developmental Disorders, 55*(7), 2377–2392. https://doi.org/10.1007/s10803-024-06355-w

Aydin, O., & Tanious, R. (2022). Performance criteria-based effect size (PCES) measurement of single-case experimental designs: A real-world data study. *Journal of Applied Behavior Analysis, 55*(3), 891–918. https://doi.org/10.1002/jaba.928

Aydin, O., & Tekin-İftar, E. (2020). Teaching math skills to individuals with autism spectrum disorder: A descriptive and meta-analysis in single case research designs. *Ankara University Faculty of Educational Sciences Journal of Special Education, 21*(2), 383–426. https://doi.org/10.21565/ozelegitimdergisi.521232

Aydin, O., Tekin-Iftar, E., & Rakap, S. (2019). Explanation of the "quality indicators of single-subject experimental research studies" rubric using studies focused on teaching mathematics skills. *Ankara University Faculty of Educational Sciences Journal of Special Education, 20*, 597–628. https://doi.org/10.21565/ozelegitimdergisi.421952

Baer, D. M., Wolf, M. M., & Risley, T. R. (1968). Some current dimensions of applied behavior analysis. *Journal of Applied Behavior Analysis, 1*(1), 91–97. https://doi.org/10.1901/jaba.1968.1-91

Baxter, A. J., Brugha, T. S., Erskine, H. E., Scheurer, R. W., Vos, T., & Scott, J. G. (2015). The epidemiology and global burden of autism spectrum disorders. *Psychological Medicine, 45*(3), 601–613. https://doi.org/10.1017/S003329171400172X

Belisle, J., Stanley, C. R., Schmick, A., Dixon, M. R., Alholail, A., Galliford, M. E., & Ellenberger, L. (2020). Establishing arbitrary comparative relations and referential transformations of stimulus function in individuals with autism. *Journal of Applied Behavior Analysis, 53*(2), 938–955. https://doi.org/10.1002/jaba.655

Bloom, B. S. (1968). Learning for mastery. *Évaluation Comment (UCLA-CSIEP), 1*(2), 1–12.

Bloom, B. S. (1971). Mastery learning. In J. H. Block (Ed.), *Mastery learning: Theory and practice* (pp. 47–63). Holt, Rinehart, and Winston.

Briggs, A. M., Dozier, C. L., Lessor, A. N., Kamana, B. U., & Jess, R. L. (2019). Further investigation of differential reinforcement of alternative behavior without extinction for escape-maintained destructive behavior. *Journal of Applied Behavior Analysis, 52*(4), 956–973. https://doi.org/10.1002/jaba.648

Brown, H. M., Oram-Cardy, J., & Johnson, A. (2013). A meta-analysis of the reading comprehension skills of individuals on the autism spectrum. *Journal of Autism and Developmental Disorders, 43*(4), 932–955. https://doi.org/10.1007/s10803-012-1638-1

Burton, C. E., Anderson, D. H., Prater, M. A., & Dyches, T. T. (2013). Video self-modeling on an iPad to teach functional math skills to adolescents with autism and intellectual disability. *Focus on Autism and Other Developmental Disabilities, 28*(2), 67–77. https://doi.org/10.1177/1088357613478829

Carlson, J. G., & Minke, K. A. (1975). Fixed and ascending criteria for unit mastery learning. *Journal of Educational Psychology, 67*(1), 96–101. https://doi.org/10.1037/h0078676

Charman, T. (2002). The prevalence of autism spectrum disorders: Recent evidence and future challenges. *European Child & Adolescent Psychiatry, 11*(6), 249–256. https://doi.org/10.1007/s00787-002-0297-8

Christopher, K., & Lord, C. (2022). Best practice assessments for autism spectrum disorders in schools. *Psychology in the Schools, 59*(7), 1454–1468. https://doi.org/10.1002/pits.22680

Cook, B. G., Tankersley, M., & Harjusola-Webb, S. (2008). Evidence-based special education and professional wisdom: Putting it all together. *Intervention in School and Clinic, 44*(2), 105–111. https://doi.org/10.1177/1053451208321566

Cordeiro, M. C., Kodak, T., Reidy, J., Stoppleworth, A., Zelinski, K., & Jainga, A. (2022). Comparison of mastery criteria applied to individual targets and stimulus sets on acquisition of tacts, intraverbals, and listener responses. *Journal of Applied Behavior Analysis, 55*(4), 1258–1279. https://doi.org/10.1002/jaba.946

Coulter, A., Entwistle, V. A., Eccles, A., Ryan, S., Shepperd, S., & Perera, R. (2015). Personalised care planning for adults with chronic or long-term health conditions. *Cochrane Database of Systematic Reviews, 2015*(3), CD010523. https://doi.org/10.1002/14651858.CD010523.pub2

Delano, M. E. (2007). Improving written language performance of adolescents with Asperger syndrome. *Journal of Applied Behavior Analysis, 40*(2), 345–351. https://doi.org/10.1901/jaba.2007.50-06

Department for Education & Department of Health. (2015). *Special educational needs and disability code of practice: 0 to 25 years: Statutory guidance for organisations which work with and support children and young people who have special educational needs or disabilities*. https://www.gov.uk/government/publications/send-code-of-practice-0-to-25

Doherty, A., Bracken, M., & Gormley, L. (2018). Teaching children with autism to initiate and respond to peer mands using picture exchange communication system (PECS). *Behavior Analysis in Practice, 11*(4), 279–288. https://doi.org/10.1007/s40617-018-00311-8

Eversole, M., Collins, D. M., Karmarkar, A., Colton, L., Quinn, J. P., Karsbaek, R., Johnson, J. R., Callier, N. P., & Hilton, C. L. (2016). Leisure activity enjoyment of children with autism spectrum disorders. *Journal of Autism and Developmental Disorders, 46*(1), 10–20. https://doi.org/10.1007/s10803-015-2529-z

Ferguson, J. L., Majeski, M. J., McEachin, J., Leaf, R., Cihon, J. H., & Leaf, J. B. (2020). Evaluating discrete trial teaching with instructive feedback delivered in a dyad arrangement via telehealth. *Journal of Applied Behavior Analysis, 53*(4), 1876–1888. https://doi.org/10.1002/jaba.773

Fethney, J. (2010). Statistical and clinical significance, and how to use confidence intervals to help interpret both. *Australian Critical Care, 23*(2), 93–97. https://doi.org/10.1016/j.aucc.2010.03.001

Fienup, D. M., & Brodsky, J. (2017). Effects of mastery criterion on the emergence of derived equivalence relations. *Journal of Applied Behavior Analysis, 50*(4), 843–848. https://doi.org/10.1002/jaba.416

Fienup, D. M., & Carr, J. C. (2021). The use of performance criteria for determining "mastery" in discrete-trial instruction: A call for research. *Behavioral Interventions, 36*(6), 756–764. https://doi.org/10.1002/bin.1827

Finnegan, E., & Accardo, A. L. (2018). Written expression in individuals with autism spectrum disorder: A meta-analysis. *Journal of Autism and Developmental Disorders, 48*(3), 868–882. https://doi.org/10.1007/s10803-017-3385-9

Frye, R. E. (2022). A personalized multidisciplinary approach to evaluating and treating autism spectrum disorder. *Journal of Personalized Medicine, 12*(3), 464. https://doi.org/10.3390/jpm12030464

Fuller, J. L., & Fienup, D. M. (2018). A preliminary analysis of mastery criterion level: Effects on response maintenance. *Behavior Analysis in Practice, 11*(1), 1–8. https://doi.org/10.1007/s40617-017-0201-0

Geiger, K. B., Carr, J. E., LeBlanc, L. A., Hanney, N. M., Polick, A. S., & Heinicke, M. R. (2012). Teaching receptive discriminations to children with autism: A comparison of traditional and embedded discrete trial teaching. *Behavior Analysis in Practice, 5*(2), 49–59. https://doi.org/10.1007/BF03391823

Gerow, S., Radhakrishnan, S., Akers, J. S., McGinnis, K., & Swensson, R. (2021). Telehealth parent coaching to improve daily living skills for children with ASD. *Journal of Applied Behavior Analysis, 54*(2), 566–581. https://doi.org/10.1002/jaba.813

Gevarter, C., Groll, M., Stone, E., & Medina Najar, A. (2021). A parent-implemented embedded AAC intervention for teaching navigational requests and other communicative functions to children with autism spectrum disorder. *Augmentative and Alternative Communication, 37*(3), 180–193. https://doi.org/10.1080/07434618.2021.1946846

Greer, B. D., Shahan, T. A., Fisher, W. W., Mitteer, D. R., & Fuhrman, A. M. (2023). Further evaluation of treatment duration on the resurgence of destructive behavior. *Journal of Applied Behavior Analysis, 56*(1), 166–180. https://doi.org/10.1002/jaba.956

Hume, K., Steinbrenner, J. R., Odom, S. L., Morin, K. L., Nowell, S. W., Tomaszewski, B., et al. (2021). Evidence-based practices for children, youth, and young adults with autism: Third generation review. *Journal of Autism and Developmental Disorders, 51*(11), 4013–4032. https://doi.org/10.1007/s10803-020-04844-2

Individuals with Disabilities Education Improvement Act of 2004 (IDEA), 20 U.S.C. § 1400 et seq. (2004). https://www.govinfo.gov/content/pkg/PLAW-108publ446/html/PLAW-108publ446.htm

Johnston, J. M., & O'Neill, G. (1973). The analysis of performance criteria defining course grades as a determinant of college student academic performance. *Journal of Applied Behavior Analysis, 6*(2), 261–268. https://doi.org/10.1901/jaba.1973.6-261

Kurt, O., & Tekin-Iftar, E. (2008). A comparison of constant time delay and simultaneous prompting within embedded instruction on teaching leisure skills to children with autism. *Topics in Early Childhood Special Education, 28*(1), 53–64. https://doi.org/10.1177/0271121408316046

Lai, M. C., Anagnostou, E., Wiznitzer, M., Allison, C., & Baron-Cohen, S. (2020). Evidence-based support for autistic people across the lifespan: Maximising potential, minimising barriers, and optimising the person–environment fit. *The Lancet Neurology, 19*(5), 434–451. https://doi.org/10.1016/S1474-4422(20)30034-X

Ledford, J. R., Lambert, J. M., Barton, E. E., & Ayres, K. M. (2021). The evidence base for interventions for individuals with ASD: A call to improve practice conceptualization and synthesis. *Focus on Autism and Other Developmental Disabilities, 36*(3), 135–147. https://doi.org/10.1177/10883576211023349

Lee, C. E., Shogren, K. A., Segal, J., Pezzimenti, F., Aleman-Tovar, J., & Taylor, J. L. (2022). Goal attainment scaling—Community-based: A method to incorporate personalized outcomes into intervention research with youth and adults on the autism spectrum. *Autism, 26*(1), 178–187. https://doi.org/10.1177/13623613211024492

LeFort, S. M. (1993). The statistical versus clinical significance debate. *Image: The Journal of Nursing Scholarship, 25*(1), 57–62. https://doi.org/10.1111/j.1547-5069.1993.tb00754.x

Lloyd, M., MacDonald, M., & Lord, C. (2013). Motor skills of toddlers with autism spectrum disorders. *Autism, 17*(2), 133–146. https://doi.org/10.1177/1362361311402230

Love, A. M., Cai, R. Y., Stephenson, J., Gallagher, E., Toland, M. D., & Gibbs, V. (2024). Adaptation of COMPASS for use in autism-specific schools in Australia: A cluster randomized trial. *Journal of Autism and Developmental Disorders, 55*, 1–14. https://doi.org/10.1007/s10803-024-06345-y

McKeown, C. A., Luczynski, K. C., & Lehardy, R. K. (2021). Evaluating the generality and social acceptability of early friendship skills. *Journal of Applied Behavior Analysis, 54*(4), 1341–1368. https://doi.org/10.1002/jaba.842

Montes, C. C., Heinicke, M. R., Guendulain, M. A., & Morales, E. (2021). A component analysis of awareness training for reducing speech disfluencies. *Journal of Applied Behavior Analysis, 54*(2), 770–782. https://doi.org/10.1002/jaba.795

Naoi, N., Yokoyama, K., & Yamamoto, J. I. (2007). Intervention for tact as reporting in children with autism. *Research in Autism Spectrum Disorders, 1*(2), 174–184. https://doi.org/10.1016/j.rasd.2006.08.005

Nygren, G., Cederlund, M., Sandberg, E., Gillstedt, F., Arvidsson, T., Gillberg, I. C., & Gillberg, C. (2012). The prevalence of autism spectrum disorders in toddlers: A population study of 2-year-old Swedish children. *Journal of Autism and Developmental Disorders, 42*(7), 1491–1497. https://doi.org/10.1007/s10803-011-1391-x

Page, P. (2014). Beyond statistical significance: Clinical interpretation of rehabilitation research literature. *International Journal of Sports Physical Therapy, 9*(5), 726–736.

Pitts, L., & Hoerger, M. L. (2021). Mastery criteria and the maintenance of skills in children with developmental disabilities. *Behavioral Interventions, 36*(2), 522–531. https://doi.org/10.1002/bin.1778

Rajagopal, S., Nicholson, K., Putri, T. R., Addington, J., & Felde, A. (2021). Teaching children with autism to tact private events based on public accompaniments. *Journal of Applied Behavior Analysis, 54*(1), 270–286. https://doi.org/10.1002/jaba.785

Randi, J., Newman, T., & Grigorenko, E. L. (2010). Teaching children with autism to read for meaning: Challenges and possibilities. *Journal of Autism and Developmental Disorders, 40*(7), 890–902. https://doi.org/10.1007/s10803-010-0938-6

Ranganathan, P., Pramesh, C. S., & Buyse, M. (2015). Common pitfalls in statistical analysis: Clinical versus statistical significance. *Perspectives in Clinical Research, 6*(3), 169–170. https://doi.org/10.4103/2229-3485.159943

Richling, S. M., Fienup, D. M., & Wong, K. (2023). Establishing performance criteria for mastery. In J. L. Matson (Ed.), *Applied behavior analysis: A comprehensive handbook*. Springer. https://doi.org/10.1007/978-3-031-19964-6_22

Richling, S. M., Williams, W. L., & Carr, J. E. (2019). The effects of different mastery criteria on the skill maintenance of children with developmental disabilities. *Journal of Applied Behavior Analysis, 52*(3), 701–717. https://doi.org/10.1002/jaba.580

Root, J. R., Browder, D. M., Saunders, A. F., & Lo, Y. Y. (2017). Schema-based instruction with concrete and virtual manipulatives to teach problem solving to students with autism. *Remedial and Special Education, 38*(1), 42–52. https://doi.org/10.1177/0741932516643592

RUPP Autism Network. (2002). Risperidone in children with autism and serious behavioral problems. *New England Journal of Medicine, 347*(5), 314–321. https://doi.org/10.1056/NEJMoa013171

Sacco, R., Camilleri, N., Eberhardt, J., Umla-Runge, K., & Newbury-Birch, D. (2022). *The prevalence of autism spectrum disorder in Europe*. IntechOpen eBooks. https://doi.org/10.5772/intechopen.108123

Schneider, A., Fienup, D. M., Gussin, R., & Moss, P. (2022). A preliminary comparison of mastery criterion frequency values: Effects on acquisition and maintenance. *Behavioral Interventions, 37*(3), 306–322. https://doi.org/10.1002/bin.1834

Semb, G. (1974). The effects of mastery criteria and assignment length on college-student test performance. *Journal of Applied Behavior Analysis, 7*(1), 61–69. https://doi.org/10.1901/jaba.1974.7-61

Simmons, C. A., Salvatore, G. L., & Zangrillo, A. N. (2022). Efficiency and preference for alternative activities during schedule thinning with functional communication training. *Journal of Applied Behavior Analysis, 55*(1), 101–120. https://doi.org/10.1002/jaba.886

Steinmetz, J. D., Seeher, K. M., Schiess, N., Nichols, E., Cao, B., Servili, C., et al. (2024). Global, regional, and national burden of disorders affecting the nervous system, 1990–2021: A systematic analysis for the global burden of disease study 2021. *The Lancet Neurology, 23*(4), 344–381. https://doi.org/10.1016/S1474-4422(24)00038-3

Sulu, M. D., Aydin, O., Martella, R. C., Erden, E., & Ozen, Z. (2024). A meta-analysis of applied behavior analysis-based interventions for individuals with autism spectrum disorders in Turkey. *Review Journal of Autism and Developmental Disorders*. Advance online publication. https://doi.org/10.1007/s40489-023-00421-2

Tan, M. J. T., Kasireddy, H. R., Satriya, A. B., Abdul Karim, H., & AlDahoul, N. (2025). Health is beyond genetics: On the integration of lifestyle and environment in real-time for hyper-personalized medicine. *Frontiers in Public Health, 12*, 1522673. https://doi.org/10.3389/fpubh.2024.1522673

Tetzlaff, L., Schmiedek, F., & Brod, G. (2021). Developing personalized education: A dynamic framework. *Educational Psychology Review, 33*(3), 863–882. https://doi.org/10.1007/s10648-020-09570-w

Tonizzi, I., & Usai, M. C. (2023). Math abilities in autism spectrum disorder: A meta-analysis. *Research in Developmental Disabilities, 139*, 104559. https://doi.org/10.1016/j.ridd.2023.104559

Tsami, L., & Lerman, D. C. (2020). Transfer of treatment effects from combined to isolated conditions during functional communication training for multiply controlled problem behavior. *Journal of Applied Behavior Analysis, 53*(2), 649–664. https://doi.org/10.1002/jaba.629

Wertalik, J. L., & Kubina, R. M., Jr. (2017). Interventions to improve personal care skills for individuals with autism: A review of the literature. *Review Journal of Autism and Developmental Disorders, 4*(1), 50–60. https://doi.org/10.1007/s40489-016-0097-6

Whyatt, C. P., & Craig, C. M. (2012). Motor skills in children aged 7–10 years diagnosed with autism spectrum disorder. *Journal of Autism and Developmental Disorders, 42*(9), 1799–1809. https://doi.org/10.1007/s10803-011-1421-8

Wilder, D. A., Ertel, H., Hodges, A. C., Thomas, R., & Luong, N. (2020). The use of auditory feedback and edible reinforcement to decrease toe walking among children with autism. *Journal of Applied Behavior Analysis, 53*(1), 554–562. https://doi.org/10.1002/jaba.607

Wolf, M. M. (1978). Social validity: The case for subjective measurement or how applied behavior analysis is finding its heart. *Journal of Applied Behavior Analysis, 11*(2), 203–214. https://doi.org/10.1901/jaba.1978.11-203

Wong, K. K., & Fienup, D. M. (2022). Units of analysis in acquisition–performance criteria for "mastery": A systematic replication. *Journal of Applied Behavior Analysis, 55*(3), 971–985. https://doi.org/10.1002/jaba.915

Wong, K. K., Fienup, D. M., Richling, S. M., Keen, A., & Mackay, K. (2022). Systematic review of acquisition mastery criteria and statistical analysis of associations with response maintenance and generalization. *Behavioral Interventions, 37*(4), 993–1012. https://doi.org/10.1002/bin.1885

Yakubova, G., & Chen, B. B. (2021). Examining the effects of parent-created and parent-implemented video prompting to teach daily living skills to an adolescent with autism. *Journal of Autism and Developmental Disorders, 51*(12), 4679–4691. https://doi.org/10.1007/s10803-021-04913-0

Yu, Y., Ozonoff, S., & Miller, M. (2024). Assessment of autism spectrum disorder. *Assessment, 31*(1), 24–41. https://doi.org/10.1177/10731911231173089

Zhao, Y., Lu, F., Ding, R., Zhu, D., Zhang, R., Sun, S., He, P., & Zheng, X. (2025). Prevalence, incidence, and characteristics of autism spectrum disorder among children in Beijing, China. *Autism: The International Journal of Research and Practice, 29*(4), 884–895. https://doi.org/10.1177/13623613241290388

Zhou, H., Xu, X., Yan, W., Zou, X., Wu, L., Luo, X., et al. (2020). Prevalence of autism spectrum disorder in China: A nationwide multi-center population-based study among children aged 6 to 12 years. *Neuroscience Bulletin, 36*(9), 961–971. https://doi.org/10.1007/s12264-020-00530-6

Chapter 2
Impact of Performance Criteria on Behaviors

Abstract Performance criteria are critical variables in determining the effectiveness, durability, and generalizability of behavioral interventions. This chapter reviews systematic analyses, empirical studies, and the author's recent review to examine how performance-criterion components—levels and frequencies—affect response maintenance and generalization of trained behaviors. Evidence consistently shows that higher performance-criterion levels (≥90% for skill acquisition; ≤10% for behavior reduction) and moderate frequencies (2–3 consecutive sessions) produce stronger and more stable behavioral outcomes. Lower levels or minimal/excessive frequencies are associated with greater variability and weaker maintenance and generalization. Performance criteria interact with participant and task characteristics, such as age, diagnosis, and skill type, suggesting that criteria must be tailored to the individual learner and the specific context. Chi-squared and regression analyses support the predictive role of stricter and moderately applied performance criteria in sustaining and transferring behavior across contexts. Collecting maintenance and generalization data, along with transparent reporting of performance-criteria components, is essential to ensure that acquired skills are durable, generalized, and socially meaningful. These findings emphasize that performance criteria are one of the functional study variables central to optimizing the outcomes of behavioral interventions.

Keywords Performance criteria · Mastery criteria · Response maintenance · Generalization · Acquisition

2.1 Effects of Performance Criteria on Changes in Behavior Under Study

In behavioral interventions, performance criteria set by researchers or practitioners can serve as a trigger factor to prompt them to provide the desired behavioral change in their customers at that level. There is some evidence in the literature that more

The original version of the chapter has been revised. A correction to this chapter can be found at https://doi.org/10.1007/978-981-95-8542-7_5

© The Author(s), under exclusive license to Springer Nature Singapore Pte Ltd. 2026, corrected publication 2026

O. Aydin, *Optimal Performance Criteria in Autism Studies*, SpringerBriefs in Modern Perspectives on Disability Research,
https://doi.org/10.1007/978-981-95-8542-7_2

stringent performance criteria have more positive effects on behavioral change. For example, in general education literature, Johnston and O'Neill (1973) found that college students performed better on unit quizzes when higher performance criteria were applied in a self-paced course based on a Personalized System of Instruction. Similarly, Semb (1974) found that college students achieved the most accurate and sustained performance when high-learning criteria were applied to short assignments. Recently, Fienup and Brodsky (2017) investigated how different performance criteria influence the development of derived equivalence relations in college students learning neuroanatomy. The findings indicated that when the performance criterion was less stringent, the effectiveness of learning was reduced.

In special education literature, performance criteria are relatively linked to the level of behavioral change. For example, Fuller and Fienup aimed to compare the impact of 50%, 80%, and 90% performance criteria on response maintenance when teaching spelling or sight word reading to three children with ASD. Although their main goal was to seek the impact of different performance criteria on response maintenance rates, their findings also indicated that the more stringent the performance criteria, the greater the skill acquisition was. Similar findings can be observed in health literature. For example, Epstein et al. (1994) examined the effects of performance criteria and contingent reinforcement in a family-based weight control program for obese children. Results showed that groups using performance criteria achieved greater short-term weight loss than controls (i.e., those without performance criteria), indicating that setting stringent, concrete performance criteria led to more positive behavioral outcomes. Collectively, these results suggest that when expectations for outcomes increase, practitioners are more likely to be bold, motivated, and enthusiastic about meeting expectations on behavioral outcomes. Conversely, when the desired behavioral level is set low or desultory, practitioners' efforts to improve behavior may also decrease.

In a notable divergence within the general education literature, several studies have reported conflicting findings regarding the impact of performance criterion levels. Carlson and Minke (1975) extended previous performance criteria research by examining both fixed and ascending criterion levels. Earlier studies had already provided evidence supporting higher performance levels (see Johnston & O'Neill, 1973; Semb, 1974). Rather than comparing only static performance levels (e.g., 80% vs. 90% accuracy), Carlson and Minke introduced a variable involving successive increases in performance criterion. Specifically, they compared three conditions: one with progressively increasing performance levels leading to a final 90% criterion and two with fixed performance levels of 80% and 90%. Contrary to previous assumptions, results showed that the fixed 80% criterion produced the most favorable student performance, suggesting that excessively stringent performance levels may not always yield superior learning outcomes.

Similarly, Reiser et al. (1986) and Reiser et al. (1987) further explored the effects of different performance criterion structures—ascending, descending, and fixed—on student performance and attitudes in mastery-oriented courses. In the 1986 study, undergraduates were assigned to one of three conditions: a criterion that gradually increased from 70% to 90%, one that decreased from 90% to 70%, or a fixed 80%

criterion across all units. Results showed that while higher performance criterion levels (e.g., 90%) improved short-term quiz performance, they did not significantly affect final examination scores. Students in the lower (70%) criterion group progressed faster, but the majority of students expressed a preference for the moderate, fixed 80% level.

To replicate and clarify these findings, Reiser et al. (1987) conducted a follow-up study comparing the same three types of performance criteria. Once again, students in the fixed 80% condition demonstrated steadier progress, achieved higher quiz performance, and expressed more positive attitudes than those in the ascending or descending conditions. Although the fixed group scored slightly higher on the final exam, the differences were not statistically significant. Across both studies, the "shaping hypothesis" (increasing the criteria improves performance more) was not supported. Together, these findings suggest that maintaining a moderate and consistent performance criterion (around 80%) is most beneficial for both student performance and motivation in mastery-oriented learning contexts.

Conflicting findings regarding the effects of performance criteria likely stem from variations in study design, participant characteristics, and task demands. Some studies have shown that higher performance criteria enhance learning and motivation because they promote greater engagement and more intensive practice. However, other studies have found no additional benefit (or even adverse effects) when criteria are set too high, as excessive demands may slow progress, increase frustration, or reduce persistence. Differences in instructional context (i.e., differences in independent variables), measurement timing (e.g., short-term quiz performance versus long-term retention), and the type of behavior targeted (simple versus complex skills) also contribute to these inconsistencies. In sum, these mixed results suggest that the effectiveness of performance criteria depends on balancing rigor with achievability; criteria that are challenging but attainable appear to yield the most consistent and positive outcomes.

2.2 Effects of Performance Criteria on Response Maintenance

This section elaborates on the impact of performance criteria on response maintenance in terms of two aspects. First, the empirical research focusing on this topic is summarized to describe the role of performance criteria on the durability of behavior over time. Second, review analyses are presented on this topic to discuss the generalization of the results of individual empirical research. Notably, empirical studies on this specific topic have been conducted recently and have been primarily found in the applied behavior analysis literature. These studies give two types of comparative information to the performance criteria literature. One is directly linked to comparing the components of performance criteria for skill maintenance, while the other is directly related to the impact of the manner of acquisition in which the skill was taught on response maintenance. The following two subsections summarize two types of comparisons related to the impact of performance criteria on skill durability. Then, the third subsection summarizes review analyses on this topic.

2.2.1 Empirical Research on Comparing the Components of Performance Criteria for Response Maintenance

Table 2.1 summarizes the empirical research on this specific topic in chronological order. As shown in the table, only five studies have been recently published in the behavior analysis literature. A total of seven empirical studies have been conducted. Richling et al. (2019) conducted three separate experiments. Six experiments sought the component "level" over the durability of the trained behavior, whereas only one study examined the component "frequency." The following paragraphs provide a detailed summary of each experiment.

Fuller and Fienup (2018) conducted a preliminary study to examine how different performance criterion levels affect response maintenance in children with autism. Three elementary-aged boys participated in discrete trial instruction involving academic tasks such as sight-word reading and spelling. The researchers compared three performance-criterion levels: 50%, 80%, and 90% accuracy in one session. Using an error-correction procedure, participants were taught until they reached the specified accuracy level, and response maintenance was assessed once weekly for 3–4 weeks. Results showed that higher performance-criterion levels produced higher response-maintenance levels: mean maintenance accuracy was 53.6% for the 50% condition, 69.1% for the 80% condition, and 88.2% for the 90% condition. The findings indicated that setting a higher performance criterion level (e.g., 90%) predicts greater response durability following instruction.

Richling et al. (2019) conducted a series of three experiments to evaluate how different performance criteria affect skill maintenance in children with developmental disabilities. In Experiment 2, one child with ASD and three children with intellectual and other developmental disabilities were taught auditory–visual conditional discriminations using a least-to-most prompting procedure. Performance criteria were set at 60%, 80%, and 100% accuracy across three consecutive sessions, followed by weekly follow-up probes for 4 weeks. Results showed that only the 100% criterion produced stable maintenance above 80% accuracy, whereas the 60% and 80% criteria yielded comparable but lower maintenance levels. In Experiment 3, the same participants were taught novel tact responses under the same conditions and at the same performance levels. Similar to Experiment 2, the 100% criterion consistently produced the highest maintenance levels, while the 60% and 80% criteria resulted in variable and often declining performance across follow-up probes. In Experiment 4, the researchers compared performance criteria of 80%, 90%, and 100% using tact training with novel stimuli, assessing maintenance 1 week after mastery. Once again, the 100% criterion produced the highest maintenance rates,

Table 2.1 Comparing the components of performance criteria for response maintenance

References	Participants	DV	IV	Comparing performance criteria	Follow-up	Outcomes
Fuller & Fienup, 2018	Three children with ASD	Sight-word reading and spelling	Error correction procedure	50%, 80%, and 90% in one session	Once per week for 3 to 4 weeks	Higher performance criterion levels yielded higher response maintenance rates.
Richling et al., 2019 Experiment 2	One child with ASD, three children with ID and ODDs	Auditory–visual conditional discrimination	Least-to-most prompting procedure	60%, 80%, and 100% across three consecutive sessions	Once per week for 4 weeks	100% criterion resulted in the highest response maintenance rates. 60% and 80% yielded comparable response maintenance rates.
Richling et al., 2019 Experiment 3	Same participants	Vocal tact	Same procedure	Same comparing performance levels	Same period	Similar results to Experiment 2 were obtained.
Richling et al., 2019 Experiment 4	Same participants	Vocal tact (for novel stimuli)	Same procedure	90% in lieu of 60%, others were same	1 week later	100% criterion resulted in the highest response maintenance rates. 80% were more successful than 90% in skill maintenance.
Pitts & Hoerger, 2021	Four children with ASD	Word-recognition	Least to most prompting procedure	80%, 90%, and 100% across three consecutive sessions	1 and 4 weeks later	Higher performance criterion levels (i.e., 90% and 100%) yielded higher response maintenance rates.
Longino et al., 2022	Two children with ASD, one typical child	Tact skills	Most to least prompting with a progressive time delay	80%, 90%, and 100% across three consecutive sessions	Once per week for 4 weeks	The performance criterion levels of 90% and 100% yielded higher response maintenance rates than those of 80%.
Schneider et al., 2022	Three children with ASD	Saying object–function relations	Most to least prompting	90% in one session/day vs. 90% across three consecutive sessions/days	Once per week for 3 to 4 weeks	More instructional sessions were required to meet the high-frequency performance criterion. However, skill maintenance rates were comparable across frequencies.

ASD: Autism spectrum disorder, DV: Dependent variable, ID: Intellectual disability, IV: Independent variable; ODDs: Other developmental disabilities whereas performance dropped sharply following the 80% and 90% criteria; interestingly, skills taught to 80% accuracy were better maintained than those taught to 90%. Overall, across the three experiments, higher performance-criterion levels, particularly 100% accuracy, were most effective at promoting durable skill maintenance over time.

Pitts and Hoerger (2021) conducted an experiment to examine how different performance-criterion levels affect response maintenance in children with developmental disabilities. Four children with autism were taught to recognize sight words using the least-to-most prompting procedure, with performance criteria set at 80%, 90%, and 100% accuracy across three consecutive sessions. After participants met the assigned criterion, follow-up probes were conducted 1 and 4 weeks later to assess maintenance. Results showed that higher performance criteria produced greater response maintenance. Responses taught under the 90% and 100% conditions were more durable over time, whereas those taught under the 80% condition deteriorated more rapidly. These findings indicate that setting higher performance criteria (e.g., 90% or 100%) enhances the long-term maintenance of learned skills following instruction.

Longino et al. (2022) conducted a replication study to examine how different performance-criterion levels affect response maintenance when using a most-to-least prompting procedure with a progressive time delay. Three children (two with ASD, one typical) participated in tact training, with performance criteria set at 80%, 90%, and 100% accuracy across three consecutive sessions. After reaching the assigned criterion, follow-up probes were conducted weekly for up to 4 weeks to assess response maintenance. Results showed that higher performance criteria produced greater maintenance: mean maintenance accuracy was approximately 71% for the 80% condition, 93% for the 90% condition, and 94% for the 100% condition. Although acquisition rates varied across participants, both 90% and 100% criteria led to more durable responding over time, whereas the 80% criterion resulted in greater performance deterioration. These findings support the use of higher performance criteria levels to promote the long-term maintenance of learned skills.

Schneider et al. (2022) conducted a study to examine how different performance-criterion frequency values affect skill acquisition and maintenance in children with autism. Three children participated in discrete trial instruction to learn object–function relations, using the most-to-least prompting procedure. Two mastery criterion frequency conditions were compared: achieving 90% accuracy in one session (1-Day) versus 90% accuracy across three consecutive sessions (3-Day). Each participant learned multiple target sets under both conditions, and maintenance probes were conducted weekly for 3–4 weeks after meeting performance criteria. Results showed that the 1-Day condition led to faster acquisition (31–56% fewer sessions to criterion) but similar levels of response maintenance compared to the 3-Day condition. The findings indicate that while increasing the frequency of consecutive performance level observations does not necessarily enhance maintenance, it reduces instructional efficiency, suggesting that a single-session performance criterion may be sufficient for learners with similar repertoires.

Across a growing body of research on this topic, particularly in the field of behavior analysis, findings consistently demonstrate that the level of performance criterion established during instruction influences the durability of learned behaviors in children with autism and other developmental disabilities. Fuller and Fienup (2018) first showed that higher performance-criterion levels (e.g., 90%) produced greater response maintenance than lower levels (50% or 80%). Building on this, Richling et al. (2019) systematically replicated and extended these findings across multiple experiments, showing that 100% accuracy criteria yielded the most stable maintenance across different skill types, whereas 60–90% criteria often led to weaker or inconsistent retention. Similarly, Pitts and Hoerger (2021) and Longino et al. (2022) confirmed that higher criteria (90–100%) consistently promote stronger maintenance of learned responses across weeks. However, Schneider et al. (2022) introduced a nuanced perspective, demonstrating that meeting a 90% criterion in a single session versus across three consecutive sessions yielded comparable response maintenance outcomes, despite the former being more instructionally efficient. In sum, these studies suggest that while increasing criterion levels (toward 90–100%) enhances response durability, extending the number of consecutive mastery sessions may not further improve maintenance and may instead reduce instructional efficiency.

2.2.2 Empirical Research on the Impact of the Manner of Skill Acquisition with a Performance Criterion on Response Maintenance

Table 2.2 summarizes the empirical studies comparing the manners of skill acquisition with a performance criterion on the durability of trained behaviors, presented in chronological order as well. As shown in the table, only six studies have been published recently in the behavior analysis literature on this topic. A total of seven empirical research studies have been conducted in these six studies. Cordeiro et al. (2022) conducted two separate experiments. Six experiments investigated the comparisons of set operant and individual operant in terms of the efficiency when acquiring skills and the evaluation of the durability of trained behaviors, whereas only one study examined the comparisons of set sizes across both conditions. The following paragraphs provide a detailed summary of each experiment.

Wong et al. (2022) conducted an experiment to compare the effects of applying performance criteria to set operant versus individual operant on sight-word acquisition and maintenance at a 100% accuracy level in one session. Four first-grade students (two with ASD, two with other developmental disabilities) were taught sight words using an error correction procedure. All participants reached the criterion more quickly when teaching individual operant rather than in sets. During 3- or 4-week follow-up sessions, set operant produced higher response maintenance for

Table 2.2 Comparing the manners of skill acquisition with a performance criterion on response maintenance

References	Participants	DV	IV	Performance criteria	Comparing manners	Follow-up	Outcomes
Wong et al., 2022	Two children with ASD, two with ODDs.	Sight-word reading	Error correction procedure	100% in one session	Set operant, individual operant	3 or 4 weeks later	Individual operant for all participants resulted in faster learning than sets. Set operant yielded more response maintenance rates than individual operant for two participants. For other two, there were similar response maintenance rates among individual operant and sets.
Wong & Fienup, 2022	One child with ASD, two with ODDs.	Sight-word reading	Error correction procedure	100% across two consecutive sessions	Set operant, individual operant	4 weeks later	Individual operant for all participants resulted in faster learning than sets. Overall, maintenance data were similar for all three participants across both conditions.
Cordeiro et al., 2022 Experiment 1	Five children with ASD	Tact skills for four, intraverbals for one	Error correction procedure	100% across two consecutive sessions	Individual targets and stimulus sets	1, 3, and 5 weeks later	Individual targets for most participants resulted in faster learning than set targets. There were similar response maintenance rates for individual and set targets
Cordeiro et al., 2022 Experiment 2	Two children with ASD from Experiment 1	Auditory–visual conditional discrimination	Error correction procedure	Same performance criteria	Same other comparable components	Same period	Similar results to Experiment 1 were obtained.
Kim et al., 2023	One child with a SLD and three typical children	Sight-word reading	Error correction procedure	100% in one session	Set operant, individual operant (3 vs. 5)	1 and 4 weeks later	Operant 3 resulted in the fastest acquisition, while operant 5 provided faster acquisition than the set operant. However, set operant were more successful than individual operant in maintaining acquired skills 1 and 4 weeks later. Individual operant were comparable in terms of response maintenance, while operant 3 was more efficient.

Zhi et al., 2023	Two children with a DD, one typical child	Sight-word reading	Error correction procedure	100% in one session	Set sizes (3, 6, and 12)	Once per 10-day intervals for up to 30 days	Set size 3 provided the fastest acquisition of sight words for all participants. However, set size 12 yielded the highest response maintenance rates for all participants.
Du et al., 2024	Eight children with ODDs	Tact skills	Error correction procedure	100% in one session	Set operant and individual operant	2 weeks later	Individual operant for most participants resulted in faster learning than sets. There were similar response maintenance rates among individual operant and sets.

DD: Developmental delay, SLD: Specific learning disability

two participants, while the other two participants showed similar maintenance across both conditions.

Wong and Fienup (2022) replicated the study of Wong et al. (2022). In this case, they used the performance criteria of 100% across two consecutive sessions. One child with ASD and two with other developmental disabilities were taught sight words in a similar format to that of Wong et al. (2022). Results were identical to those of Wong et al., except for response maintenance rates, which resulted in comparable rates for all three children across both conditions.

Cordeiro et al. (2022) conducted two experiments to examine the effects of applying performance criteria to stimulus sets versus individual targets on skill acquisition and response maintenance. In both experiments, the performance criterion required 100% correct responding across two consecutive sessions. In Experiment 1, they taught tact to four children with ASD and intraverbal skills to one child using an error correction procedure. After meeting the criterion, follow-up probes were conducted 1 to 5 weeks later. Three of five participants acquired skills faster in the individual target condition, whereas response maintenance was similar across conditions, with 75% or greater correct responding at follow-up. In Experiment 2, they extended the comparison to auditory–visual conditional discrimination (AVCD) training with two participants from Experiment 1. Both participants acquired targets more rapidly in the individual target condition, and similar response maintenance rates were observed across conditions; however, over-selecting responses produced false positives for 20% of targets in the individual target condition. Similarly, Du et al. (2024) investigated the impact of applying performance criteria to stimulus sets and individual operant on tact acquisition and response maintenance in eight preschoolers with developmental disabilities. Using an error correction procedure, researchers taught tact until participants achieved 100% accuracy in a single session. Six of eight participants demonstrated faster acquisition in the individual operant condition, whereas response maintenance after 2 weeks was comparable across conditions (51–52%).

Kim et al. (2023) conducted an experiment to examine the effects of applying varying teaching trial doses on sight word acquisition and maintenance at the 100% accuracy level in a single session. Four second-grade students with and without disabilities were taught sight words under three conditions: Set Analysis 5 (a set of four words with five trials per word); Operant Analysis 5 (individual four words with five trials per word); and Operant Analysis 3 (individual four words with three trials per word). Operant 3 resulted in the fastest acquisition, followed by Operant 5, whereas Set 5 produced the slowest acquisition. However, Set 5 led to better response maintenance at 1- and 4-week follow-ups compared to both operant conditions. Response maintenance levels were comparable across Operant 3 and Operant 5, although Operant 3 was more efficient overall, requiring fewer teaching trials to reach criterion.

Zhi et al. (2023) conducted a systematic replication study to examine how different stimulus set sizes affect both skill acquisition and response maintenance in young children. Three preschoolers (two with developmental delays, one typically developing) participated in tact-training of sight words under three set-size conditions: sets of 3 stimuli (3 per session), 6 stimuli, and 12 stimuli taught simultaneously (each stimulus presented three times per session). The performance criterion was set at the 100% accuracy in a single session and defined on an individual operant basis. When a specific sight-word target met the criterion, it was replaced with a novel target in the same set. After meeting the criterion for all sight words, maintenance probes were conducted every 10 days for up to 30 days. Results showed that the smallest set size (3) yielded the fastest acquisition compared to set sizes 6 and 12. However, the largest set size (12) reliably produced the highest maintenance accuracy.

Du et al. (2024) conducted a systematic replication comparing the effects of applying performance criteria to set operant versus individual operant on tact acquisition and response maintenance in eight preschoolers with developmental disabilities. Using an error-correction procedure and a performance criterion of 100% accuracy in one session, the researchers taught up to 20 tacts under both conditions. Results showed that six of the eight children acquired tact more efficiently in the individual operant condition, requiring 20–40% fewer learning opportunities; one participant learned faster under the set operant and one showed minimal differences. Response maintenance assessed 2 weeks after instruction was comparable across conditions, averaging 51% for the set operant and 52% for the individual operant. Overall, applying performance criteria to the individual operant improved acquisition efficiency without compromising maintenance.

Across these studies, researchers examined how applying performance criteria to set versus individual operant influences both acquisition efficiency and response maintenance, typically using high performance criterion levels. Most studies assigned the performance criterion at 100% accuracy, either in a single session (Du et al., 2024; Kim et al., 2023; Wong et al., 2022; Zhi et al., 2023) or across two consecutive sessions (Cordeiro et al., 2022; Wong & Fienup, 2022). Participants were primarily young children with autism or other developmental disabilities, often engaged in academic or verbal learning tasks such as sight-word reading, tact training, or auditory–visual discrimination. Across studies, teaching individual operant consistently resulted in faster acquisition, reflecting greater instructional efficiency. However, set-based instruction—though slower—was frequently associated with equal or superior response maintenance during follow-up probes conducted 1–4 weeks after meeting performance criteria. Zhi et al. (2023) also demonstrated that larger set sizes (e.g., 12 stimuli) resulted in stronger maintenance, whereas smaller sets accelerated learning. Collectively, findings suggest that when high performance criteria (near or at 100% accuracy) are used, instructional frequency (one vs. multiple consecutive sessions) has little impact on maintenance outcomes, and that educators must balance acquisition speed with long-term skill durability when deciding between individual- and set-based teaching formats.

2.2.3 Systematic Review Analyses on the Impact of Performance Criteria on Response Maintenance

This section details two systematic reviews published on this topic and also supplements the literature with a part of the results of a systematic review conducted by the author of this book (Aydin, n.d.). Across the published reviews, both McDougale et al. (2020) and Wong et al. (2022) examined how the stringency and structure of performance criteria in skill-acquisition research relate to response maintenance following training. Together, these studies highlight a consistent pattern: higher set performance criteria tend to be associated with stronger maintenance outcomes, whereas lower assigned criteria often fail to support sustained responding after instruction ends. The following paragraphs provide a detailed summary of these two reviews, focusing on the impact of performance criteria on response maintenance.

As a first review on this topic, McDougale et al. (2020) provided a descriptive analysis of 157 skill-acquisition studies published between 2015 and 2017 in *Journal of Applied Behavior Analysis (JABA)*, *Behavior Analysis in Practice*, and *Behavioral Interventions*. Although no further statistical analyses were conducted, descriptive data revealed that only 41% of studies included maintenance probes. Among those, 61% reported durable responding, 33% showed idiosyncratic outcomes, and 3% reported no maintenance. Critically, the study identified that researchers most often used 90% or 100% accuracy as the performance criterion, typically across one or two sessions, whereas practitioners in comparable surveys (Richling et al., 2019) commonly used 80% accuracy across three sessions. The authors interpreted this conflict as a potential explanation for why clinical maintenance outcomes are often weaker: the lower performance criteria typically used in practice may not yield stable post-training performance. Despite its central theoretical importance in the behavioral analysis literature, they concluded that response maintenance data are not reported in studies to the desired extent and that empirical studies manipulating performance criteria as independent variables are needed to identify which combinations of level and frequency best predict durable behavior change.

Wong et al. (2022) advanced this line of inquiry by conducting a systematic review and statistical analysis of 212 skill-acquisition studies (2017 to 2019) compiled from the same three journals as those in McDougale et al. (2020) and their associated maintenance and generalization data (the impact of performance criteria on generalization is presented in the later subsection). Maintenance was assessed in 83% of the reviewed studies. Drawing on 759 participant-level cases, they quantitatively tested the relation between performance-criterion levels and response maintenance rates using chi-squared statistics. Results showed a significant positive association between higher performance criteria and response maintenance; participants taught to ≥90–100% accuracy were substantially more likely to maintain responding compared to those trained to ≤80–89%. In addition to the criterion level, Wong et al. also examined the frequency with which the performance criterion was required to be met (e.g., one observation vs. two or more consecutive observations).

They found that higher criterion-level frequencies generally produced stronger maintenance outcomes, except when the performance criterion itself was already set at 90–100%.

In sum, these two studies provide converging evidence that response maintenance is directly influenced by the performance-criteria parameters used during acquisition. McDougale et al. (2020) found that maintenance data reporting in the field was not at a desirable level. Wong et al. (2022) demonstrated, with empirical data, that higher performance-criterion levels (≥90–100%) reliably predict better response maintenance outcomes. In addition, Wong et al. showed that requiring the criterion to be met across two or three consecutive sessions generally strengthened maintenance, except when the performance criterion was already set at 90 to 100%, at which point the effect of frequency diminished. Both studies emphasize the need to treat performance criteria as a functional component among study variables rather than as arbitrary decisions and to incorporate planned maintenance probes to evaluate the long-term effectiveness of behavioral changes.

As a supplement to the two existing systematic reviews, I also conducted a systematic review and analysis study (Aydin, n.d.)[1] to evaluate the impact of performance criteria components on response maintenance and generalization (the results of generalization are presented in the later sub-section). One hundred seventy-six studies compiled from JABA between the issues of 2019 and 2023 were examined and coded in terms of several aspects. Sorting through 2661 participant-level cases from 176 studies, I conducted descriptive and a series of statistical analyses to examine the relationships between study variables and response maintenance, as well as to predict the factors associated with greater durability of trained behaviors across cases. Figure 2.1 presents the descriptive findings from the studies in which maintenance data were collected. As shown in the figure, maintenance data were reported in only 40% (n = 70) of the reviewed studies, which contained a total of 717 cases (27% out of the 2661 cases), after excluding unanalyzable data from the sample. The majority of the studies collected the first maintenance data between 0 and 2 weeks after the interventions ended, and conducted one or two sessions to evaluate maintenance of trained behaviors. Response maintenance rates generally met the performance criteria levels set in the studies, and some even exceeded the studied levels. However, a substantial number of studies yielded lower outcomes in response maintenance when compared to performance criteria levels. As a note, although the previous two review studies and recent experimental research examined only skill acquisition behaviors to determine the impact of performance criteria components on skill maintenance, this study included studies that aimed to both increase and decrease behaviors. Seven studies out of 70, collectively involving 40 cases, aimed to decrease problem behaviors at a predetermined performance criterion level. In line with this expanded sample, the review seeks to enhance the generalizability of previous findings.

---

[1] Some of the data reported in this chapter are also included in a single-authored manuscript submitted to a peer-reviewed journal. The analyses and interpretations are presented here in an expanded and integrative form.

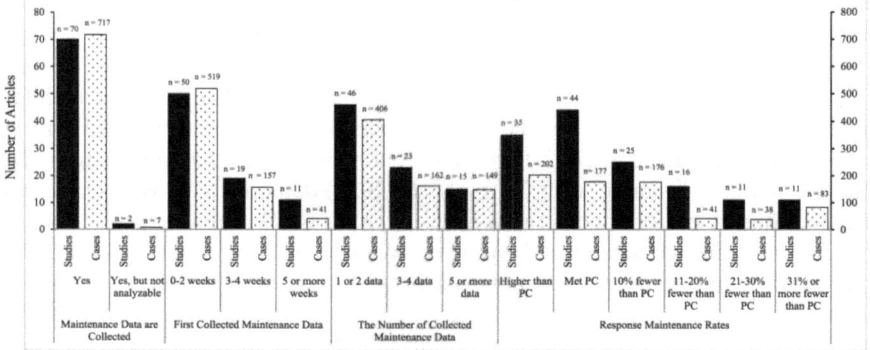

Fig. 2.1 Descriptive features of response maintenance data of the included studies from JABA issues between 2019 and 2023. PC = Performance Criteria/Criterion

As conducted in the Wong et al. (2022) study, I performed chi-squared analysis to determine the impact of performance criteria components on response maintenance rates. Wong et al. (2022) employed chi-squared analyses with a 4 × 2 crosstab for response maintenance and generalization outcomes, using two skill acquisition criteria (below 80% and 80% or above), and excluding destructive behavior performances. I expanded chi-squared analyses by categorizing response maintenance rates and generalization outcomes (in the later subsection) based on meeting performance criteria levels and frequencies, including studies involving destructive behavior performances. In this context, I coded performance criteria levels into four categories: 100% or 0%; 90–99% or 1–10%; 80–89% or 11–20%; <80% or > 20%, for increasing behaviors or reducing behaviors, respectively. Performance criteria frequency values were also coded into four categories: 1, 2, 3, and more than 3. I coded response maintenance rates into six categories, considering their meeting rates of performance criteria levels: higher, met, 1–10% fewer, 11–20% fewer, 21–30% fewer, and 31% or more fewer.

Table 2.3a presents the chi-squared analysis examining the relationship between performance criteria levels and response maintenance rates. The association was statistically significant, $\chi^2(15, N = 706) = 244.41$, $p < .001$, with a moderate effect size (Cramer's $V = .340$, $p < .001$). Adjusted residuals highlighted several key patterns. Lenient performance criteria levels (<80% for increasing behaviors or > 20% for decreasing behaviors) were associated with fewer cases meeting the criterion than expected, but also a higher-than-expected proportion of cases exceeding the criterion. Mid-range performance criteria levels (80–89% or 11–20%) showed fewer cases than expected meeting the criterion and substantially fewer cases 1–10% below the criterion, while the proportion of cases exceeding the criterion was higher than expected. Stricter performance criteria levels (90–99% or 1–10%) yielded significantly fewer cases meeting the criterion, yet more cases performed 31% or more below the criterion and exceeded the criterion. Finally, the strictest performance criteria level (100% or 0%) produced more cases meeting the criterion than expected but fewer cases exceeding it. Overall, these findings suggest that

Table 2.3a Chi-squared analysis for response maintenance rates vs. performance criteria levels

PC levels		Response maintenance rates: Met PC	1–10% fewer than PC	11–20% fewer than PC	21–30% fewer than PC	31% or more fewer than PC	Higher than PC	Total cases
<80% or >20%	Count	6	24	1	1	5	35	72
	Expected count	16.4	17.9	4.0	4.1	8.5	21.1	72.0
	Adjusted residual	−3.1*	1.7	−1.6	−1.7	−1.3	3.8*	
80–89% or 11–20%	Count	18	7	9	12	10	80	136
	Expected count	31.0	33.9	7.5	7.7	16.0	39.9	136.0
	Adjusted residual	−3.0*	−5.9*	6	1.8	−1.8	8.4*	
90–99% or 1–10%	Count	10	32	6	6	33	70	157
	Expected count	35.8	39.1	8.7	8.9	18.5	46.0	157.0
	Adjusted residual	−5.6*	−1.5	−1.1	−1.1	4.1*	4.8*	
100% or 0%	Count	127	113	23	21	35	22	341
	Expected count	77.8	85.0	18.8	19.3	40.1	100.0	341.0
	Adjusted residual	8.8*	4.9*	1.4	5	−1.2	−12.9*	
Total	Count	161	176	39	40	83	207	706
	Expected count	161.0	176.0	39.0	40.0	83.0	207.0	706.0

Note: 2 cells (8.3%) have expected count less than 5. The minimum expected count is 3.98. In line with these findings, Pearson chi-squared resulted in X^2 (15, N = 706) = 244.405, p < .001. Cramer's V resulted in .340, p < .001. Cells with adjusted residual values equal to or exceeding an absolute value of 1.96 were marked with an asterisk

stricter performance criteria tend to ensure higher rates of response maintenance. In contrast, more lenient criteria increase variability, with a mixture of both underperformance and overperformance of response maintenance relative to the set criterion.

Table 2.3b presents the chi-squared analysis examining the relationship between performance criteria frequencies and response maintenance rates. The association was statistically significant, $\chi^2(15, N = 699) = 97.91$, $p < .001$, with a small-to-moderate effect size (Cramer's $V = .216$, $p < .001$). Adjusted residuals indicated meaningful deviations across performance criteria frequencies. Single observation of the criterion showed fewer cases performing 11–20% below the target than expected, but fewer cases performing 31% or more below the target. Observing the criterion twice was associated with fewer cases meeting the criterion than expected (adjusted residual = −2.2), more cases 1–10% below the criterion, and more cases 31% or more below the criterion. Three successive observations of the criterion

Table 2.3b Chi-squared analysis for response maintenance rates vs. performance criteria frequencies

PC frequencies		Response maintenance rates: Met PC	1–10% fewer than PC	11–20% fewer than PC	21–30% fewer than PC	31% or more fewer than PC	Higher than PC	Total cases
1	Count	14	16	11	7	3	22	73
	Expected count	16.8	18.4	4.1	4.2	8.7	20.9	73.0
	Adjusted residual	−.8	−.7	3.7*	1.5	−2.2*	.3	
2	Count	77	122	14	18	58	97	386
	Expected count	88.9	97.2	21.5	22.1	45.8	110.4	386.0
	Adjusted residual	−2.2*	4.3*	−2.5*	−1.3	2.9*	−2.3*	
3	Count	62	14	11	15	22	73	197
	Expected count	45.4	49.6	11.0	11.3	23.4	56.4	197.0
	Adjusted residual	3.3*	−6.9*	.0	1.3	−.4	3.1*	
More than 3	Count	8	24	3	0	0	8	43
	Expected count	9.9	10.8	2.4	2.5	5.1	12.3	43.0
	Adjusted residual	−.7	4.8*	.4	−1.7	−2.5*	−1.5	
Total	Count	161	176	39	40	83	200	699
	Expected count	161.0	176.0	39.0	40.0	83.0	200.0	699.0

Note: 4 cells (16.7%) have expected count less than 5. The minimum expected count is 2.40. In line with these findings, Pearson chi-squared resulted in X^2 (15, $N = 699$) = 97.905, $p < .001$. Cramer's V resulted in .216, $p < .001$. Cells with adjusted residual values equal to or exceeding an absolute value of 1.96 were marked with an asterisk

resulted in significantly more cases meeting the criterion than expected and fewer cases 1–10% below the criterion, while the proportion of cases exceeding the criterion was also higher than expected. In contrast, more than three observations produced fewer cases performing 31% or more below the criterion, but also more cases 1–10% below the criterion. Overall, these findings suggest that three successive observations of performance criteria tend to optimize response maintenance, balancing the proportion of cases meeting the criterion while minimizing extreme underperformance. Both minimal (one to two) and excessive (>3) applications appear less effective in producing consistent maintenance outcomes.

I also performed a regression analysis to identify the predictive effect of performance criteria levels on response maintenance rates (using continuous variable coding of the levels and response maintenance rates), as in the Fuller and Fienup (2018) study. All performance criteria across 70 studies were converted to percentages whenever possible. Figure 2.2 shows the linear regression analysis of performance criteria levels on response maintenance rates. The results revealed a statistically significant model, $F(1, 700) = 133.008$, $p < .001$, indicating that higher performance criteria levels can play a significant role in achieving higher response maintenance rates of behaviors after intervention is terminated ($\beta_1 = .636$, $p < .001$). However, the $R^2 = .16$ indicates that the model explains only 16% of the variance in response maintenance rates.

When viewed collectively, findings from both empirical research and systematic reviews converge on the conclusion that performance criteria represent a pivotal variable influencing the durability of behavior change. Experimental studies manipulating performance criterion levels (e.g., Fuller & Fienup, 2018; Longino et al., 2022; Pitts & Hoerger, 2021; Richling et al., 2019) have consistently demonstrated that higher accuracy standards, typically 90% to 100%, yield stronger and more stable response maintenance than lower criteria (≤80%). These results align closely with large-scale review data (McDougale et al., 2020; Wong et al., 2022), which similarly identified higher and clearly defined criteria as predictors of robust post-intervention performance. The present review builds upon this foundation by incorporating both skill-acquisition and behavior-reduction studies, demonstrating that the predictive role of performance criteria extends beyond acquisition tasks also to influence the long-term suppression or reduction of target behaviors. Although separate data are not presented, it can be stated that the function of performance criteria in response maintenance follows a similar pattern across increasing and decreasing targets. Furthermore, although findings on the frequency component remain mixed, empirical work (e.g., Schneider et al., 2022) suggests minimal added benefit of

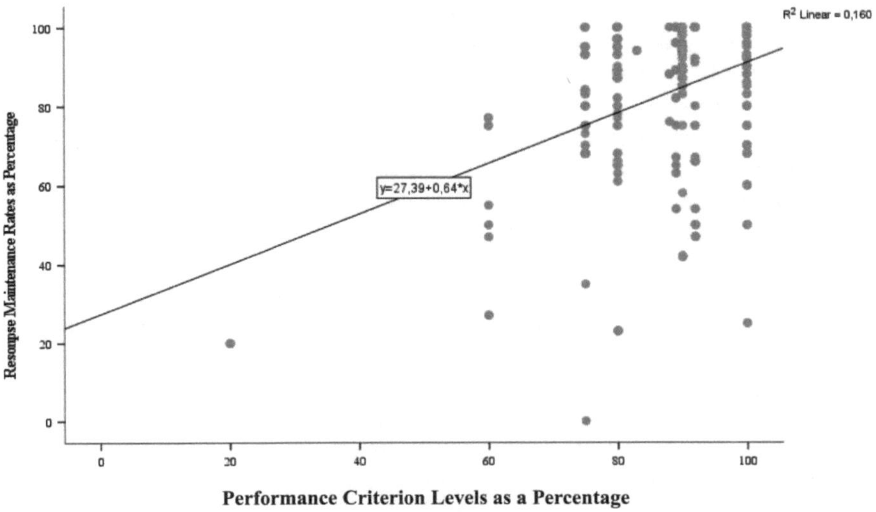

Fig. 2.2 Regression analysis of performance criteria levels on response maintenance (*Source*: Aydin, n.d.)

multi-session criteria, while the present analysis and the Wong et al. (2022) study identified higher response maintenance under moderate frequencies (2 or 3), both studies indicate that performance criteria frequency interacts with practitioner and task characteristics in shaping behavioral durability. Chi-squared and regression analyses further confirmed that stricter criteria levels significantly predict maintenance outcomes; however, the variance explained remains modest (R^2 = .16). In sum, these results reinforce that performance criteria are not arbitrary procedural decisions but rather functional study variables that determine the persistence of behavioral change across both skill acquisition and behavior reduction domains.

2.3 Effects of Performance Criteria on Generalization

This section elaborates on the impact of performance criteria on the generalization rates of trained behavior to new contexts. Regarding this topic, there is no specific empirical study; however, the previous two systematic reviews and my recent review focus on this topic, as well as response maintenance, as explained in the previous subsection. These reviews have compiled studies in the field of behavior analysis.

Remember that McDougale et al. (2020) reviewed 157 skill-acquisition studies (2015–2017) from *JABA*, *Behavior Analysis in Practice*, and *Behavioral Interventions* to identify how researchers report performance criteria and whether they include generalization probes. The findings revealed that only 41% of studies were programmed or tested for generalization. Among these, the most frequent generalization type was across stimuli (17%), followed by across environments (10%), across therapists (6%), across behaviors (5%), and across clients (5%). The majority of studies (59%) included no explicit programming for, or measurement of, generalization following skill acquisition. In sum, generalization was under-assessed and under-reported in the reviewed studies, and its relationship to performance criteria levels was not questioned in the McDougale et al. study.

Recall that Wong et al. (2022) conducted a systematic and statistical review of 212 skill-acquisition studies (2017–2019), examining 759 participant-level cases. Their goal was to evaluate whether performance criterion levels predicted the strength of generalization after training. Across studies, generalization was reported in approximately two-thirds of cases, most often assessed across stimuli, settings, or individuals, and typically within 4 weeks of reaching performance criterion. Using chi-squared analyses, Wong et al. found a significant positive association between higher performance criteria (≥90–100%) and the occurrence of generalization across participant groups. Practitioners who had been treated to stricter performance criteria levels were more likely to demonstrate the target response in novel contexts or with untreated exemplars. In contrast, studies employing lower criteria (≤80–89%) were less likely to report successful generalization.

Importantly, Wong et al. also examined the frequency component of performance criteria and found that multi-session meeting level (e.g., meeting criterion across two or more consecutive sessions) was significantly more likely to yield generalization than a single session. In other words, not only higher accuracy levels but also greater stability in performance levels across sessions predicted stronger generalization outcomes. These results extended prior findings on maintenance by showing that the same pattern applies to generalization. Both higher performance levels and repeated attainment of those criteria increase the likelihood of behavior transfer beyond the treatment context. Wong et al. interpreted this as evidence that the performance-criteria components function as meaningful independent variables influencing generalization outcomes, rather than serving solely as procedural thresholds of trained behaviors.

Consequently, the two studies highlight that generalization is not underrepresented in behavioral literature. Wong et al. (2022) also reported that generalization is closely tied to the performance criteria employed during acquisition. McDougale et al. (2020) exposed the field's descriptive requirements; most notably, the frequent absence of generalization assessment and performance criteria documentation, while Wong et al. (2022) provided empirical confirmation that higher performance criteria promote broader and more reliable generalization. Both highlight that systematic programming for generalization and transparent reporting of criterion components are essential for ensuring that acquired skills are not only acquired but also functionally meaningful and generalized across contexts.

As with the analyses conducted for response maintenance, I performed both descriptive and inferential statistical analyses to examine the relationships between study variables and generalization rates and to identify factors associated with greater generalizability of trained behaviors across novel contexts. Figure 2.3 presents the descriptive findings from the studies in which generalization data were collected. As shown in the figure, generalization data were reported in only 25% ($n = 44$) of the reviewed studies ($n = 176$), encompassing a total of 302 cases (11% of the 2661 cases), after excluding unanalyzable data from the sample. More studies conducted one or two sessions to evaluate the generalizability of trained behaviors to novel contexts, while a substantial number conducted three or more sessions to

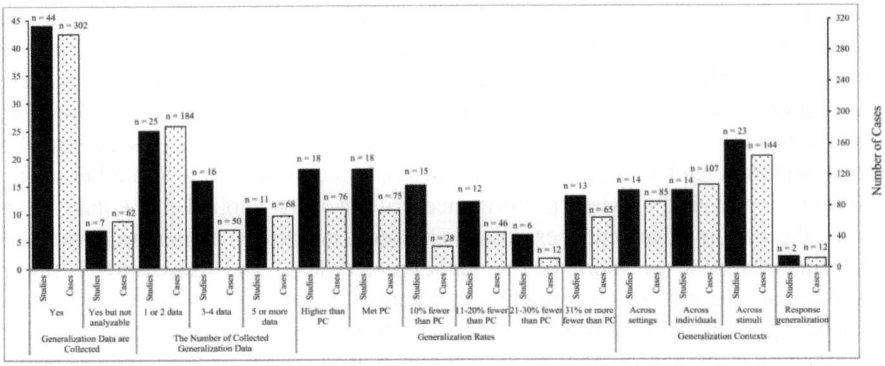

Fig. 2.3 Descriptive features of generalization data of the included studies from JABA issues between 2019 and 2023. PC: Performance Criteria

collect generalization data. Generalization rates generally met or exceeded the performance criteria levels set in the studies. However, a substantial number of studies reported lower generalization outcomes than performance criteria levels. Generalization contexts occurred across four main domains: settings, individuals, stimuli, and responses. The most favored condition was generalization across stimuli, while the least preferred condition was response generalization. Notably, four of the 44 studies, encompassing a total of 43 cases, targeted the reduction of problem behaviors based on predetermined performance criterion levels. By including these studies, the present review broadens the sample and aims to strengthen the generalizability of prior findings stemming from two previous review and analysis studies.

Tables 2.4a and 2.4b show the results of chi-squared analyses in terms of the relationship between generalization rates and performance criteria components. As shown in Table 2.4a, performance criteria levels were significantly associated with generalization rates, $\chi^2(15, N = 291) = 222.01$, $p < .001$ (Fisher's exact test), with a moderate-to-strong effect size (Cramer's $V = .473$, $p < .001$). Specifically, studies using lenient performance criteria levels (i.e., <80% for increasing behaviors or >20% for decreasing behaviors) showed disproportionately higher rates of generalization that exceeded the established criteria than expected. However, these levels also corresponded to a higher-than-expected proportion of cases (31% or more) that performed below the intended criteria. In contrast, stricter criteria (100% or 0%) were associated with significantly more cases meeting the set performance criteria. The mid-range performance criteria levels (80–89% or 11–20%, and 90–99% or 1–10%) generally aligned with expected distributions, showing no substantial deviations. Overall, these findings suggest that lenient performance criteria may promote broader generalization beyond the treatment context, albeit at the cost of reduced consistency in meeting target performance levels. In contrast, stricter performance criteria ensure higher fidelity to performance goals but may limit generalization across contexts.

As shown in Table 2.4b, the association between performance criteria frequencies and generalization rates was statistically significant, $\chi^2(15, N = 289) = 86.36$, $p < .001$ (Fisher's exact test), with a moderate effect size (Cramer's $V = .338$, $p < .001$). The adjusted residuals indicated notable deviations across performance criteria frequency levels. Specifically, studies that applied performance criteria twice exhibited higher-than-expected rates of generalization exceeding the criterion and slightly more cases that fell 11–20% below the target. By contrast, observing the criterion three consecutive times resulted in significantly more cases meeting the target performance levels and fewer instances of outcomes 31% or more below the criterion. Interestingly, when performance criteria were applied more than three times, the pattern reversed; these cases showed a markedly higher proportion of performances 31% or more below the expected level and substantially fewer instances of meeting or exceeding the set criteria. Consequently, these findings suggest that applying performance criteria two or three consecutive times may optimize generalization and target attainment, whereas both minimal (single) and excessive (more than three) applications appear less effective, either due to insufficient

Table 2.4a Chi-squared analysis for generalization rates vs. performance criteria levels

		Generalization rates						
PC levels		Met PC	1–10% fewer than PC	11–20% fewer than PC	21–30% fewer than PC	31% or more fewer than PC	Higher than PC	Total cases
<80% or >20%	Count	0	4	0	0	22	37	63
	Expected count	16.2	5.8	9.7	2.6	13.2	15.4	63.0
	Adjusted residual	−5.3*	−.9	−3.8*	−1.9	3.1*	7.2*	
80–89% or 11–20%	Count	7	6	10	5	11	20	59
	Expected count	15.2	5.5	9.1	2.4	12.4	14.4	59.0
	Adjusted residual	−2.7*	.3	.4	1.9	−.5	1.9	
90–99% or 1–10%	Count	2	10	4	0	20	14	50
	Expected count	12.9	4.6	7.7	2.1	10.5	12.2	50.0
	Adjusted residual	−3.9*	2.9*	−1.6	−1.6	3.6*	.7	
100% or 0%	Count	66	7	31	7	8	0	119
	Expected count	30.7	11.0	18.4	4.9	24.9	29.0	119.0
	Adjusted residual	9.6*	−1.7	4.2*	1.3	−5.0*	−8.1*	
Total	Count	75	27	45	12	61	71	291
	Expected count	75.0	27.0	45.0	12.0	61.0	71.0	291.0

Note: 5 cells (20.8%) have an expected count of less than 5. The minimum expected count is 2.06. In line with these findings, Fisher's exact test resulted in X^2 (15, N = 291) = 222.010, $p < .001$. Cramer's V resulted in .473, $p < .001$. Cells with adjusted residual values equal to or exceeding an absolute value of 1.96 were marked with an asterisk

observation of the trained behaviors in a single context at a pre-determined level or to potential overtraining effects that reduce performance consistency across contexts.

As I did with response maintenance rates, I also performed a regression analysis to explore the predictive effect of performance criteria levels on generalization rates. Figure 2.4 shows the linear regression analysis of performance criteria levels on generalization rates. The results revealed a statistically significant model, $F(1, 288) = 43.223$, $p < .001$, indicating that higher performance criteria levels can play a significant role in achieving higher generalization rates of trained behaviors across various contexts ($\beta_1 = .680$, $p < .001$). However, the $R^2 = .13$ indicates that the model explains only 13% of the variance in generalization rates.

When examining the three reviews collectively, the convergent evidence from systematic reviews and the present analysis underscores that performance criteria

Table 2.4b Chi-squared analysis for generalization rates vs. performance criteria frequencies

PC frequencies		Generalization rates: Met PC	1–10% fewer than PC	11–20% fewer than PC	21–30% fewer than PC	31% or more fewer than PC	Higher than PC	Total cases
1	Count	3	2	6	0	5	9	25
	Expected count	6.5	2.2	3.9	1.0	5.3	6.1	25.0
	Adjusted residual	−1.7	−.1	1.2	−1.1	−.1	1.4	
2	Count	26	15	29	2	29	44	145
	Expected count	37.6	12.5	22.6	6.0	30.6	35.6	145.0
	Adjusted residual	−3.1*	1.0	2.1*	−2.4*	−.5	2.3*	
3	Count	44	7	9	6	6	16	88
	Expected count	22.8	7.6	13.7	3.7	18.6	21.6	88.0
	Adjusted residual	6.2*	−.3	−1.7	1.5	−3.9*	−1.7	
More than 3	Count	2	1	1	4	21	2	31
	Expected count	8.0	2.7	4.8	1.3	6.5	7.6	31.0
	Adjusted residual	−2.6*	−1.1	−2.0*	2.6*	6.7*	−2.5*	
Total	Count	75	25	45	12	61	71	289
	Expected count	75.0	25.0	45.0	12.0	61.0	71.0	289.0

Note: 7 cells (29.2%) have an expected count of less than 5. The minimum expected count is 1.04. In line with these findings, Fisher's exact test resulted in X^2 (15, N = 289) = 86.356, $p < .001$. Cramer's V resulted in .338, $p < .001$. Cells with adjusted residual values equal to or exceeding an absolute value of 1.96 were marked with an asterisk

can be a decisive factor not only for maintaining but also for generalizing trained behaviors across contexts. Although the number of generalization assessments remains low in the published intervention studies, the available data consistently indicate that higher criteria (≥90–100%) facilitate stronger and more consistent transfer of learning to novel settings, stimuli, individuals, or responses. Findings from the present review further indicate that while higher performance criteria for levels and moderate criteria for frequencies (e.g., 2 or 3) are positively associated with generalization. However, this relation appears to be influenced by additional procedural and participant characteristics, rather than reflecting a purely direct or linear effect. The inclusion of behavior-reduction studies further strengthens this conclusion, demonstrating that stricter performance-criterion levels (e.g., 0 to 20%) are equally critical for ensuring the durable suppression of maladaptive responses across contexts. At the same time, the modest proportion of variance explained by performance criteria (R^2 = .13) implies that while performance criterion level is a

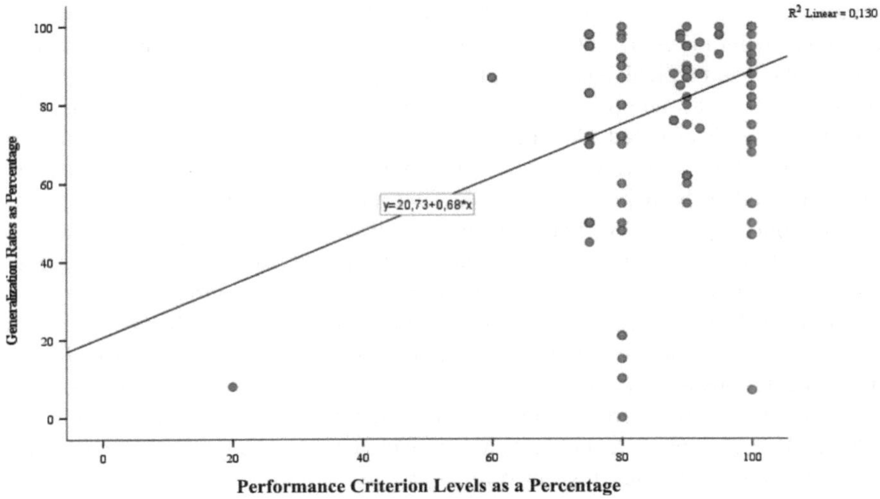

Fig. 2.4 Regression analysis of performance criteria levels on generalization rates (*Source*: Aydin, n.d.)

necessary condition for generalization, it is not a sufficient one; other procedural and participant variables likely moderate this relationship. Overall, these findings reinforce the conceptual parallel between response maintenance and generalization: both can reflect the durability of learning, and both can systematically be shaped by how "performance criteria" are defined during acquisition. Therefore, the establishment and transparent reporting of rigorous, empirically validated performance criteria should be regarded as central features of intervention design and evaluation in behavioral intervention studies.

2.4 Potential Variables to Be Considered in Determining Performance Criteria

Both systematic reviews and analyses, as well as empirical studies, clearly indicate that setting performance criteria at higher levels (90% and more for increase, 10% or lower for decrease) and moderate frequencies (2 or 3) produces more durable and generalizable behavioral change than setting criteria at lower levels or at very low (single) or very high (more than 3) frequencies. However, as emphasized in Chap. 1, identifying optimal performance criteria can vary depending on participant characteristics and the type of dependent variables being studied. Although both maintenance and generalization are indicators of socially meaningful behavioral change, we also need to focus on these variables to observe a clear, socially meaningful behavioral change.

To my knowledge, no study to date has evaluated the relationships between other study variables and the assignment of performance criteria. Using the same data sample from my review, I coded participant characteristics in terms of diagnosis category, including ASD, intellectual disability (ID), other developmental disabilities (ODDs), and typical; age ranges, including preschool (0–5), elementary (6–13), secondary (14–18), and post-secondary (19 or older); and gender, including male, female, and undetermined. Note that I coded diagnoses with more than one category (e.g., ASD + ID) separately, that is, within both ASD and ID categories. I also separated and coded the dependent variables as follows: academic skills, social communication/social skills, verbal language, safety skills, daily living skills, treatment skills, destructive/reducing behaviors, and health-related skills. Each of these categories was cross-tabulated with the performance-criteria components using chi-squared analysis to examine relationships between the performance-criteria components and other potential study variables. Since there was no statistically significant relationship between gender and performance criteria components, these crossed comparisons were excluded. Other comparisons were presented in Tables 2.5a, 2.5b, 2.6a, 2.6b, 2.7a and 2.7b, accompanied by a and b for performance criteria levels and frequencies, respectively.

As shown in Table 2.5a, the chi-squared analyses indicated that certain performance criteria levels were significantly associated with specific task types. Overall, these findings suggest that certain task types are more closely associated with specific performance criteria levels. For instance, social communication and social skills were more often targeted using lower performance criteria levels (<80%) and less frequently with the highest performance criteria levels (100%). Verbal language skills tended to involve mid-range performance criteria levels (80–89%) more frequently, whereas the highest performance criteria levels were applied less often. Behavior reduction tasks were less commonly addressed at the highest performance-criteria level (0%), whereas health-related skills were more frequently associated with this top-level criterion (100%). Overall, the chi-squared test was significant, $X^2(24, N = 238) = 47.458$, $p < .001$, and Cramer's $V = .262$ indicated a moderate association. These results demonstrate that task types meaningfully influence the selection and distribution of performance criteria levels in published studies.

Table 2.5b showed that certain task types were also associated with specific performance criteria frequencies. Mid-range frequencies (2 or 3) were statistically significant in several tasks. Verbal language skills were more often targeted using three consecutive sessions than expected, whereas behavior reduction tasks were more frequently addressed at the two frequencies. Health-related skills, in contrast, were less commonly associated with the three frequencies but more often targeted using the highest frequency level (more than three). Other skill types, including academic, social communication, daily living, safety, and treatment skills, did not show statistically significant associations with specific performance criteria frequencies. Overall, the chi-squared test was significant, $X^2(24, N = 228) = 34.434$, $p < .05$, while Cramer's $V = .224$ indicated a weak to moderate association. These results demonstrate that task types meaningfully influence the frequency with which performance criteria are applied.

As shown in Table 2.6a, the chi-squared analyses indicated that certain performance criteria levels were significantly associated with participant diagnosis. Overall, these findings suggest that different participant groups are more closely associated with specific performance criteria levels. For instance, participants with ASD were more often targeted using mid-range performance criteria levels (80–89% or 11–20%) and less frequently with the highest performance criteria levels (100%

Table 2.5a Chi-squared analysis for dependent variables vs. PC (performance criteria) levels

Dependent variables		PC levels				
		<80% or > 20%	80–89% or 11–20%	90–99% or 1–10%	100% or 0%	Total
Academic skills	Count	0	6	3	15	24
	Expected count	2.0	7.4	4.0	10.5	24.0
	Adjusted residual	−1.6	−.7	−.6	1.9	
Social communication/ Social skills	Count	8	16	12	16	52
	Expected count	4.4	16.1	8.8	22.8	52.0
	Adjusted residual	2.0*	.0	1.3	−2.1*	
Verbal language	Count	5	23	8	15	51
	Expected count	4.3	15.8	8.6	22.3	51.0
	Adjusted residual	.4	2.5*	−.3	−2.3*	
Safety skills	Count	1	0	0	4	5
	Expected count	.4	1.5	.8	2.2	5.0
	Adjusted residual	.9	−1.5	−1.0	1.6	
Daily living skills	Count	3	3	2	8	16
	Expected count	1.3	4.9	2.7	7.0	16.0
	Adjusted residual	1.5	−1.1	−.5	.5	
A training for a treatment skill	Count	1	7	5	18	31
	Expected count	2.6	9.6	5.2	13.6	31.0
	Adjusted residual	−1.1	−1.1	−.1	1.7	
Destructive/reducing behaviors	Count	3	17	10	10	40
	Expected count	3.4	12.4	6.7	17.5	40.0
	Adjusted residual	−.2	1.7	1.5	−2.6*	
Health-related skills	Count	0	1	2	16	19
	Expected count	1.6	5.9	3.2	8.3	19.0
	Adjusted residual	−1.4	−2.5*	−.8	3.7*	

(*continued*)

Table 2.5a (continued)

Dependent variables		PC levels <80% or > 20%	80–89% or 11–20%	90–99% or 1–10%	100% or 0%	Total
Total	Count	21	73	42	102	238
	Expected count	21.0	73.0	42.0	102.0	238.0

Note: 19 cells (59.4%) have expected count less than 5. The minimum expected count is .42. In line with these findings, Fisher's exact test resulted in X^2 (24, $N = 238$) = 47.458, $p < .001$. Cramer's V resulted in .262, $p < .001$. Cells with adjusted residual values equal to or exceeding an absolute value of 1.96 were marked with an asterisk

Table 2.5b Chi-squared analysis for dependent variables vs. PC frequencies

Dependent variables		PC frequencies 1	2	3	More than 3	Total
Academic skills	Count	5	10	8	0	23
	Expected count	2.7	10.2	9.3	.8	23.0
	Adjusted residual	1.6	−.1	−.6	−.9	
Social communication/social skills	Count	7	27	16	2	52
	Expected count	6.1	23.1	21.1	1.7	52.0
	Adjusted residual	.4	1.2	−1.6	.2	
Verbal language	Count	3	20	28	0	51
	Expected count	6.0	22.6	20.7	1.7	51.0
	Adjusted residual	−1.5	−.8	2.3*	−1.5	
Safety skills	Count	0	2	3	0	5
	Expected count	.6	2.2	2.0	.2	5.0
	Adjusted residual	−.8	−.2	.9	−.4	
Daily living skills	Count	0	5	10	1	16
	Expected count	1.9	7.1	6.5	.5	16.0
	Adjusted residual	−1.5	−1.1	1.8	.7	
A training for a treatment skill	Count	4	10	12	2	28
	Expected count	3.3	12.4	11.4	.9	28.0
	Adjusted residual	.5	−1.0	.3	1.2	
Destructive/reducing behaviors	Count	2	22	11	1	36
	Expected count	4.2	16.0	14.6	1.2	36.0
	Adjusted residual	−1.2	2.2*	−1.3	−.2	
Health-related skills	Count	4	8	3	2	17
	Expected count	2.0	7.5	6.9	.6	17.0
	Adjusted residual	1.6	.2	−2.0*	2.0*	
Total	Count	25	104	91	8	228
	Expected count	25.0	104.0	91.0	8.0	228.0

Note: 20 cells (62.5%) have expected count less than 5. The minimum expected count is .17. In line with these findings, Fisher's exact test resulted in X^2 (24, $N = 228$) = 34.434, $p < .05$. Cramer's V resulted in .224, $p > .05$. Cells with adjusted residual values equal to or exceeding an absolute value of 1.96 were marked with an asterisk

Table 2.6a Chi-squared analysis for participant diagnosis vs. PC levels

Participant diagnosis		PC levels <80% or >20%	80–89% or 11–20%	90–99% or 1–10%	100% or 0%	Total
ASD	Count	36	161	76	166	439
	Expected count	33.0	115.3	69.5	221.2	439.0
	Adjusted residual	.7	6.6*	1.1	−7.0*	
ID	Count	5	8	9	17	39
	Expected count	2.9	10.2	6.2	19.7	39.0
	Adjusted residual	1.3	−.8	1.3	−.9	
ODDs	Count	1	6	1	10	18
	Expected count	1.4	4.7	2.8	9.1	18.0
	Adjusted residual	−.3	.7	−1.2	.4	
Typical	Count	35	94	76	323	528
	Expected count	39.7	138.7	83.5	266.1	528.0
	Adjusted residual	−1.1	−6.4*	−1.3	7.1*	
Total	Count	77	269	162	516	1024
	Expected count	77.0	269.0	162.0	516.0	1024.0

Note: Four cells (25%) have an expected count of less than 5. The minimum expected count is 1.35. In line with these findings, Fisher's exact test resulted in X^2 (9, N = 1024) = 66.110, $p < .001$. Cramer's V resulted in .146, $p < .001$. Cells with adjusted residual values equal to or exceeding an absolute value of 1.96 were marked with an asterisk

Table 2.6b Chi-squared analysis for participant diagnosis vs. PC frequencies

Participant diagnosis		PC frequencies 1	2	3	More than 3	Total
ASD	Count	26	258	136	13	433
	Expected count	64.4	210.6	147.6	10.3	433.0
	Adjusted residual	−7.1*	6.3*	−1.6	1.1	
ID	Count	6	11	22	0	39
	Expected count	5.8	19.0	13.3	.9	39.0
	Adjusted residual	.1	−2.6*	3.0*	−1.0	
ODDs	Count	5	5	8	0	18
	Expected count	2.7	8.8	6.1	.4	18.0
	Adjusted residual	1.6	−1.8	.9	−.7	
Typical	Count	100	174	148	9	431
	Expected count	64.1	209.7	146.9	10.3	431.0
	Adjusted residual	6.7*	−4.7*	.1	−.6	
Total	Count	137	448	314	22	921
	Expected count	137.0	448.0	314.0	22.0	921.0

Note: Three cells (18.8%) have an expected count of less than 5. The minimum expected count is .43. In line with these findings, Pearson chi-squared resulted in X^2 (9, N = 921) = 76.087, $p < .001$. Cramer's V resulted in .166, $p < .001$. Cells with adjusted residual values equal to or exceeding an absolute value of 1.96 were marked with an asterisk

Table 2.7a Chi-squared analysis for participant ages vs. PC levels

Participant ages		PC levels <80% or > 20%	80–89% or 11–20%	90–99% or 1–10%	100% or 0%	Total
Preschool (0–5)	Count	24	99	54	85	262
	Expected count	18.8	71.3	39.9	132.1	262.0
	Adjusted residual	1.5	4.5*	2.8*	−6.8*	
Elementary (6–13)	Count	19	86	50	128	283
	Expected count	20.3	77.0	43.1	142.7	283.0
	Adjusted residual	−.3	1.4	1.4	−2.1*	
Secondary (14–18)	Count	1	16	10	11	38
	Expected count	2.7	10.3	5.8	19.2	38.0
	Adjusted residual	−1.1	2.1*	1.9	−2.7*	
Post-secondary (19 or older)	Count	26	65	35	269	395
	Expected count	28.3	107.4	60.2	199.1	395.0
	Adjusted residual	−.6	−6.2*	−4.6*	9.1*	
Total	Count	70	266	149	493	978
	Expected count	70.0	266.0	149.0	493.0	978.0

Note: 1 cell (6.3%) has an expected count less than 5. The minimum expected count is 2.72. In line with these findings, Pearson chi-squared resulted in X^2 (9, N = 978) = 100.487, $p < .001$. Cramer's V resulted in .185, $p < .001$. Cells with adjusted residual values equal to or exceeding an absolute value of 1.96 were marked with an asterisk

or 0%). In contrast, typically developing participants were less often addressed at mid-range levels but more frequently targeted at the highest performance criteria levels. Participants with ID and ODDs did not show statistically significant associations with specific performance criteria levels. Overall, the chi-squared test was significant, $X^2(9, N = 1024) = 66.110$, $p < .001$, and Cramer's $V = .146$ indicated a weak to moderate association. These results demonstrate that participant diagnosis meaningfully influences the selection and distribution of performance criteria levels in published studies.

Table 2.6b showed that participant diagnosis was also associated with specific performance criteria frequencies. Participants with ASD were less often targeted using a single observation but more frequently with two repetitions. Participants with ID were more frequently targeted at three repetitions and less frequently at two repetitions. Typically developing participants were more often targeted using a single repetition and less frequently with two repetitions. ODDs did not show

Table 2.7b Chi-squared analysis for participant ages vs. PC frequencies

Participant ages		PC frequencies 1	2	3	More than 3	Total
Preschool (0–5)	Count	11	142	83	4	240
	Expected count	35.9	113.0	85.0	6.0	240.0
	Adjusted residual	−5.3*	4.4*	−.3	−1.0	
Elementary (6–13)	Count	59	121	87	1	268
	Expected count	40.1	126.2	94.9	6.7	268.0
	Adjusted residual	3.9*	−.8	−1.2	−2.7*	
Secondary (14–18)	Count	2	14	13	9	38
	Expected count	5.7	17.9	13.5	1.0	38.0
	Adjusted residual	−1.7	−1.3	−.2	8.5*	
Post-secondary (19 or older)	Count	59	135	127	8	329
	Expected count	49.3	154.9	116.6	8.3	329.0
	Adjusted residual	1.9	−2.8*	1.5	−.1	
Total	Count	131	412	310	22	875
	Expected count	131.0	412.0	310.0	22.0	875.0

Note: 1 cell (6.3%) has an expected count less than 5. The minimum expected count is .96. In line with these findings, Pearson chi-squared resulted in X^2 (9, $N = 875$) = 116.539, $p < .001$. Cramer's *V* resulted in .211, $p < .001$. Cells with adjusted residual values equal to or exceeding an absolute value of 1.96 were marked with an asterisk

statistically significant associations with specific performance criteria frequencies. Overall, the chi-squared test was significant, $X^2(9, N = 921) = 76.087$, $p < .001$, while Cramer's $V = .166$ indicated a weak to moderate association. These results demonstrate that participant diagnosis meaningfully influences the frequency with which performance criteria are applied.

Table 2.7a presents the chi-squared analysis examining the relationship between participant age groups and performance criteria levels. The results indicate that different age groups are associated with specific performance criteria levels. Preschool-aged participants (0–5 years) were more frequently targeted using mid-range performance criteria levels (80–89% or 11–20% and 90–99% or 1–10%) and less often with the highest level (100% or 0%). Elementary-aged participants (6–13 years) largely followed expected distributions, with a slight underrepresentation at the highest level. Adolescents (14–18 years) were more often addressed at mid-range levels and less frequently at the highest level. Post-secondary participants (19 years or older) showed the opposite pattern, with less frequent use of mid-range levels but more frequent targeting at the highest performance criteria level. The chi-squared test was significant, $X^2(9, N = 978) = 100.487$, $p < .001$, and Cramer's $V = .185$, indicating a weak to moderate association. These findings suggest that participant age plays a meaningful role in determining the performance criteria assigned in intervention studies.

Table 2.7b shows the relationship between participant age groups and the frequencies accompanying the performance-criteria levels. Preschool-aged participants (0–5 years) were less often targeted with a single observation but more frequently with two repetitions. Elementary-aged participants (6–13 years) were more frequently addressed with one repetition and less often with more than three repetitions. Adolescents (14–18 years) were more commonly involved in interventions using higher repetition frequencies (more than three), while post-secondary (19 or older) participants were less frequently targeted at mid-range frequencies (two repetitions). Overall, the chi-squared test was significant, $X^2(9, N = 875) = 116.539, p < .001$, with a Cramer's V of .211, indicating a weak to moderate association. These results highlight that age influences the frequency with which performance criteria levels are applied in practice, reflecting tailored approaches that depend on participants' developmental stage.

2.5 Concluding Remarks

The evidence reviewed in this chapter demonstrates that performance criteria play a pivotal role in determining both the durability and generalization of treated behaviors. Across systematic reviews, empirical studies, and the present analyses, higher performance-criterion levels (≥90% for skill acquisition; ≤10% for behavior reduction) and moderate frequencies (typically 2 or 3 consecutive sessions) were consistently associated with stronger response maintenance and broader generalization. Conversely, lower levels or minimal/excessive frequencies of performance criteria tended to produce less reliable and more variable outcomes. Performance-criteria components interact with participant and task characteristics, such as age, diagnosis, and task type, highlighting that optimal criteria are changeable, not standardizable, and should be tailored to the practitioner and context. For instance, younger participants or those acquiring social communication skills may benefit from moderate criterion levels and repetitions, whereas older participants require the highest levels (i.e., 100% or 0%). Even when targeting health-related skills, the highest performance criteria components (i.e., 100% with more than three consecutive sessions) are often required. Accurately defining and applying performance criteria is therefore critical, not only for evaluating the effectiveness of interventions but also for ensuring that behavioral changes are durable, generalizable, and socially meaningful. Collecting maintenance and generalization data, alongside transparent reporting of criterion components, strengthens the technological and empirical foundations of behavioral research. By recognizing performance criteria as functional study variables rather than arbitrary procedural decisions, researchers and practitioners can optimize intervention outcomes, supporting long-term behavior acquisition, behavior reduction, and overall developmental progress across diverse populations.

References

Aydin, O. (n.d.). *Impact of performance criteria assignments on response maintenance and generalization: an investigation across study variables.*

Carlson, J. G., & Minke, K. A. (1975). Fixed and ascending criteria for unit mastery learning. *Journal of Educational Psychology, 67*(1), 96–101. https://doi.org/10.1037/h0078676

Cordeiro, M. C., Kodak, T., Reidy, J., Stoppleworth, A., Zelinski, K., & Jainga, A. (2022). Comparison of mastery criteria applied to individual targets and stimulus sets on acquisition of tacts, intraverbals, and listener responses. *Journal of Applied Behavior Analysis, 55*(4), 1258–1279. https://doi.org/10.1002/jaba.946

Du, L., Speckman, J., & Fienup, D. M. (2024). Applying "mastery" criteria to sets and individual operants: A replication with preschoolers with disabilities. *Journal of Behavioral Education*, 1–21. https://doi.org/10.1007/s10864-024-09564-6

Epstein, L. H., McKenzie, S. J., Valoski, A., Klein, K. R., & Wing, R. R. (1994). Effects of mastery criteria and contingent reinforcement for family-based child weight control. *Addictive Behaviors, 19*(2), 135–145. https://doi.org/10.1016/0306-4603(94)90038-8

Fienup, D. M., & Brodsky, J. (2017). Effects of mastery criterion on the emergence of derived equivalence relations. *Journal of Applied Behavior Analysis, 50*(4), 843–848. https://doi.org/10.1002/jaba.416

Fuller, J. L., & Fienup, D. M. (2018). A preliminary analysis of mastery criterion level: Effects on response maintenance. *Behavior Analysis in Practice, 11*(1), 1–8. https://doi.org/10.1007/s40617-017-0201-0

Johnston, J. M., & O'Neill, G. (1973). The analysis of performance criteria defining course grades as a determinant of college student academic performance. *Journal of Applied Behavior Analysis, 6*(2), 261–268. https://doi.org/10.1901/jaba.1973.6-261

Kim, J. Y., Fienup, D. M., Draus, C. J., & Wong, K. K. (2023). Differential mastery criteria impact sight word acquisition and maintenance: Application to individual operants and teaching trial doses. *Journal of Applied Behavior Analysis, 56*(2), 388–399. https://doi.org/10.1002/jaba.970

Longino, E., Richling, S. M., McDougale, C. B., & Palmier, J. M. (2022). The effects of mastery criteria on maintenance: A replication with most-to-least prompting. *Behavior Analysis in Practice, 15*(2), 397–405. https://doi.org/10.1007/s40617-021-00562-y

McDougale, C. B., Richling, S. M., Longino, E. B., & O'Rourke, S. A. (2020). Mastery criteria and maintenance: A descriptive analysis of applied research procedures. *Behavior Analysis in Practice, 13*(2), 402–410. https://doi.org/10.1007/s40617-019-00365-2

Pitts, L., & Hoerger, M. L. (2021). Mastery criteria and the maintenance of skills in children with developmental disabilities. *Behavioral Interventions, 36*(2), 522–531. https://doi.org/10.1002/bin.1778

Reiser, R. A., Driscoll, M. P., Farland, D. S., Vergara, A., & Tessmer, M. C. (1986). The effects of various mastery criteria on student performance and attitude in a mastery-oriented course. *ECTJ, 34*(1), 31–38. https://doi.org/10.1007/BF02768360

Reiser, R. A., Driscoll, M. P., & Vergara, A. (1987). The effects of ascending, descending, and fixed criteria on student performance and attitude in a mastery-oriented course. *ECTJ, 35*(4), 195–202. https://doi.org/10.1007/BF02766964

Richling, S. M., Williams, W. L., & Carr, J. E. (2019). The effects of different mastery criteria on the skill maintenance of children with developmental disabilities. *Journal of Applied Behavior Analysis, 52*(3), 701–717. https://doi.org/10.1002/jaba.580

Schneider, A., Fienup, D. M., Gussin, R., & Moss, P. (2022). A preliminary comparison of mastery criterion frequency values: Effects on acquisition and maintenance. *Behavioral Interventions, 37*(3), 306–322. https://doi.org/10.1002/bin.1834

Semb, G. (1974). The effects of mastery criteria and assignment length on college-student test performance. *Journal of Applied Behavior Analysis, 7*(1), 61–69. https://doi.org/10.1901/jaba.1974.7-61

Wong, K. K., Bajwa, T., & Fienup, D. M. (2022). The application of mastery criterion to individual operants and the effects on acquisition and maintenance of responses. *Journal of Behavioral Education, 31*(3), 461–483. https://doi.org/10.1007/s10864-020-09420-3

Wong, K. K., & Fienup, D. M. (2022). Units of analysis in acquisition–performance criteria for "mastery": A systematic replication. *Journal of Applied Behavior Analysis, 55*(3), 971–985. https://doi.org/10.1002/jaba.915

Wong, K. K., Fienup, D. M., Richling, S. M., Keen, A., & Mackay, K. (2022). Systematic review of acquisition mastery criteria and statistical analysis of associations with response maintenance and generalization. *Behavioral Interventions, 37*(4), 993–1012. https://doi.org/10.1002/bin.1885

Zhi, H., Fienup, D. M., Greer, R. D., & Henderson, S. S. (2023). A comparison of stimulus set sizes: Systematic replication with operant analysis acquisition criteria. *Behavior Analysis in Practice, 16*(4), 1138–1150. https://doi.org/10.1007/s40617-023-00793-1

Chapter 3
Optimal Performance Criteria in Autism Intervention Studies

Abstract This chapter focuses specifically on autism intervention research to identify empirically supported thresholds for performance criteria and to clarify how their components function as study variables. Drawing on 161 studies published in leading behavioral journals and two meta-analyses, the chapter synthesizes data from 1407 cases involving 546 autistic participants. Performance-criteria components were examined to assess their relationships with task domains, participant characteristics, response maintenance, generalization, and instructional efficiency. Published autism interventions have shown that specific performance criterion levels are assigned depending on task type and age group. Higher performance-criteria levels were a consistent predictor of higher maintenance and generalization outcomes, but explained only a small portion of the variance. Performance-criteria frequency exerted higher frequencies were associated with longer instructional timelines rather than with superior outcomes. Analyses of trial intensity per session showed that more intensive instruction formats were associated with more intervention time; however, they did not make a difference in achieving criterion levels. This section highlights evidence-based recommendations for selecting and reporting performance criteria in autism studies, offering suggestions for performance-criterion levels that balance efficiency and long-term outcome sustainability, taking into account the characteristics of autistic participants and the types of behaviors being intervened on.

Keywords Performance criteria · Autism · Behavioral interventions · Maintenance · Generalization

---

The original version of the chapter has been revised. A correction to this chapter can be found at https://doi.org/10.1007/978-981-95-8542-7_5

© The Author(s), under exclusive license to Springer Nature Singapore Pte Ltd. 2026, corrected publication 2026

O. Aydin, *Optimal Performance Criteria in Autism Studies*, SpringerBriefs in Modern Perspectives on Disability Research,
https://doi.org/10.1007/978-981-95-8542-7_3

3.1 Determining Optimal Performance Criteria Thresholds for Autism Studies

Considering the general literature, without distinguishing between autism and other developmental disabilities or even typical individuals, Chap. 2 presents valuable evidence on the impact of performance criteria on response maintenance and generalization, and on the optimal selection of performance criteria based on statistically significant indicators for the study variables, such as participant characteristics and dependent variable categories. Chapter 2 indicates that moderate performance-criterion levels (81–90% for increasing behaviors and 11–20% for decreasing behaviors) with two frequencies are generally preferred for autistic participants in autism-related studies, and that this preference is statistically significant. In addition, Chap. 2 suggests that higher performance criteria yield higher response maintenance and generalization in the behavioral intervention field. These provide valuable information to the autism literature, but there is a need to investigate the impact and choice of performance criteria, with a more closely focused examination of autism studies. This investigation will allow us to justify, with evidentiary support, which performance-criterion components to choose when conducting studies with specific study variables in autism research. Therefore, it will also be possible to clarify, based on autism intervention literature, which performance criteria choice may be optimal for the benefit of students with autism spectrum disorder (ASD) in the studied subjects.

This chapter investigates how the performance criteria assigned in autism behavioral intervention studies impact outcomes related to response maintenance and generalization. Additionally, this chapter explores prevailing trends among researchers in the autism field regarding the selection of performance criteria components, analyzing these patterns in relation to key study variables and their statistical significance. Through a meta-analytic synthesis of data derived from the published literature, this chapter aims to provide guidance for researchers, practitioners, and authorities working in autism interventions. It is expected that this synthesis will help illuminate evidentiary thresholds for identifying socially meaningful behavioral change and support the determination of truly evidence-based practices in autism studies, the relevance of which is highlighted in more detail in Chap. 1. To conduct repetitive analyses of Chap. 2 for autism-related intervention studies, the following section first describes the data source used in the analyses. Then, the characteristics of performance criteria and other study variables in autism studies are given. The chapter further provides evidence for selecting appropriate performance criteria components and for the impact of performance criteria on response maintenance and the generalization of trained behaviors. Based on these findings, general recommendations on the selection of optimal performance criteria in autism studies are provided, accounting for key study variables.

3.2 Data Source of the Analyses Conducted for Empirical Evidence

The present study drew on behavioral intervention research in the field of autism to conduct the relevant analyses. Data were obtained from three highly reputable behavioral intervention journals focused on autism, along with also the autism-related data set described in Chap. 2, and studies reporting performance criteria in two autism-focused meta-analyses (Aydin et al., 2025; Sulu et al., 2024) that used performance criteria-based effect size (PCES) suggested by Aydin & Tanious (2022) to calculate effect sizes. The three journals were the *Journal of Autism and Developmental Disorders* (JADD), *Behavioral Interventions* (BI), and the *Journal of Behavioral Education* (JoBE). The autism-related data set from Chap. 2, which includes studies from the *Journal of Applied Behavior Analysis* (JABA), was also incorporated into the current analyses. Issues of JADD, BI, and JoBE were reviewed for a 1-year period, from November 2024 through November 2025, whereas the JABA data set covered studies published between December 2019 and December 2023. In contrast, the two meta-analyses did not impose publication-year restrictions for the beginning year when identifying the included studies; one synthesized daily living skills interventions for autistic individuals (cf. Aydin et al., 2025), and the other synthesized applied behavior analysis–based interventions conducted in Türkiye (cf. Sulu et al., 2024). In total, 161 studies were included: 102 from JABA, 14 from BI, 6 from JADD, 4 from JoBE, and the remaining 35 from the two meta-analyses. Across these studies, 546 individuals with ASD were identified, yielding 1407 analyzable cases, each representing distinguishable data.

3.3 Characteristics of Performance Criteria in Autism Studies

Figures 3.1a and 3.1b show the distributions of performance criteria components in autism studies: levels and frequencies, respectively. In addition, Fig. 3.1c shows the distributions of performance criteria types used in autism studies. As in the analyses of Chap. 2, all performance criteria types were converted to percentages to enable comparisons and statistical analyses of performance criteria set in the included studies. For example, if there is a maximum frequency value in behavior measurements, this value is accepted as 100%. The frequency values performed via intervention are contrasted with the maximum frequency as a percentage. Another example is that if a study has a targeted duration, that duration is treated as 100%. The duration of the target behavior across the intervention phase is compared with the goal duration as a percentage (100%). When reducing behaviors, if a percentage reduction from the baseline average is targeted, the baseline average is treated as 100%. Assume that a study aims to decrease the problem behaviors of autistic individuals by 80% from the baseline average. In this case, the baseline average is set to 100%, and the target is to reduce the problem behavior to 20%. Note that if there were more than 100%

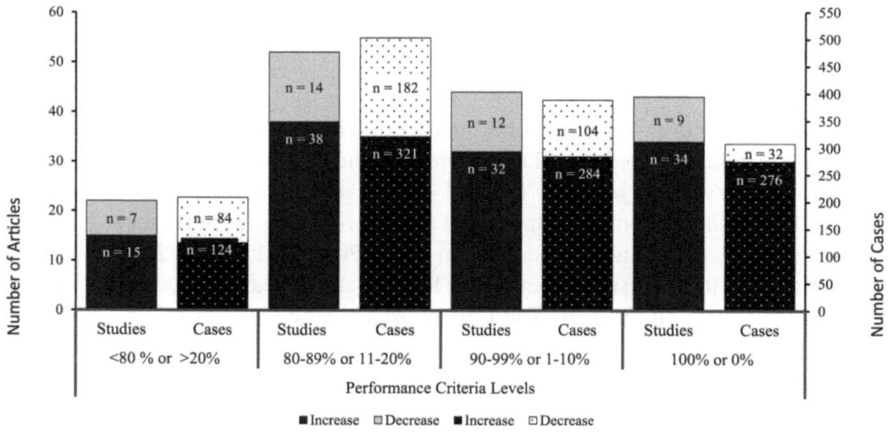

Fig. 3.1a Distributions of performance criteria levels in autism studies

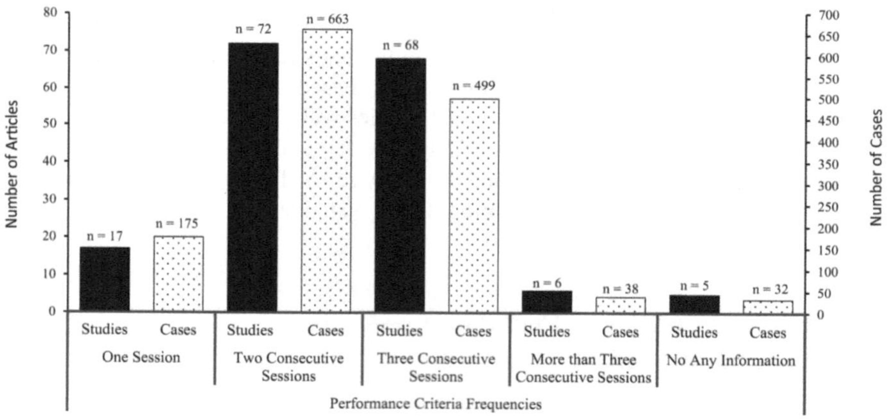

Fig. 3.1b Distributions of performance criteria frequencies in autism studies

in intervention sessions in this case, these data were also accepted as fulfilling the performance criteria at 100%. Accordingly, calculations and evaluations are performed to determine whether performance was met.

Figure 3.1a shows the percentage distribution of performance-criterion levels for both increasing and decreasing behaviors, based on the number of observations under the study and case conditions. For behaviors that are desired to be increased in autism research, the lowest assigned performance criteria were < 80%, and the highest utilized levels were 80–89%. 90 to 99% and full level (100%) were also frequently preferred performance criterion levels in autism studies for increasing behaviors. In behavior-reduction autism studies, the lowest preferred performance criterion was 0%, whereas the highest utilized levels were 11–20%. On the other hand, 1–10% levels were also frequently used as performance-criterion levels in behavior-reduction autism studies.

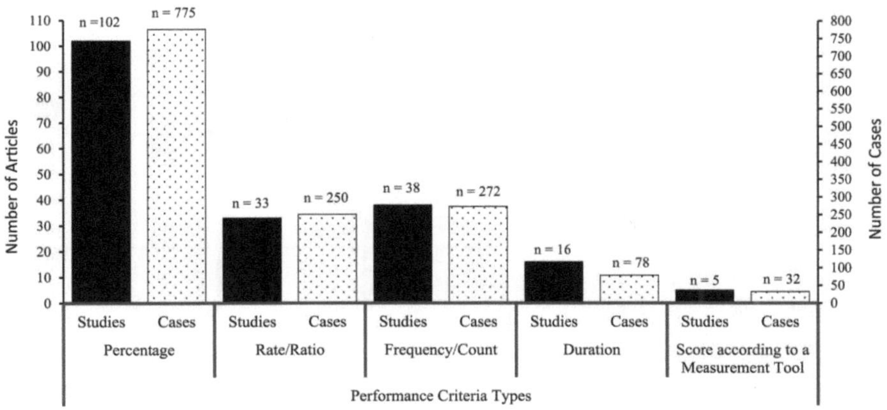

Fig. 3.1c Distributions of performance criteria types in autism studies

Figure 3.1b shows the distribution of performance criterion frequencies. Frequencies two (45% of the reviewed articles) and three (42% of them) were the most frequently observed frequencies associated with performance criteria levels in behavioral interventions in autism studies. Although the figure does not distinguish between increasing and decreasing behaviors, the same frequencies (i.e., 2 or 3) were most common in both. One or more than three frequencies were the least common number of repeated observations used to accompany performance-criteria levels in autism studies.

Figure 3.1c shows the distribution of performance-criterion types for behavioral interventions in autism studies. As shown in this figure, the percentage was the most frequently used performance criterion level (63% of the included studies), whereas the score according to a measurement tool was the least frequently used level in autism studies (3% of the included studies). As in the data of Fig. 3.1b, although the figure does not distinguish between increasing and decreasing behaviors, the same types were observed in similar portions in both.

3.4 Evidence for Dependent and Independent Variable Categories

Before introducing the relationships between the performance criteria components and the dependent/independent variable categories, descriptive distribution information is presented in Fig. 3.2. Among the dependent variable categories, the most studied were social communication/social skills, verbal language, and disruptive behaviors. Safety, daily living, and health skills were the least-studied categories of dependent variables. On the other hand, among the independent variable categories, six defined categories are distributed in similar proportions, especially in terms of cases. This is a clear indicator that these six independent variable categories are often used to train a variety of behaviors of individuals with ASD.

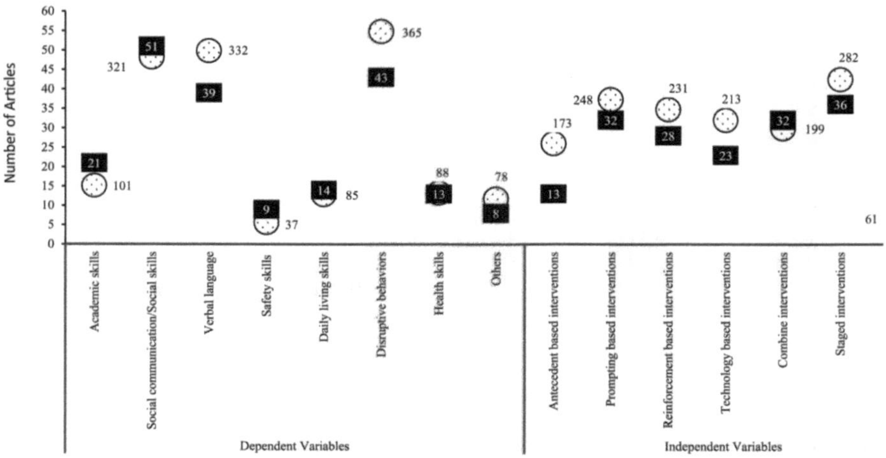

Fig. 3.2 Descriptive distributions of dependent and independent variable categories in autism studies

To determine relationships between components of performance criteria assigned and the dependent variable categories studied in autism research, I conducted a series of chi-squared analyses. As in Chap. 2, I coded autism intervention studies by dependent variable category. These dependent variable categories were cross-tabulated with the categories of performance criteria components: level and frequency, respectively. As shown in Table 3.1a, performance-criterion levels were differentially associated with dependent variable categories. Academic skills and social communication/social skills were more frequently targeted using higher mid-range performance criteria (90–99%), whereas the use of the highest criteria levels (100%) or lower levels (<80%) was used less frequently. Verbal language skills were more frequently associated with mid-range performance criteria, notably the 80–89% range, while the highest criteria levels were applied less often than expected. Daily living skills also showed a greater use of higher mid-range criteria (90–99%), with no significant deviation observed for the highest criterion level. Safety skills were highly associated with the highest performance-criterion level (100%) and were used less frequently at lower and mid-range levels.

In contrast, behavior-reduction targets displayed a distinct pattern, with significantly greater representation at lower and mid-range performance-criterion levels and markedly fewer applications of the highest criterion level (0%). Health-related skills followed a pattern similar to other acquisition targets, with more frequent use of higher mid-range performance criteria and reduced use of the highest criteria levels. Overall, the chi-squared analysis indicated a statistically significant association between dependent variable categories and performance-criterion levels, $\chi^2(18, N = 1199) = 271.41, p < .001$. Cramer's $V = .274$ indicated a moderate association, suggesting that performance-criterion selection varied meaningfully as a function of the type of task targeted in published autism intervention studies rather than reflecting arbitrariness.

Table 3.1a Chi-squared analysis for dependent variables vs. PC (performance criteria) levels

Dependent variables		PC levels <80% or > 20%	80–89% or 11–20%	90–99% or 1–10%	100% or 0%	Total
Academic skills	Count	12	30	28	25	95
	Expected count	13.0	29.9	25.6	26.5	95.0
	Adjusted residual	−0.5	0.2	2.0*	−0.3	
Social communication/ social skills	Count	28	92	96	104	320
	Expected count	43.8	100.9	86.2	89.1	320.0
	Adjusted residual	−3.1*	−1.2	3.2*	1.8	
Verbal language	Count	45	120	85	81	331
	Expected count	45.3	104.4	89.2	92.2	331.0
	Adjusted residual	−0.1	2.2*	−0.6	−2.0*	
Safety skills	Count	1	1	7	32	41
	Expected count	5.6	12.9	11.1	11.4	41.0
	Adjusted residual	−2.1*	−4.1*	−1.4	7.3*	
Daily living skills	Count	8	20	22	23	73
	Expected count	10.0	23.0	19.7	20.3	73.0
	Adjusted residual	−0.7	−0.8	2.0*	0.7	
Disruptive behaviors	Count	60	90	60	45	255
	Expected count	34.9	80.4	68.7	71.0	255.0
	Adjusted residual	5.2*	1.5	−1.4	−4.1*	
Health-related skills	Count	10	25	25	24	84
	Expected count	11.5	26.5	21.6	23.4	84.0
	Adjusted residual	−0.5	−0.4	2.1*	−0.2	
Total	Count	166	378	323	334	1199
	Expected count	166.0	378.0	323.0	334.0	1199.0

Note: All expected cell counts exceeded 5, with the minimum expected frequency being 5.7. A Pearson chi-squared test of independence indicated a statistically significant association between dependent variable categories and performance-criterion levels, $\chi^2(18, N = 1199) = 271.41$, $p < .001$. Cramer's V indicated a moderate effect size ($V = .274$, $p < .001$). Cells with adjusted residual values equal to or exceeding an absolute value of 1.96 were marked with an asterisk

Table 3.1b presents the chi-squared analysis examining the relationship between performance criteria frequencies and dependent variables. Overall, the association was not statistically significant, $\chi^2(18, N = 1329) = 13.52$, $p > .05$, with a very weak effect size (Cramer's $V = .058$, $p > .05$). Adjusted residuals indicated that most cells did not deviate meaningfully from expected counts, suggesting minimal association between performance criteria frequency and dependent variable distribution. However, one notable deviation was observed for "Health-related skills" in the "More than 3" performance-criteria frequency, which had fewer cases than expected. This indicates that in this category, participants were underrepresented relative to expectations, suggesting that applying more than three successive performance criteria may be less common for health-related skill outcomes. Other dependent variables and performance-criteria frequencies showed adjusted residuals within ±1.96,

Table 3.1b Chi-squared analysis for dependent variables vs. PC frequencies

		PC frequencies				
Dependent variables		1	2	3	More than 3	Total
Academic skills	Count	14	49	36	2	101
	Expected count	12.85	48.7	36.7	2.79	101
	Adjusted residual	0.3	0.1	−0.1	−0.5	
Social communication/social skills	Count	41	155	121	4	321
	Expected count	40.9	154.7	116.3	8.88	321
	Adjusted residual	−0.0	−0.0	0.4	−1.2	
Verbal language	Count	42	160	123	7	332
	Expected count	42.25	159.9	120.5	8.18	332
	Adjusted residual	−0.0	−0.0	0.2	−0.6	
Safety skills	Count	5	18	13	1	37
	Expected count	4.71	17.8	13.4	1.02	37
	Adjusted residual	0.1	0.1	−0.1	0.0	
Daily living skills	Count	12	41	31	1	85
	Expected count	10.83	40.95	30.8	2.35	85
	Adjusted residual	0.4	0.0	0.2	−0.9	
Destructive/reducing behaviors	Count	53	176	130	6	365
	Expected count	46.5	176.0	132.4	10.1	365
	Adjusted residual	0.9	0.0	−0.2	−1.3	
Health-related skills	Count	13	42	32	1	88
	Expected count	8.9	35.1	27.0	6.0	88
	Adjusted residual	1.3	1.2	0.9	−2.0*	
Total	Count	180	641	486	22	1329
	Expected count	180	641	486	22	1329

Note: One cell (14.3%) had an expected count below 5, with the minimum being 1.02. A Pearson chi-squared test of independence indicated that the association between dependent variable categories and performance criteria frequencies was not statistically significant, $\chi^2(18, N = 1329) = 13.52$, $p > .05$. Cramer's V indicated a very weak association ($V = 0.058$, $p > .05$). Cells with adjusted residual values equal to or exceeding an absolute value of 1.96 were shaded and marked with an asterisk indicating no significant deviations from expected counts. Overall, these findings suggest that the general relationship between performance criterion frequencies and dependent variables in autism studies is weak and that frequencies typically accompany performance criterion levels with two or three consecutive sessions across studies.

Because no statistically significant relationships were found between the performance criterion components and the independent variable categories, these cross-tabulations are not presented here. These findings indicate that the overall and individual relationships between the performance-criterion components and the independent variable categories in autism research are statistically insignificant. In other words, there is no relationship between the performance-criterion values assigned by researchers in the studies and the independent variables they used.

Overall, the findings from this subsection suggest that researchers in autism intervention studies tend to differentiate *how strictly* performance is defined depending on the type of skill being taught, rather than *how often* the criterion must be met. Across most task domains—academic, social communication, verbal language, daily living, and health-related skills—performance criteria were most commonly set at mid-to-high levels (80–89% or 11–20% and 90–99% or 1–10%), whereas the strictest criteria (100% or 0%) were used far less frequently than expected. Behavior reduction targets, however, followed a noticeably different pattern, relying more heavily on lower and mid-range criteria levels (≥21% and 11–20%), with comparatively limited use of the highest criteria (i.e., 0%). This contrast likely reflects practical and functional considerations, as expectations for consistency and response variability naturally differ between skill acquisition and behavior reduction targets. Although performance-criterion frequency was not statistically associated with dependent variable categories, the distributional patterns indicate that moderate frequencies (two or three consecutive observations) were used most often across task domains, whereas both single-observation criteria and more stringent frequencies (more than three consecutive observations) were comparatively less common. The moderate association between dependent variable categories and performance-criterion levels supports the view that decisions about criterion *stringency* are not arbitrary but reflect implicit judgments about task complexity and stability. In contrast, the absence of meaningful relationships involving performance-criterion frequency (e.g., single observation, two or three consecutive observations, or more than three) suggests that frequency functions more as a routine methodological choice than as a skill-specific design decision. Overall, these results indicate that while researchers adapt the stringency of performance criteria to the nature of the targeted behavior, they most commonly require that these criteria be met across two or three consecutive sessions.

3.5 Evidence for Participant Characteristics

Figure 3.3 shows descriptive statistics for the characteristics of autistic participants. Among 546 individuals with ASD, 95% were diagnosed with autism solely. Preschool and elementary-age groups accounted for 87% of the entire sample. And there were four times as many male participants as female participants.

Since there were no statistically significant links between the performance criteria components and diagnosis or gender categories, only age groups cross-tabulated with the performance criteria components are shown here. Tables 3.2a and 3.2b show the relationships between age groups and performance criteria components: level and frequency, respectively. As shown in Table 3.2a, the chi-squared analysis indicated that performance criteria levels were differentially associated with participant age groups $\chi^2(9, N = 546) = 17.96, p = .035$, with a small effect size ($V = 105$, $p = .035$). Preschool-aged participants (0–5 years) were significantly less likely to receive the highest performance criteria levels, suggesting that more flexible or moderate criteria were commonly applied in early childhood. In contrast, elementary-aged participants (6–13 years) and post-secondary participants (19+ years) were more frequently taught using the most stringent criteria levels (100% or 0%), whereas mid-range levels were used less often than expected in older groups. Secondary-aged participants (14–18 years) showed no notable deviations across performance criteria levels. Overall, these findings indicate that, while effect sizes were small, performance-criterion level selections varied systematically by age: younger participants were more often taught under moderate criteria, and older participants were more often taught under strict criteria.

Table 3.2b presents the chi-squared analysis examining the relationship between participant age groups and performance criteria frequencies. Overall, the association was not statistically significant, $\chi^2(9, N = 534) = 9.53, p > .05$, with a very weak

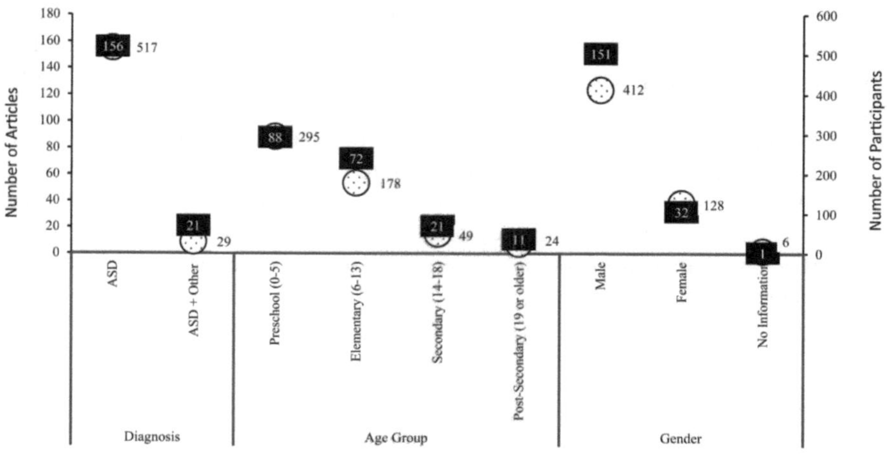

Fig. 3.3 Descriptive distributions of participant characteristics in autism studies

Table 3.2a Chi-squared analysis for participant ages vs. PC levels

Participant ages		PC levels <80% or > 20%	80–89% or 11–20%	90–99% or 1–10%	100% or 0%	Total
Preschool (0–5)	Count	27	111	61	96	295
	Expected count	25.2	113.2	59.7	96.9	295
	Adjusted residual	1.41	1.58	0.62	−2.83*	
Elementary (6–13)	Count	12	54	32	80	178
	Expected count	12.1	53.7	31.1	81.1	178
	Adjusted residual	−0.59	−1.51	−0.82	2.48*	
Secondary (14–18)	Count	1	21	13	14	49
	Expected count	1.2	20.9	12.6	14.3	49
	Adjusted residual	−1.34	1.11	1.25	−1.37	
Post-secondary (19 or older)	Count	1	4	2	17	24
	Expected count	1.5	4.3	2.0	16.2	24
	Adjusted residual	−0.21	−1.96*	−1.36	3.13*	
Total	Count	41.0	190.0	108.0	207.0	546
	Expected count	41.0	190.0	108.0	207.0	546

Note: Four cells (25%) had an expected count below 5, with the minimum being 1.2. Fisher's exact test was used to confirm the findings. The Pearson chi-squared test indicated a statistically significant association between participant ages and performance criteria levels, $\chi^2(9, N = 546) = 17.96$, $p = .035$. Cramer's V indicated a small effect size ($V = .105, p = .035$). Cells with adjusted residual values equal to or exceeding an absolute value of 1.96 were marked with an asterisk

effect size (Cramer's $V = .077, p > .05$). Adjusted residuals indicated that most cells did not meaningfully deviate from expected values, suggesting that performance criteria frequencies were applied similarly across age groups. A notable deviation emerged only for the "Secondary (14–18)" age group at the "More than 3" frequency level, which showed a higher-than-expected count, indicating somewhat greater use of more intensive performance criteria within this age group.

These results contrast with the descriptive findings reported earlier in Chap. 2, in which performance criteria frequencies of 2 and 3 were more prominently used with autistic participants (similar descriptive results were also obtained in this chapter). In fact, Chap. 2 analyses demonstrated that frequency 2 was significantly more common among autistic individuals. The lack of significant age-related differences in the current analysis suggests that although 2 and 3 frequencies are generally preferred in autism intervention research, this preference does not systematically vary by participant age. Instead, the use of mid-range performance-criterion frequencies

Table 3.2b Chi-squared analysis for participant ages vs. PC frequencies

		PC frequencies				
Participant ages		1	2	3	More than 3	Total
Preschool (0–5)	Count	41	129	115	4	289
	Expected count	43.30	133.13	107.16	5.41	289
	Adjusted residual	−0.56	−0.72	1.41	−0.90	
Elementary (6–13)	Count	28	81	63	2	174
	Expected count	26.07	80.16	64.52	3.26	174
	Adjusted residual	0.50	0.16	−0.29	−0.86	
Secondary (14–18)	Count	7	24	14	3	48
	Expected count	7.19	22.11	17.80	0.90	48
	Adjusted residual	−0.08	0.57	−1.19	2.35*	
Post-secondary (19 or older)	Count	4	12	6	1	23
	Expected count	3.45	10.60	8.53	0.43	23
	Adjusted residual	0.33	0.60	−1.12	0.90	
Total	Count	80	246	198	10	534
	Expected count	80.0	246.0	198.0	10.0	534.0

Note: Four cells (25%) have an expected count less than 5. The minimum expected count is 0.43. In line with these findings, Fisher's exact test was used to confirm the results. The chi-square yielded $\chi^2(9, N = 534) = 9.53$, $p = .390$. Cramer's V resulted in .077, $p = .390$. Cells with adjusted residual values equal to or exceeding an absolute value of 1.96 were marked with an asterisk

(2 or 3) appears consistent across age groups, aligning with earlier population-level findings but not indicating differential application across specific developmental stages. Overall, these results imply that while performance criteria frequency selection is influenced by participant characteristics such as diagnostic category, age itself exerts little effect on performance-criteria frequency decisions.

Considered collectively, the findings from this subsection suggest that participant age plays a modest yet meaningful role in how *performance-criterion levels* are selected in autism intervention research, while exerting little influence on *performance-criterion frequency*. Across the sample, autistic participants were predominantly young (preschool and elementary age groups), male, and diagnosed solely with autism; however, neither diagnosis nor gender showed meaningful associations with performance-criterion components. In contrast, age-related differences emerged for performance-criterion *levels*, albeit with a small effect size. Preschool-aged children (0–5 years) were less likely to be taught using the strictest criteria (100% or 0%), instead receiving instruction under more flexible, mid-range levels (80–89% or 11–20% and 90–99% or 1–10%), consistent with developmental expectations in early learning. Elementary-aged (6–13 years) and post-secondary (19+) participants, by comparison, were more frequently taught under the highest performance criteria, suggesting higher expectations for consistency at later developmental stages. Secondary-aged adolescents (14–18 years) did not show a distinct pattern, indicating a more heterogeneous application of criteria within this group. By contrast, performance-criterion frequency showed no statistically reliable association with age. Although a single deviation indicated somewhat greater use of higher frequencies (more than three consecutive observations) among secondary-aged participants, overall patterns remained stable across age groups. Importantly, this stability aligns with earlier descriptive findings showing a general preference for moderate frequencies (two or three consecutive observations) in autism research, a pattern that appears to reflect a field-wide convention rather than age-specific tailoring. In sum, these results suggest that researchers are more likely to adjust the *stringency of* performance expectations based on developmental considerations, while relying on relatively consistent, mid-range expectations (2 or 3 times) for *how often* performance must be demonstrated, regardless of participant age.

3.6 Evidence for Response Maintenance of Trained Behaviors

Figure 3.4 presents descriptive statistics for maintenance data collected in autism intervention studies. Approximately 39% (n = 62) of the reviewed studies reported maintenance outcomes, and these studies represented 39% (n = 553) of all cases included in the data set (N = 1407). Maintenance measurements were typically conducted shortly after participants met the performance criteria during intervention; specifically, 72% of the maintenance assessments occurred within 0–2 weeks. More than half of the cases with maintenance data (54%) included only one or two follow-up measurements. Many cases maintained performance at or above the original performance-criterion levels. A considerable proportion of cases also demonstrated maintenance within 1–10% below the criterion, indicating that behavior change was largely sustained following intervention.

Tables 3.3a and 3.3b shows the relationships between performance-criteria components (level and frequency, respectively) and response maintenance rates. Table 3.3a displays the chi-squared analysis evaluating the association between performance-criterion levels and response maintenance rates. The association reached statistical significance, $\chi^2(15, N = 553) = 89.42$, $p < .001$, with a small-to-moderate effect size (Cramer's $V = .201$). Examination of adjusted residuals revealed several localized deviations from expected frequencies.

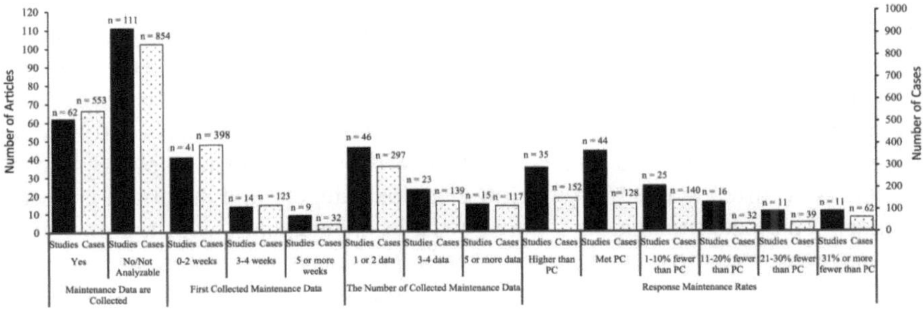

Fig. 3.4 Descriptive distributions of maintenance data collected in autism studies

Table 3.3a Chi-squared analysis for response maintenance rates vs. performance criteria levels

PC levels		Met PC	1–10% Fewer than PC	11–20% fewer than PC	21–30% fewer than PC	31% or more fewer than PC	Higher than PC	Total cases
		Response maintenance rates						
<80% or >20%	Count	15	11	8	11	9	32	86
	Expected count	19.91	21.77	4.98	6.07	9.64	23.64	86
	Adjusted residual	−1.36	−2.91*	1.52	2.26*	−0.24	2.20	
80–89% or 11–20%	Count	43	38	11	9	17	83	201
	Expected count	46.52	50.89	11.63	14.18	22.54	55.25	201
	Adjusted residual	−0.74	−2.62*	−0.24	−1.79	−1.55	5.50*	
90–99% or 1–10%	Count	29	47	7	12	21	37	153
	Expected count	35.41	38.73	8.85	10.79	17.15	42.05	153
	Adjusted residual	−1.45	1.81	−0.75	0.45	1.16	−1.08	
100% or 0%	Count	41	44	6	7	15	0	113
	Expected count	26.16	28.61	6.54	7.97	12.67	31.06	113
	Adjusted residual	3.71*	3.73*	−0.24	−0.40	0.78	−7.34*	
Total	Count	128	140	32	39	62	152	553
	Expected count	128	140	32	39	62	152	553

Note. One cell (4.2%) had an expected count less than 5, and the minimum expected count was 4.98. In line with these findings, the Pearson chi-square test indicated a statistically significant association between performance-criterion levels and response maintenance rates, $\chi^2(15, N = 553) = 89.42$, $p < .001$. The effect size, measured by Cramer's V, was .201 ($p < .001$). Cells with adjusted residual values equal to or exceeding an absolute value of 1.96 were shaded and marked with an asterisk

For the most lenient performance-criteria levels (<80% for increasing behaviors or >20% for decreasing behaviors), cases were significantly underrepresented in the 1–10% below-criterion category and overrepresented in the 21–30% below-criterion category. These levels also produced more instances than expected of cases exceeding the performance criterion, reflecting considerable score dispersion following intervention. Within the mid-range levels (80–89% or 11–20%), the only significant deviations occurred in the 1–10% below criterion category and the above-criterion category. This pattern suggests relatively stable maintenance, with a pronounced tendency to exceed the trained criterion levels. For the stricter performance-criteria level range (90–99% or 1–10%), none of the residuals were statistically significant, although the 1–10% below-criterion category showed a mild elevation (adjusted

Table 3.3b Chi-squared analysis for response maintenance rates vs. performance criteria frequencies

PC frequencies		Response maintenance rates: Met PC	1–10% fewer than PC	11–20% fewer than PC	21–30% fewer than PC	31% or more fewer than PC	Higher than PC	Total cases
1	Count	12	26	5	3	5	18	69
	Expected count	15.88	17.79	4.07	4.96	7.88	18.43	69
	Adjusted residual	−1.19	2.42*	0.51	−0.98	−1.17	−0.12	
2	Count	65	73	13	16	26	73	266
	Expected count	61.23	68.58	15.68	19.10	30.37	71.03	266
	Adjusted residual	0.77	0.87	−0.98	−1.03	−1.18	0.38	
3	Count	43	39	12	19	31	48	192
	Expected count	44.20	49.50	11.31	13.79	21.92	51.27	192
	Adjusted residual	−0.26	−2.16*	0.26	1.81	2.56*	−0.66	
More than 3	Count	5	2	2	1	0	6	16
	Expected count	3.68	4.13	0.94	1.15	1.83	4.27	16
	Adjusted residual	0.79	−1.23	1.14	−0.15	−1.46	0.99	
Total	Count	125	140	32	39	62	145	543
	Expected count	125	140	32	39	62	145	543

Note: 8 cells (33.3%) have an expected count less than 5. The minimum expected count is 0.94. In line with these findings, Fisher's exact test was used to confirm the results. The chi-square yielded $\chi^2(15, N = 543) = 22.48$, $p = .096$. Cramer's V resulted in .117, $p = .096$. Cells with adjusted residual values equal to or exceeding an absolute value of 1.96 were shaded and marked with an asterisk

residual = 1.81). This distribution indicates that maintenance performance for this level clustered close to the targeted criterion levels, with limited extreme deviations. The strictest performance criteria level (100% or 0%) exhibited strong and interpretable deviations. Cases were significantly overrepresented in both meeting the criterion and performing 1–10% below it, while cases performing above the targeted criterion were markedly underrepresented. These results are consistent with a ceiling effect inherent in a 100% requirement, constraining upward variability during maintenance. Collectively, these findings indicate that stricter performance criteria narrow the distribution of maintenance outcomes and promote clustering around the criterion level, whereas lenient criteria produce broader variability—including both substantial decrements and performance gains—during follow-up.

Table 3.3b presents the chi-squared analysis assessing the association between performance-criterion frequencies and response maintenance rates. Although the overall test did not reach statistical significance, $\chi^2(15, N = 543) = 22.48, p = .096$, the effect size was small (Cramer's $V = .117$), and several adjusted residuals indicated localized deviations worth interpreting. A single observation of the performance criterion level was associated with more cases than expected falling within the 1–10% below-criterion range, suggesting slight decreases in performance during maintenance for this frequency. For two consecutive observations, no adjusted residuals exceeded the significance threshold, indicating that maintenance outcomes for this frequency largely aligned with expected distributions. Three consecutive observations, however, showed a different pattern. Cases were underrepresented in the 1–10% below-criterion category, while cases performing 31% or more below the targeted criterion levels were overrepresented. This suggests that although performance remained stable at times, a subset of individuals showed more substantial declines at this frequency level. Finally, frequencies exceeding three observations did not yield significant deviations, although slight trends toward fewer cases in the 31% or more below-criterion category and modest increases in the above targeted criterion levels were observed. Overall, these findings indicate that while performance-criterion frequency was not strongly associated with response maintenance outcomes in the autism-only data set, particularly at one and three observations, there are specific tendencies toward either slight underperformance or more pronounced decreases during follow-up. Frequency 2 may be a more optimal option to sustain the trained behavior.

Figure 3.5 shows the linear regression analysis of performance criteria levels on response maintenance rates in autism studies. The results revealed a statistically significant model, $F(1, 551) = 121.271, p < .001$, indicating that higher performance criteria levels can play a significant role in achieving higher response maintenance

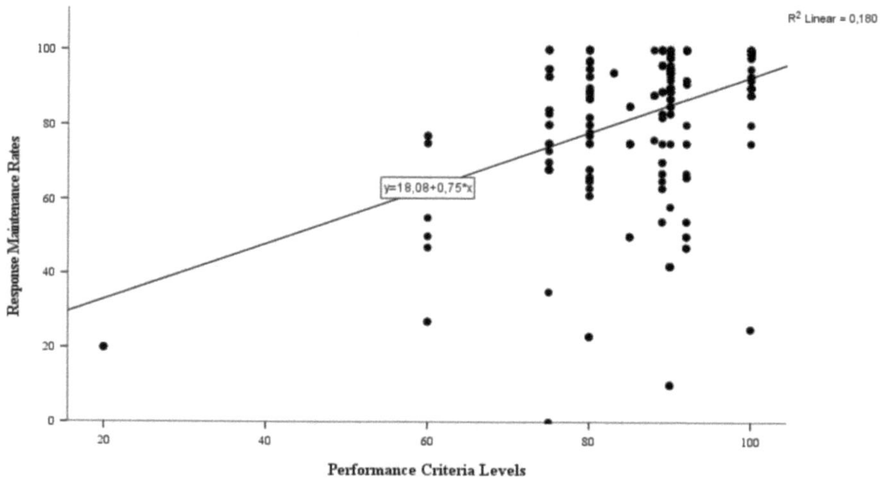

Fig. 3.5 Regression analysis of performance criteria levels on response maintenance rates in autism studies

rates after the intervention is terminated (β_1 = 0.747, $p < .001$; 95% CI [0.614, 0.880]). However, the $R^2 = .18$ indicates that the model explains only 18% of the variance in response maintenance rates.

Collectively, the findings from this subsection highlight performance criteria components, particularly the targeted levels, as a meaningful determinant of response maintenance following intervention in autism studies. Descriptively, maintenance assessments were most often conducted shortly after meeting performance criteria was attained and were typically based on a limited number of follow-up observations, yet the majority of cases showed maintenance at or near the original performance criterion levels. Inferential analyses further demonstrated that performance-criterion levels were significantly associated with maintenance outcomes, with stricter performance-criterion levels producing more stable and tightly clustered post-intervention performance. Specifically, the highest criteria (100% or 0%) promoted maintenance outcomes concentrated around the targeted level itself, reflecting both reduced downward loss and a ceiling-related constraint on upward variability. In contrast, more lenient criteria (<80% or >20%) were linked to substantially greater dispersion during maintenance, including both notable declines and performance exceeding the targeted criterion levels. Mid-to-high ranges (80–89% or 11–20% and 90–99% or 1–10%) tended to yield more balanced patterns, with maintenance outcomes remaining close to the targeted criterion levels and fewer extreme deviations. Performance-criterion frequency, by comparison, showed a weaker and less consistent relationship with response maintenance. While the overall association did not reach statistical significance, the obtained patterns suggested that single observations were more often followed by slight performance decrements, and three consecutive observations were occasionally associated with more pronounced declines in a subset of cases. Two consecutive observations, however, showed the most stable alignment with expected maintenance outcomes across categories. Finally, regression results converged with these findings, indicating that higher criterion levels predict stronger response maintenance, albeit with a modest proportion of explained variance ($R^2 = .18$). In sum, these results suggest that setting higher performance expectations during acquisition can enhance the durability of behavior change, while performance-criterion frequency plays a comparatively secondary and fine-tuning role—potentially optimizing response maintenance when moderate values (2 or 3) are used.

3.7 Evidence for Generalization of Trained Behaviors

Figure 3.6 presents descriptive statistics for generalization data reported in autism intervention studies. Approximately 25% ($n = 41$) of the reviewed studies included generalization outcomes, representing 21% ($n = 299$) of all cases in the data set ($N = 1407$). Among these cases, more than half (62%) involved only one or two generalization observations for the trained behaviors, and in the cases with two data points, typically one observation during the baseline phase and another during the

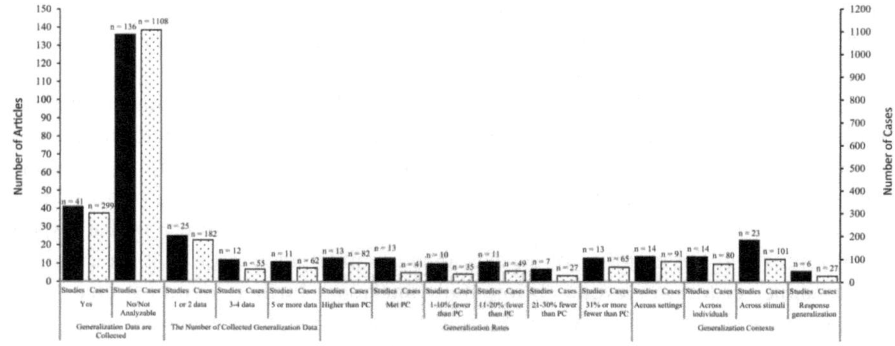

Fig. 3.6 Descriptive distributions of generalization data collected in autism studies

intervention phase. A substantial portion of cases (41%) demonstrated generalization of the target behavior across contexts at or above the original performance-criterion levels. Notably, a considerable number of cases generalized behaviors at 11–20% below and at 31% or more below the specified performance criteria levels. Overall, the distribution of generalization conditions appeared largely consistent across the examined contexts. Response generalization emerged as the least-studied generalization context within autism intervention research.

Tables 3.4a and 3.4b show the relationships between performance-criteria components (level and frequency, respectively) and generalization rates. Table 3.4a presents the chi-squared analysis examining the association between performance-criterion levels and generalization outcomes. The relationship was statistically significant, $\chi^2(15, N = 299) = 115.35, p < .001$, with a moderate effect (Cramer's $V = .359$). Adjusted residuals showed distinct generalization patterns across performance-criterion levels, with important implications for intervention planning. For the most lenient performance criteria (<80% or >20%), cases were substantially overrepresented in the 1–10% below-criterion category and in the above-criterion category (i.e., higher than the targeted performance criteria levels), whereas the 31% or more below-criterion category was significantly underrepresented. This pattern indicates highly variable generalization outcomes, with many autistic participants outperforming the originally targeted performance-criterion levels and others demonstrating only minimal decrements.

Within the mid-range performance-criterion levels (80–89% or 11–20%), generalization performance showed a more polarized pattern. Cases met the performance-criterion levels less often than expected and displayed a large positive deviation in the above-criterion category. Conversely, the 31% or more below-criterion category was markedly underrepresented. These findings suggest that moderate performance criteria tend to produce generalization outcomes skewed toward higher-than-trained performance levels, with fewer instances of substantial performance losses. For

Table 3.4a Chi-squared analysis for generalization rates vs. performance criteria levels

PC levels		Generalization rates: Met PC	1–10% fewer than PC	11–20% fewer than PC	21–30% fewer than PC	31% or more fewer than PC	Higher than PC	Total cases
<80% or >20%	Count	7	9	3	3	0	16	38
	Expected count	5.2	4.4	6.2	3.4	8.3	10.4	38.0
	Adjusted residual	.9	2.5*	−1.5	−.3	−3.5*	2.2*	
80–89% or 11–20%	Count	9	8	16	9	12	59	113
	Expected count	15.5	13.2	18.5	10.2	24.6	31.0	113.0
	Adjusted residual	−2.3*	−1.9	−.8	−.5	−3.6*	7.5*	
90–99% or 1–10%	Count	12	7	9	7	10	7	52
	Expected count	7.1	6.1	8.5	4.7	11.3	14.3	52.0
	Adjusted residual	2.2*	.4	.2	1.2	−.5	−2.5*	
100% or 0%	Count	13	11	21	8	43	0	96
	Expected count	13.2	11.2	15.7	8.7	20.9	26.3	96.0
	Adjusted residual	−.1	−.1	1.8	−.3	6.6*	−7.3*	
Total	Count	41	35	49	27	65	82	299
	Expected count	41.0	35.0	49.0	27.0	65.0	82.0	299.0

Note: 3 cells (12.5%) have an expected count of less than 5. The minimum expected count is 3.43. In line with these findings, the Pearson chi-squared test yielded $\chi^2(15, N = 299) = 115.350$, $p < .001$. Cramer's V resulted in .359, $p < .001$. Cells with adjusted residual values equal to or exceeding an absolute value of 1.96 were marked with an asterisk

stricter performance criteria (90–99% or 1–10%), deviations were more constrained. The only statistically significant departures occurred in the "Met PC" and above-criterion categories, where cases were, respectively, overrepresented and underrepresented. This distribution reflects a tighter clustering of generalization around the targeted criterion levels, with limited upward variability and minimal extreme decrements. The strictest performance criterion (100% or 0%) yielded the most pronounced deviations. Cases performing 31% or more below the criterion were strongly overrepresented, whereas cases performing above the criterion were sharply underrepresented. As in maintenance comparisons, these results are consistent with a ceiling effect inherent in a 100% requirement, constraining upward variability during generalization. In sum, these results show that stricter criteria constrain generalization variability and concentrate outcomes around or below the

Table 3.4b Chi-squared analysis for generalization rates vs. performance criteria frequencies

PC frequencies		Generalization rates						
		Met PC	1–10% fewer than PC	11–20% fewer than PC	21–30% fewer than PC	31% or more fewer than PC	Higher than PC	Total cases
1	Count	3	6	5	7	6	1	28
	Expected count	3.8	3.3	4.6	2.5	6.1	7.7	28.0
	Adjusted residual	−.48	1.68	.22	3.10*	−.04	−2.97*	
2	Count	13	10	11	9	21	58	122
	Expected count	16.7	14.3	20.0	11.0	26.5	33.5	122.0
	Adjusted residual	−1.28	−1.57	−2.86*	−.83	−1.58	6.47*	
3	Count	23	17	31	11	38	21	141
	Expected count	19.3	16.5	23.1	12.7	30.7	38.7	141.0
	Adjusted residual	1.23	.18	2.47*	−.70	2.06*	−4.59*	
More than 3	Count	2	2	2	0	0	2	8
	Expected count	1.1	.94	1.3	.72	1.7	2.2	8.0
	Adjusted residual	.94	1.19	.67	−.90	−1.51	−.16	
Total	Count	41	35	49	27	65	82	299
	Expected count	41.0	35.0	49.0	27.0	65.0	82.0	299.0

Note: 10 cells (41.7%) have an expected count of less than 5. The minimum expected count is 0.72. In line with these findings, Fisher's exact test was used

The chi-squared test yielded $\chi^2(15, N = 299) = 147.83$, $p < .001$. Cramer's V resulted in .315, $p < .001$. Cells with adjusted residual values equal to or exceeding an absolute value of 1.96 were marked with an asterisk

targeted criterion levels, whereas more lenient criteria allow a wider range of generalization, including both substantial gains and noticeable decrements.

Table 3.4b presents the chi-squared analysis assessing the association between performance-criterion frequencies and generalization rates. Although the overall association was statistically significant, $\chi^2(15, N = 299) = 147.83$, $p < .001$, the effect size was moderate (Cramer's $V = .315$). Several adjusted residuals revealed distinct and practically relevant deviations from expected distributions. For a single observation of the performance-criterion level, cases were significantly overrepresented in the 21–30% below-criterion category, while cases performing above the criterion were underrepresented. This suggests that when performance criteria levels are evaluated only once, generalization tends to be weaker and more variable, with autistic participants more prone to moderate performance losses rather than exceeding trained levels. For two consecutive observations, the most notable deviations occurred in the 11–20% below-criterion category, which was underrepresented, and in the above-criterion category, which was strongly overrepresented. This pattern indicates that two observations may provide a more stable foundation for generalization, reducing moderate decrements while promoting higher-than-expected performance for many cases. Three consecutive observations produced a mixed pattern. Cases were overrepresented in both the 11–20% below-criterion category and the 31% or more below-criterion category, while they were underrepresented in the above-criterion range. This suggests that although some individuals generalized adequately, others showed substantial performance drops, reflecting uneven outcomes at this frequency level. Finally, frequencies exceeding three observations did not yield statistically significant deviations, with no adjusted residuals surpassing the ±1.96 threshold. The pattern for this group suggests generally expected generalization outcomes, with no strong tendency toward either improvement or decline. Overall, these findings indicate that performance-criterion frequency plays a meaningful but variable role in generalization. In particular, two observations appear to support stronger generalization, while a single observation and three observations show more vulnerability to performance decreases. In line with these results, as with maintenance outcomes, frequency two may be a more optimal option to generalize the trained behavior across different contexts.

Figure 3.7 presents the linear regression examining the extent to which performance-criteria levels predict generalization rates. The model was statistically significant, $F(1, 297) = 43.456$, $p < .001$. Higher performance-criteria levels were associated with higher generalization outcomes following intervention ($\beta_1 = 0.703$, $p < .001$; 95% CI [0.493, 0.913]). The model accounted for a small portion of variance, with an R^2 of .13, indicating that performance-criteria levels explain about 13% of the variability in generalization rates.

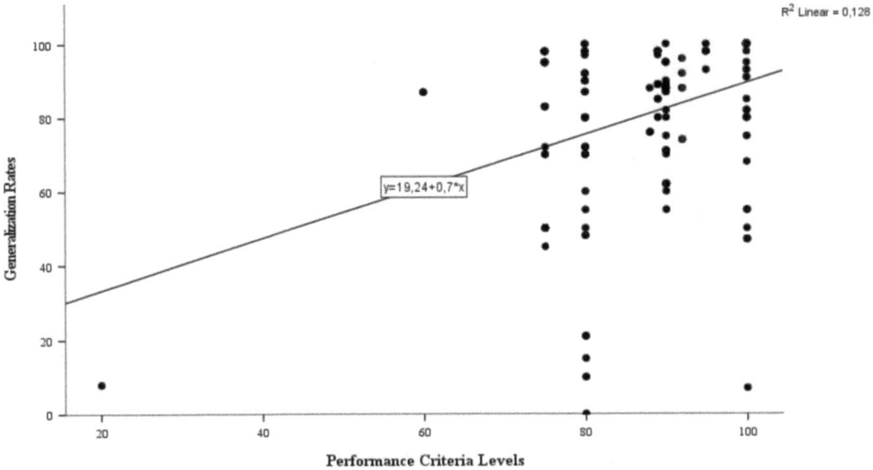

Fig. 3.7 Regression analysis of performance criteria levels on generalization rates in autism studies

Collectively, the findings from this subsection indicate that both components of performance criteria—*level* and *frequency*—play meaningful, yet distinct, roles in shaping generalization outcomes in autism intervention research. Descriptively, generalization remains underreported, is often assessed using a limited number of probes, and shows substantial variability in the extent to which trained behaviors transfer across different contexts. Inferential analyses nonetheless revealed several clear patterns. Performance-criterion *levels* were moderately associated with generalization outcomes, such that more lenient criteria (<80% or >20%) allowed a broader range of generalization performance, including both marked improvements beyond the taught criterion and noticeable decrements. In contrast, stricter criteria (90–99% or 1–10% and especially 100% or 0%) constrained variability, producing generalization outcomes clustered closer to—or below—the targeted performance-criterion levels, consistent with ceiling-related limitations. Mid-range criteria (80–89% or 11–20%) tended to favor stronger-than-expected generalization while minimizing large performance losses, suggesting a balance between flexibility and stability in transfer of behavioral change. Performance-criterion *frequency* also demonstrated a statistically meaningful association with generalization, but with more differentiated effects across levels. Two consecutive observations were most consistently associated with favorable generalization outcomes, reducing moderate performance losses and increasing the likelihood of above-criterion performance. In contrast, single observations and three consecutive observations were more often linked to vulnerability in generalization, including moderate to substantial performance decrements for some cases. Frequencies exceeding three observations showed no strong directional tendency, yielding generally expected outcomes. Regression analyses further supported these patterns, indicating that higher performance-criterion levels predict stronger generalization, although they account for only a modest proportion of variance ($R^2 = .13$). In sum, these findings suggest that while rigorous performance expectations can strengthen generalization, optimal transfer of behavioral change is most likely when criterion *levels* and *frequencies* are carefully calibrated—particularly favoring moderately high criteria combined with moderate verification of performance (frequency 2)—rather than maximized indiscriminately.

3.8 Evidence for the Efficiency in Meeting Performance Criteria

To evaluate the efficiency of performance-criterion components used in autism intervention research, three complementary analyses were conducted. First, two Spearman's rank-order correlation analyses examined the strength and direction of monotonic associations between performance-criterion specifications and the amount of instruction required to meet those criteria. The first analysis tested the relationship between the levels of performance criteria and the number of sessions needed to reach the criteria (treated as continuous variables). The second analysis assessed the relationship between the frequencies of performance criteria and the number of sessions required to meet the criteria, again using continuous variables. In addition, a chi-squared analysis was performed to examine the association between the number of instructional trials delivered per session and the number of sessions needed to meet the performance criteria, with these variables coded as categorical. Before introducing the results of the correlational analyses, descriptive findings on the sessions collected to meet the performance criteria and on the number of trials per session are presented.

Figure 3.8 shows the distribution of sessions collected while meeting performance criteria. According to the findings, no study was found that did not meet the performance criteria in all its cases. However, 27 studies covered both cases that met performance criteria and those that did not. 77% (n = 1086) of all cases across the sample met performance criteria set in the autism intervention research. The remaining portion (n = 321) did not achieve the criteria. Five or fewer sessions were required for 69% (n = 752) of the cases that met performance criteria. As the number of required sessions increased, the incidence decreased, suggesting that the interventions in autism studies were generally efficient in terms of time consumption.

In 71% of cases that met the performance criteria, intervention sessions were not continued after the criteria were met, whereas in the remaining cases, practitioners continued the intervention, which was either due to the natural flow of the intervention or due to the structure of the research design (i.e., single-case experimental designs).

Figure 3.9 indicates the distribution of the number of trials conducted in a session. Generally, five or fewer trials (n = 428) and six to ten trials (n = 364) were planned to be conducted in a session in autism interventions that met performance criteria. And as the number of trials conducted in a session increased, the frequency

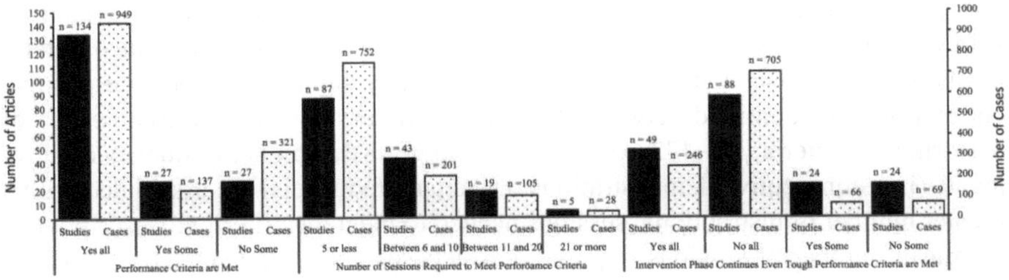

Fig. 3.8 Descriptive information on sessions collected while meeting performance criteria in autism studies

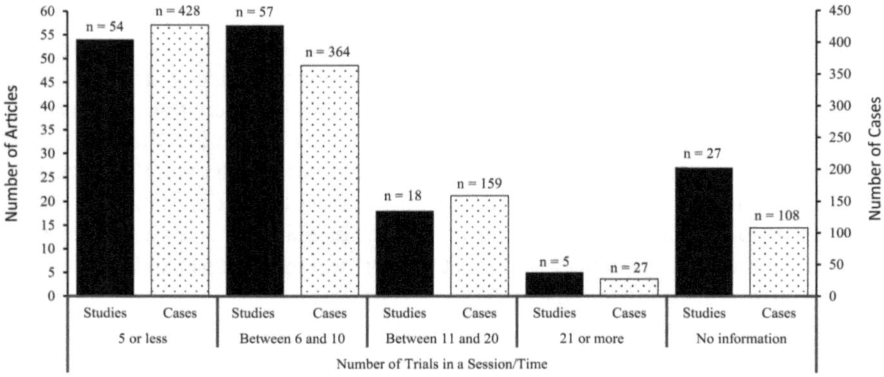

Fig. 3.9 Descriptive information for the number of trials conducted in a session in autism interventions that met performance criteria

Table 3.5 Results of correlation analyses

Variables		PC levels	PC frequencies
The number of sessions required to meet PC	Mean	88.51	2.21
	SD	12.54	0.521
	Spearman's ρ	.021	.472
	p (2-tailed)	.724	.001*
	N	1086	1032

Note: Mean and SD of the required sessions were 7.22 and 6.21, respectively. Required sessions have a total of 1086 data points. The asterisk indicates a statistically significant correlation with required sessions. SD: Standard deviation

of cases decreased. Notably, a substantial number of studies (and cases) did not include any information on trial numbers per session.

Table 3.5 summarizes the results of the correlation analyses examining the associations between the number of sessions required to meet performance criteria and both performance criteria levels and frequencies. No significant monotonic relationship was found between the required number of sessions and performance criteria levels, $\rho = .021$, $p = .724$. In contrast, a statistically significant moderate positive correlation was identified between the number of sessions and the frequencies of performance criteria, $\rho = .472$, $p = .001$. This suggests that higher frequency requirements (i.e., consecutive demonstrations of the targeted levels) are associated with a greater number of instructional sessions needed to meet the criterion. Descriptively, the mean number of sessions required across cases was 7.22 (SD = 6.21), with a total of 1086 data points contributing to this analysis.

Table 3.6 presents the chi-squared analysis examining the association between the number of instructional trials conducted per session and the number of sessions required to meet the performance criterion. The overall association was statistically significant, $\chi^2(9, N = 978) = 50.06, p < .001$. Although the effect size was small (Cramer's $V = .13$), several adjusted residuals indicate meaningful localized deviations that help clarify how instructional dosage relates to acquisition efficiency.

Autistic participants who met the performance criterion within five or fewer sessions were taught with lower trial densities, as reflected by the near-expected frequencies in the 5-or-less and 6–10 trial conditions and the significant underrepresentation in the 21+ trial range. This pattern indicates that low trial intensity is often sufficient for rapid responders. In the group achieving the criterion in 6–10 sessions, a different trend appears. Although this group still trained efficiently, they were disproportionately represented in the 11–20 and 21+ trial conditions. Given that trial density is determined before instruction begins, this suggests that cases assigned to moderately intensive teaching formats tend to require slightly more instructional time to meet the criterion, though not to the extent seen in slower responding groups.

For autistic participants who required 11–20 sessions, the pattern becomes clearer. These cases were significantly overrepresented in the highest trial-density condition (21+ trials). This indicates that instructional programs designed with higher initial intensity are often used for students or behaviors that are expected to require more sustained training, and indeed, these cases did take longer to meet the criterion. The strongest deviation was observed among autistic participants who

Table 3.6 Chi-squared analysis for number of required sessions to meet PC vs. number of trials used in a session

Number of required sessions to meet PC		Number of trials in a session				
		5 or less	6–10	11–20	21+	Total
5 or less	Count	332	283	107	11	733
	Expected count	320.78	272.81	119.17	20.24	733.0
	Adjusted residual	0.66	0.66	−1.43	−2.20*	
6–10	Count	60	47	44	8	159
	Expected count	69.58	59.18	25.85	4.39	159.0
	Adjusted residual	−1.62	−1.58	4.26*	2.33*	
11–20	Count	31	29	6	5	71
	Expected count	31.07	26.43	11.54	1.96	71.0
	Adjusted residual	−0.02	0.51	−1.79	2.18*	
21+	Count	5	5	2	3	15
	Expected count	6.56	5.58	2.44	0.41	15.0
	Adjusted residual	−0.61	−0.24	−0.31	3.97*	
Total	Count	428	364	159	27	978
	Expected count	428.0	364.0	159.0	27.0	978.0

Note: 4 cells (25.0%) have an expected count of less than 5. The minimum expected count is 0.41. In line with these findings, Fisher's exact test was used to confirm the results. The chi-squared analysis yielded $\chi^2(9, N = 978) = 50.06, p < .001$. Cramer's V resulted in .13, indicating a small effect size. Cells with adjusted residual values equal to or exceeding an absolute value of 1.96 were marked with an asterisk required more than 21 sessions. This group showed a marked overrepresentation in the 21+ trial condition, suggesting that tasks assigned to the most intensive instructional formats from the outset generally require the longest training durations.

In sum, the findings show that different trial densities are associated with different session requirements for meeting performance criteria. Lower trial densities (5 or fewer per session) were most common among autistic participants who met the criterion in the fewest sessions, whereas higher trial densities (11–20 and 21+ per session) were more frequent among cases who required additional instructional sessions. Although the effect size for this association was small, the pattern indicates a clear correspondence between the number of trials delivered per session and the total number of sessions required to meet performance criteria.

3.9 General Recommendations for Selecting Appropriate Performance Criteria in Autism Studies

Based on the converging evidence across analyses of task domains, participant characteristics, response maintenance, generalization, and instructional efficiency, the following recommendations are offered for researchers and practitioners designing autism interventions:

Differentiate performance-criterion levels by task type:

- Performance-criteria levels should be selected considering task types. Academic, verbal language, social skills, daily living, and health-related skills are most commonly and effectively targeted using moderate-to-high criteria (80–89% or 90–99%). In contrast, safety skills show a distinct pattern, with a greater reliance on the strictest performance criteria (100% accuracy) to address higher demands for risk minimization. Behavior-reduction targets are more frequently associated with lower or mid-range criteria (11–20% or >20%), depending on functional goals and the acceptance range of response variability.

Use higher performance-criterion levels strategically to support maintenance and generalization:

- Higher performance-criterion levels are consistently associated with better response maintenance and generalization outcomes; however, they should be interpreted as a facilitating condition rather than a standalone solution. Given the modest proportion of variance explained, the presence of other factors (e.g., intervention type; Aydin, n.d.) influencing response sustainability and generalization should also be considered. Durable behavior change requires deliberate programming for both maintenance and generalization beyond performance thresholds alone.

Favor moderate criteria levels to balance both durability and generalizability of behavioral change:

- Mid-range criteria (80–89% for acquisition; 11–20% for reduction) often yield the most balanced performance profiles, supporting responding that remains close to, or occasionally exceeds, the trained criterion levels while reducing the risk of sharp performance loss across diverse contexts and over time.

Treat performance-criterion frequency as a fine-tuning variable rather than a primary lever:

- Across analyses, frequency demonstrated weaker, less domain-specific associations than performance-criteria levels. Its function appears supportive, shaping confirmation of responding rather than independently guiding outcomes; it shapes the validation of the responses.

Prefer moderate frequencies (two or three consecutive observations) in most instructional contexts:

- These frequencies were most commonly used across the field and were associated with more favorable maintenance and generalization outcomes (in particular for frequency two), while avoiding the vulnerabilities observed with single observations or overly repeated demonstrations.

Be cautious with single-observation criteria when the durability of behavior is a primary goal:

- Single observations were more often associated with performance declines during maintenance and weaker generalization, suggesting that *they may reflect momentary success rather than durable behavioral change.*

Higher performance-criterion frequencies are associated with longer instructional timelines rather than increased efficiency:

- Higher frequency requirements are associated with longer instructional timelines, even when the performance-criterion level remains constant. Accordingly, increased frequency should be reserved for situations where consistency verification is clinically, socially, or methodologically essential.

Align trial density with realistic expectations about response pace:

- Lower trial densities are often sufficient for cases that meet the criteria rapidly, whereas higher trial densities tend to be assigned to and correspond with more extended acquisition periods. Trial density should be planned intentionally, considering the timeline.

Adjust criterion stringency across developmental stages, but keep frequency relatively stable:

- Younger participants are more often trained using flexible, moderate criteria levels, whereas older participants are more commonly expected to meet stricter thresholds. Frequency, however, appears appropriately standardized across age groups (generally 2 or 3 consecutive sessions) and should not be heavily age-dependent.

Report performance criteria components transparently:

- Performance-criterion levels and frequencies, and trial densities should be clearly specified, justified, and reported, as each plays a distinct role in shaping acquisition, response maintenance, generalization, and efficiency outcomes.

3.10 Concluding Remarks

The findings presented in this chapter extend the conclusions of Chap. 2 by clarifying *how* and *why* different components of performance criteria function across autism intervention contexts. Rather than treating performance criteria as uniform performance thresholds, this chapter demonstrates that criterion levels, criterion frequencies, and instructional density operate as distinct yet interrelated study variables that shape acquisition efficiency, maintenance, and generalization in different ways. Across analyses, performance-criterion *levels* emerged as the primary driver of durable outcomes. Criterion levels were assigned statistically significant levels by task domain and participant age, indicating that researchers implicitly adjust performance stringency based on developmental expectations and behavioral demands. Moderately high levels were most often associated with stable response maintenance and favorable generalization patterns, whereas the strictest criteria promoted consistency by constraining variability more.

In contrast, performance-criterion *frequencies* showed weaker domain-specific differentiation but clear implications for instructional efficiency and outcome stability. Moderate frequencies (typically two or three consecutive observations) were most commonly observed across autism studies and were associated with more favorable response maintenance and generalization profiles. Higher frequencies were consistently linked to longer instructional timelines without corresponding improvements in outcomes, indicating that frequency functions more as a verification mechanism than as a determinant of training quality. Analyses of instructional trials further reinforced this distinction. Trial density per session was strongly aligned with the number of instructional sessions required to meet criteria. Together, these patterns demonstrate that performance criteria are embedded within broader instructional design choices that balance efficiency, rigor, and outcome durability.

Importantly, neither response maintenance nor generalization was fully explained by performance-criterion level rigor alone. The modest variance across models highlights the necessity of explicit programming for long-term outcomes beyond performance-criteria definitions. In sum, the findings of this chapter underscore the importance of conceptualizing performance criteria as multidimensional, context-sensitive parameters. When selected intentionally and reported transparently, performance criteria can serve not only as evaluative benchmarks but also as powerful tools to optimize training efficiency, durability, and meaningful behavioral change in autism intervention research and to accurately identify evidence-based interventions.

References

Aydin, O. (n.d.). *Impact of performance criteria assignments on response maintenance and generalization: An investigation across study variables.*

Aydin, O., Sulu, M. D., & Ari-Arat, C. (2025). A meta-analysis of self-management interventions in teaching daily living skills to autistic individuals. *Journal of Autism and Developmental Disorders, 55*(7), 2377–2392. https://doi.org/10.1007/s10803-024-06355-w

Aydin, O., & Tanious, R. (2022). Performance criteria-based effect size (PCES) measurement of single-case experimental designs: A real-world data study. *Journal of Applied Behavior Analysis, 55*, 891. https://doi.org/10.1002/jaba.928

Sulu, M. D., Aydin, O., Martella, R. C., Erden, E., & Ozen, Z. (2024). A meta-analysis of applied behavior analysis-based interventions for individuals with autism spectrum disorders (ASD) in Turkey. *Review Journal of Autism and Developmental Disorders*, 1–31. Advanced online publication. https://doi.org/10.1007/s40489-023-00421-2

Chapter 4
Selecting Optimal Performance Criteria for Autism Interventions: A Practical Guide

Abstract This chapter addresses a practical yet often overlooked question in autism intervention research: how to select performance criteria that are both meaningful and defensible. Rather than treating performance criteria as arbitrary benchmarks, the chapter argues that these decisions should be guided by the type of behavior being targeted and the functional significance of change for the individual and their environment. For behaviors targeted for increase, a structured rubric is introduced to support performance-criterion selection by jointly considering participant characteristics, task features, and measurement factors. Task-specific interpretation tables translate rubric scores into recommended criterion levels and frequencies, allowing flexibility when response variability is functional and greater stringency when skills are safety- or risk-sensitive. For behaviors targeted for reduction, the chapter presents a separate rubric that reflects the functions of disruptive behaviors. This framework emphasizes various parameters such as severity, risk to self or others, contextual pervasiveness, and the acceptability of residual behavior. Both rubrics were refined through focus group interviews with six experts and written feedback from two additional experts, strengthening their relevance to social validity. Overall, this chapter offers a practical and transparent guide to selecting performance criteria, supporting empirically informed, functionally appropriate, and socially valid decision-making in autism interventions.

Keywords Performance criteria · Rubrics · Decreasing behaviors · Increasing behaviors · Autism

© The Author(s), under exclusive license to Springer Nature Singapore Pte Ltd. 2026
O. Aydin, *Optimal Performance Criteria in Autism Studies*, SpringerBriefs in Modern Perspectives on Disability Research,
https://doi.org/10.1007/978-981-95-8542-7_4

4.1 Autism Intervention Domains

As discussed in previous chapters, there are two distinct behavioral types studied in the intervention literature. One category, called "increasing behaviors," represents behaviors in which interventions aim to raise the behavior to a higher level than its current level, while the other category, called "decreasing behaviors," represents behaviors in which interventions aim to lower the behavior to a lower level than its current level. The following subsections detail these two distinct behavioral types studied in autism literature. Then, two separate rubrics based on a scoring system are recommended to establish optimal performance criteria for autism interventions.

4.1.1 Increasing Behaviors

A desirable behavioral change, dependent on performance criteria, is a key to ensuring socially important effects in the community (Aydin & Tanious, 2022; Baer et al., 1968; Wolf, 1978). As realized in Chap. 3's coding processes, although the skills examined in the autism intervention literature spanned diverse domains, the core effort for each skill focused on achieving outcomes that benefit the student/participant, family, teacher, or other members of the community. Within the studies reviewed, skill-acquisition targets, particularly those involving response increases, were clustered into several functionally distinct areas. Across the autism literature, behaviors targeted for increases can be grouped into six primary domains: (a) academic tasks, (b) social communication/social skills, (c) verbal language, (d) daily living skills, (e) safety skills, and (f) health-related skills. The following definitions detail which types of skills are meant in each domain.

Academic Tasks: Academic tasks encompass a wide range of skills aligned with the formal school curriculum and essential for successful engagement in educational settings. These include foundational literacy skills such as reading fluency, comprehension, decoding, and written expression; numerical skills such as number sense, calculation, problem-solving, and logical reasoning; and content domain competencies in subjects such as science and social studies. Beyond separate academic outcomes, academic tasks also include behavioral prerequisites necessary for effective engagement in instruction; these are often referred to as on-task or academic engagement behaviors. These behaviors include paying attention to instructional materials, following teacher directions, initiating and completing tasks, maintaining effort during independent work, and transitioning appropriately between academic activities.

Social Communication/Social Skills: Social communication and social skills encompass a broad range of behaviors that enable individuals to initiate, maintain, and respond appropriately during interactions in various social settings. Social communication refers to the use of verbal and nonverbal behaviors in natural social contexts, including classroom settings, peer groups, community settings, and family interactions, such as initiating conversation, maintaining reciprocal dialogue, greeting others, expressing needs or opinions, or answering questions. These skills also encompass pragmatic language components such as taking turns, maintaining a topic, taking perspective, and adjusting communication to the listener's needs. Social skills, on the other hand, include broader socially mediated behaviors that support participation and social integration. These range from everyday social interactions (e.g., sending emails, sharing materials, asking for help) to play skills (e.g., cooperative play, rule-based games), emotional and behavioral regulation, and following group routines. Social skills also encompass behaviors important for conforming to social norms, such as waiting, negotiating, resolving conflicts, understanding the feelings of others, and showing empathy.

Verbal Language: Verbal language, or verbal behavior, encompasses a wide range of skills related to the production, comprehension, and functional use of spoken language. These skills include basic operant behaviors such as mand (requests), tact (labeling), echoing, and intraverbals, as well as more advanced linguistic repertoires. Verbal behavior also includes auditory-visual conditional discrimination, phonological awareness, and letter–sound matching; these collectively also support early reading and academic skill development. Additional components include speech fluency, articulation, expressive vocabulary, grammar, and second-language acquisition, depending on the learner's environments and instructional goals. Social communication, while closely related, differs, in that it involves the application of verbal language in socially meaningful contexts. In other words, social communication requires verbal language skills but goes beyond mere speech production. It consists of using language appropriately to initiate and maintain interactions, interpret social cues, take turns speaking, adapt speech to different partners or settings, and participate in complex social interactions. Therefore, while verbal language represents the foundational linguistic repertoire, social communication differs, in that it reflects how this repertoire is used functionally and contextually in real-world social interactions.

Daily Living Skills: Daily living skills encompass a broad set of adaptive behaviors that enable individuals to function independently in personal, home, and community settings. Personal daily living skills include activities such as eating, dressing, personal care, toileting, personal hygiene, and managing leisure time. These basic routines support self-care and are critical for autonomy in both home and school settings. Domestic skills involve responsibilities within the living environment, such as housekeeping, organizing personal belongings, doing laundry, preparing meals, and safely using household appliances or devices. These behaviors facilitate participation in family routines and contribute to readiness for independent living. In addition, community living skills extend adaptive functionality beyond the home, encompassing abilities such as navigating public spaces, understanding and following community rules, managing time and money, shopping, using public transportation, accessing community services, and using the phone in the context of functional interaction with others.

Safety Skills: Safety skills encompass a range of adaptive behaviors that enable individuals to recognize, avoid, and respond appropriately to potentially harmful or dangerous situations in their daily environments. These skills include personal safety behaviors such as recognizing unsafe interactions with strangers, identifying inappropriate physical contact, responding to bullying or threats, and knowing when and how to seek help from trusted adults. Safety skills also include environmental safety behaviors such as navigating streets and pedestrian areas, recognizing hazardous vehicles, understanding traffic signs, avoiding sharp or hot objects, and following rules regarding water, fire, or electrical hazards. In addition, safety skills include emergency response behaviors such as understanding what an emergency is, knowing how to call emergency services, following evacuation procedures, and applying basic problem-solving steps to stay safe during unexpected events.

Health-related Skills: Health-related skills encompass a broad range of behaviors that support an individual's physical well-being, disease prevention, and overall healthy lifestyle. These skills include preventative health behaviors such as attending routine medical and dental checkups, understanding basic health information, recognizing symptoms requiring medical attention, and adhering to medication or treatment plans. They also include health-protective behaviors such as engaging in regular physical activity, maintaining a balanced diet, controlling body weight, practicing good sleep hygiene, and avoiding harmful substances (e.g., quitting smoking, limiting alcohol consumption). Furthermore, health-related skills include personal health management and safety practices such as correctly using personal protective equipment (e.g., masks, gloves, helmets), following hygiene routines to prevent illness, managing chronic health conditions, and understanding how lifestyle choices impact long-term health outcomes.

4.1.2 Decreasing Behaviors

Decreasing or reducing behaviors refer to classes of observable and measurable behaviors that are intentionally targeted for reduction because they hinder learning, social participation, safety, or overall quality of life. Reducing behaviors are generally functionally defined; that is, they are classified according to their negative impact on the individual or environment. The goal of intervention may be to reduce the frequency, duration, intensity, or likelihood of the behavior, rather than to eliminate it entirely. In many cases, reduction goals are addressed in conjunction with teaching appropriate alternative or substitution desirable behaviors that serve similar functions. Examples of decreasing behaviors include compulsive behaviors such as aggression, self-harm, property damage, tantrums, disobedience, and escape, which may pose safety risks or significantly disrupt educational routines. This category also includes disruptive or inhibiting behaviors such as extracurricular behavior, stereotypical behaviors that hinder learning, excessive vocalization, or refusal to participate in academic tasks. In academic and social contexts, behavior reduction may include reducing inappropriate verbal behaviors (e.g., yelling, interrupting, repetitive speech), socially inappropriate actions, or behaviors that limit peer interaction and classroom cohesion.

In autism intervention research, behavior reduction is often addressed in conjunction with skill acquisition goals, and performance criteria are typically specified in terms of responses that remain acceptable (e.g., reduced occurrence rather than complete absence). In summary, behavior reduction for undesirable behaviors of autistic persons represents a critical area of intervention focused on enhancing adaptive functioning, promoting safety, and supporting meaningful participation in home, school, and community settings.

4.2 Rubric Development Study to Set Optimal Performance Criteria in Autism Interventions

To develop two separate rubrics to establish optimal performance criteria for autism interventions targeting behavior acquisition and behavior reduction, two complementary approaches were followed. First, based on the results of Chap. 3 and the author's own experiences, two candidate rubrics were generated: one for increasing behaviors and one for decreasing behaviors, considering potential parameters that have relationships between study variables and performance criteria components (i.e., level and frequency) assigned in studies. Because Chap. 3 identified meaningful differences in how performance criteria were applied across dependent variable categories for behaviors targeted for increase, separate recommendation tables were also constructed for each skill domain to support domain-specific interpretation and application of the rubric for the behavior acquisition interventions. In contrast, because behavioral reduction efforts were not categorized by dependent variable area, a single recommendation table was deemed sufficient for these interventions.

After constructing these two rubrics and the corresponding recommendation tables, a complementary validation step was undertaken through a focus group interview conducted via a scheduled Zoom meeting. The focus group consisted of six experts, although eight experts initially intended to participate. The remaining two experts who were invited to the focus group, but were unable to attend for various reasons, also submitted their opinions in writing. All experts held PhD degrees in autism-related fields, such as special education and applied behavior analysis. Almost all experts also had experience implementing various interventions for autistic participants to improve their behavioral outcomes. Following these discussions and feedback, the rubrics and interpretation tables were finalized. Tables 4.1a and 4.2a present the finalized rubrics, including the scoring systems used to determine optimal performance criteria for behaviors to be increased and those to be decreased, respectively.

Table 4.1a Performance criteria setting rubric for increasing behaviors in autism interventions

A. Participant characteristics		Scores	Notes
Age group	0 to 5 years (Preschool)	1	
	6 to 13 years (Elementary)	2	
	14 to 18 years (Secondary)	2	
	19 or older (Post-secondary)	3	
Intellectual disability	Severe	1	
	Moderate	2	
	Mild or no intellectual disability	3	
Other comorbid conditions (CCs)	Multiple CCs (e.g., ADHD + SLD)	1	
	Single CC (e.g., ADHD or SLD)	2	
	No other comorbidity/ high-functioning autism	3	
B. Skill characteristics			
Prerequisite conditions			
1. *Is the target skill a prerequisite for skills in that field?*	Yes	1	
	No	0	
2. *Is the target skill a prerequisite for skills in other areas?*	Yes	1	
	No	0	
3. *Does the targeted skill represent a behavioral cusp?*	Yes	1	
	No	0	
4. *Does the targeted skill represent a pivotal behavior?*	Yes	1	
	No	0	
Task complexity	Multiple operations/ chained skills	2	
	Single-step/discrete	3	
Daily use	Low (1 to 3 times)	1	
	Moderate (4 to 6)	2	
	High (7 or more)	3	
Practitioner perspective	Low instructional priority	1	
	Moderately important	2	
	Instructionally critical	3	
Participant perspective	Low functional relevance	1	
	Moderate impact	2	
	High autonomy impact	3	
Family perspective	Low everyday relevance	1	
	Situationally useful	2	
	Daily life essential	3	

(*continued*)

Table 4.1a (continued)

		Scores	Notes
C. Measurement details			
Planned instructional intensity (e.g., probe intensity)	Low (1 to 3 sessions per week)	1	
	Moderate (4 to 6)	2	
	High (7 or more)	3	
Critical steps percentage of total task in multiple/chained skills	Not applicable or 0–33%	1	
	34–66%	2	
	67–100%	3	
Mean of baseline level	Zero	1	
	1–30%	2	
	31 and more %	3	
Total score			

ADHD: Attention-deficit/hyperactivity disorder, SLD: Specific learning disability

Explanatory information for the increasing behaviors rubric

Participant characteristics

1. The age range of school periods may vary from country to country. In such cases, it is advisable to consider whether the participant falls within the specified age range.
2. Because intellectual disability was highly common in individuals with ASD, intellectual disability and other comorbid conditions were given as separate items of the sub-scale. Other comorbid conditions should be evaluated independently of intellectual disability.

Skill characteristics

1. Prerequisite conditions of the targeted skills are examined into four aspects. One of these relates to the field of study. For example, if a targeted mathematical skill constitutes a prerequisite for acquiring another mathematical skill, this item is scored as "yes." Another is related to skills outside the field of study. For example, if a mathematical skill being studied constitutes a prerequisite for skills to be studied in areas such as facilitating daily life or strengthening social skills, this item is scored as "yes." Thirdly, the skill is examined to determine whether it has a behavioral cusp feature. A *behavioral cusp*, as defined by Rosales-Ruiz and Baer (1997), is "a behavior change that has consequences for the organism beyond the change itself, some of which may be considered important" (p. 534) and "cusps are behavior changes, sometimes simple, sometimes complex, that systematically cause other, further, not formally programmed behavior changes that are significant either because of their breadth or because of their importance to the organism or its species" (p. 537). For example, eye contact or the use of a communication device can function as a behavioral cusp (see Rosales-Ruiz & Baer, 1997, for details). Lastly, the targeted behavior is evaluated to determine whether it has a pivotal behavior feature. A pivotal behavior leads to changes across a wide range of areas without the need for additional training (Koegel & Frea, 1993; Mahoney et al., 2007; Stahmer, 1995). For example, number sense or social interaction can be conceptualized as pivotal behaviors.
2. In daily use, using the skill 1 to 3 times can be considered "low," 4 to 6 times "moderate," and 7 or more times "high."
3. Perspective categories may include subjective assessments. While open to interpretation, it is recommended that these items be carefully considered and scored to determine an accurate performance criterion based on task type. If the participant is unable to respond, the practitioner or family can give a score on the importance of the skill being studied for the participant. As a side note, "practitioner" can refer to a teacher, therapist, or medical practitioner.

(*continued*)

Table 4.1a (continued)

Measurement details
1. In terms of planned instructional intensity, 1 to 3 intervention sessions per week can be considered "low," 4 to 6 sessions "moderate," and 7 or more sessions "high."
Other details
• Notes column: This column allows notes to be taken for unspecified or unforeseen circumstances of the scored items. • Ranges below 80% were not considered a recommended range for behaviors that are desired to be improved, as they are generally underreported in the literature. However, given the nature of targeted behaviors and the characteristics of the participants, a target below 80% is better than not working at all. Even increasing a behavior from 0% to 70% or even 50% can have meaningful consequences for participants and their environments. • If the study will set another type performance criterion (e.g., count, score, frequency, duration), that type can be considered as percentage. For example, maximum count and score can be considered 100% and the targeted count or score can be converted to the targeted percentage. On the other hand, if there is a maximum frequency value in behavior measurements, this value can be accepted as 100%. Another example is if there is a targeted duration in a study, this duration can be considered 100%.

4.2.1 Rubric for Increasing Behaviors

Three sub-scales were constructed to influence the setting of performance criteria: (a) participant characteristics, (b) skill characteristics, and (c) measurement details. Participant characteristics include: (a) age-group, (b) intellectual disability, and (c) other comorbid conditions. Skill characteristics contain: (a) prerequisite conditions, (b) task complexity, (c) daily use, (d) practitioner perspective, (e) participant perspective, and (f) family perspective. And lastly, measurement details cover: (a) planned instructional intensity, (b) critical steps percentage of total task in multiple/chained skills, and (c) mean of baseline level. To interpret the obtained scores in various skill domains, separately, skill-based interpretation tables were also presented. Interpretation tables were given for the six domains of desirable behaviors (as highlighted in the "increasing behaviors") and finalized after the focus group interview. Table 4.1a shows the rubric scale for increasing behaviors, whereas Tables 4.1b, 4.1c, 4.1d, 4.1e, 4.1f and 4.1g present the interpretation of the obtained scores by skill domain. To provide a more transparent and objective assessment, explanatory information has been added below the rubric score table for each sub-scale category.

4.2.2 Rubric for Decreasing Behaviors

Three sub-scales were also used when setting performance criteria for the behaviors targeted for reduction: (a) participant characteristics, (b) functional characteristics of behavior, and (c) measurement details. Like in the increasing behaviors rubric, participant characteristics include: (a) age-group, (b) intellectual disability, and (c) other comorbid conditions. On the other hand, functional characteristics of behavior

Table 4.1b Domain 1: Academic tasks

Total score range	Recommended PC level	Recommended PC frequency	Suggestive information
≤ 20	Mid-range (80–89%)	2	Academic performance may fluctuate due to task demands or learner characteristics. A moderate acquisition level supports acquisition without inhibiting the variability necessary for fluency development.
21–29	Mid to high (90–99%)	2 or 3	The optimal balance between instructional rigor and transfer of academic skills. Most academic skills are acquired steadily, which can facilitate generalization across contexts and continued durability of the academic skills after instruction ends. *The heavily favored performance criteria for academic skills in the autism literature, as shown in Chap.* 3.
≥ 30	High/strict (100%)	3	Appropriate when academic skill is a prerequisite, safety-related, or instructionally critical. Monitor for ceiling effects and the generalization and retention of skills acquired with the highest criterion.

Table 4.1c Domain 2: Social communication/social skills

Total score range	Recommended PC level	Recommended PC frequency	Suggestive information
≤ 20	Mid-range (80–89%)	2	A moderately stringent criterion can be appropriate during early stages of skill acquisition or for exploratory social targets, where allowing variability and spontaneity in responding can be essential for supporting naturalistic generalization.
21–29	Mid to high (90–99%)	2 or 3	Suitable for structured social objectives (e.g., scripted initiations). In structured environments, durability can be maintained around the pre-determined performance criterion level. Incorporate with explicit generalization programming. *The heavily favored performance criteria for social communication/ social skills in the autism literature, as shown in Chap.* 3.
≥ 30	High/strict (100%)	3	Use cautiously, as excessive stringency may suppress spontaneous responding and constrain generalization across contexts.

Table 4.1d Domain 3: Verbal language

Total score range	Recommended PC level	Recommended PC frequency	Suggestive information
≤ 20	Mid-range (80–89%)	2	Language emergence often involves response variability. Lower stringency can support shaping and expansion of language acquisition. *The heavily preferred performance criteria for verbal language in the autism literature, as shown in Chap.* 3
21–29	Mid to high (90–99%)	2 or 3	It can support stable language use while maintaining flexibility in generalization across contexts and interlocutors.
≥ 30	High/strict (100%)	3	Use cautiously. High stringency may restrict spontaneous responding and limit generalization across different contexts.

Table 4.1e Domain 4: Daily living skills

Total score range	Recommended PC level	Recommended PC frequency	Suggestive information
≤ 20	Mid-range (80–89%)	2	Partial independence may be functionally sufficient; mid-range criteria permit acceptable variability without functional breakdown across daily routines.
21–29	Mid to high (90–99%)	2 or 3	Best balance between independence, maintenance, and transfer across settings. *The heavily favored performance criteria for daily living skills in the autism literature, as shown in Chap. 3.*
≥ 30	High/strict (100%)	3	Suitable for safety-critical steps or chained routines where negligence would compromise function.

cover: (a) severity of problem behavior, (b) risk to self or others, (c) acceptability of the targeted residual behavior after the intervention ended, (d) contextual pervasiveness, (e) practitioner perspective, and (f) family perspective. Last, measurement details contain: (a) planned treatment density, (b) baseline stability of the targeted decreasing behavior, and (c) mean of baseline level. An interpretation table for the scores obtained from the rubric for undesirable behaviors was constructed and finalized after the focus group interview. Table 4.2a shows the rubric scale for decreasing behaviors, whereas Table 4.2b presents the interpretation of the obtained scores for undesirable behaviors. Explanatory information has also been added below the rubric score table for the sub-scale categories to ensure a more transparent and objective assessment.

Table 4.1f Domain 5: Safety skills

Total score range	Recommended PC level	Recommended PC frequency	Suggestive information
≤ 20	Mid-range (80–89%)	2	Not recommended. Consider risks for the safety of an autistic person when performing these skills in real environments at this range level. However, rather than abandoning instruction due to the perceived difficulty of achieving perfect performance, some safety skills (e.g., protection from digital environments) may be targeted around a criterion level of 80%.
21–29	Mid to high (90–99%)	2 or 3	Use cautiously. It may be suitable only for safety-critical steps in cases where the skills are crucial in real settings but do not pose any life-threatening risks.
≥ 30	High/strict (100%)	3	Suitable for safety-critical steps in cases where the skills are crucial in real settings and have various life-threatening risks. *The heavily preferred performance criteria for safety skills in the autism literature, as shown in Chap.* 3

Table 4.1g Domain 6: Health-related skills

Total score range	Recommended PC level	Recommended PC frequency	Suggestive information
≤ 20	Mid-range (80–89%)	2	Functional adequacy may be sufficient for non-critical health routines (e.g., basic hygiene sequences, hydration behaviors, or scheduled wellness activities); mid-range criteria allow minor, non-hazardous variability without compromising overall health outcomes.
21–29	Mid to high (90–99%)	2 or 3	Behavioral consistency with maintenance and generalization while minimizing health-related risk. *The heavily favored performance criteria for health skills in the autism literature, as shown in Chap.* 3.
≥ 30	High/strict (100%)	3	Recommended for safety-critical or risk-sensitive health behaviors (e.g., medication administration, medical hygiene), where errors may lead to harmful consequences.

4.3 Concluding Remarks

This chapter addressed a longstanding but under-specified methodological issue in autism intervention research: how to set performance criteria in a principled, transparent, and functionally meaningful manner. Building on the empirical patterns

Table 4.2a Performance criteria setting rubric for decreasing behaviors in autism interventions

A. Participant characteristics		Scores	Notes
Age group	0 to 5 years (Preschool)	1	
	6 to 13 years (Elementary)	2	
	14 to 18 years (Secondary)	2	
	19 or older (Post-secondary)	3	
Intellectual disability	Severe	1	
	Moderate	2	
	Mild or no intellectual disability	3	
Other comorbid conditions (CCs)	Multiple CCs (e.g., ADHD + SLD)	1	
	Single CC (e.g., ADHD or SLD)	2	
	No other comorbidity/ high-functioning autism	3	
B. Functional characteristics of behavior			
Severity of problem behavior	Mild (1 to 5 occurrences per day)	1	
	Moderate (6 to 10)	2	
	Severe (11 or more)	3	
Risk to self or others	Low (1 to 2 occurrences per day)	1	
	Moderate (3 to 5)	2	
	High (6 or more)	3	
Acceptability of the targeted residual behavior (after the intervention ended)	Acceptable	1	
	Partially acceptable	2	
	Unacceptable	3	
Contextual pervasiveness	A single context-specific	1	
	Multiple contexts (more than one)	2	
	Pervasive across conditions (consistently across diverse conditions)	3	
Practitioner perspectives	Partial reduction acceptable	1	
	Strong reduction desirable	2	
	Near-zero occurrence required	3	
Family perspective	Residual behavior manageable (after the intervention ended)	1	
	Creates moderate daily burden	2	
	Severely disrupts family life / safety	3	

(*continued*)

Table 4.2a (continued)

		Scores	Notes
C. Measurement details			
Planned treatment intensity (e.g., probe intensity)	Low (1 to 5 sessions per week)	1	
	Moderate (6 to 10)	2	
	High (11 or more)	3	
Baseline stability of the targeted decreasing behavior	Highly variable	1	
	Moderately stable	2	
	Highly stable	3	
Mean of baseline level	Top level	1	
	1–30% lower than the top level	2	
	31 or more % lower than the top level	3	
Total score			

Explanatory information for the decreasing behaviors rubric

Participant characteristics

1. The age range of school periods may vary from country to country. In such cases, it is advisable to consider whether the participant falls within the specified age range.
2. Because intellectual disability was highly common in individuals with ASD, intellectual disability and other comorbid conditions were given as separate items of the sub-scale. Other comorbid conditions should be evaluated independently of intellectual disability.

Functional characteristics of behavior

1. In terms of the severity of problem behavior, frequencies of 1 to 5 occurrences per day may be scored as "low," 6 to 10 occurrences as "moderate," and 11 or more occurrences per day as "high."
2. With respect to the risk to self or others, frequencies of 1 to 2 occurrences per day may be scored as "low", 3 to 5 occurrences as "moderate," and 6 or more occurrences per day as "high."
3. As for the acceptability of the targeted residual behavior after the intervention ended, a 1–20% reduction from mean baseline level of the targeted disruptive behavior (i.e., remaining behavior is 80% or upper of the mean baseline level) might be considered "unacceptable"; a 21–49% reduction "partially acceptable" (i.e., remaining behavior is 51–79% of the mean baseline level), and a 50% or greater reduction "acceptable" (i.e., remaining behavior is 0–49% of the mean baseline level).
4. In terms of the contextual pervasiveness of disruptive behavior, single context–specific refers to situations in which the target disruptive behavior occurs only under one clearly defined condition, such as in the presence of a particular person or within a specific setting. In contrast, multiple contexts indicate that the disruptive behavior occurs across more than one context, for example, when the behavior is observed with both the practitioner and a family member, or across different settings. Pervasive across conditions, on the other hand, refers to situations in which the disruptive behavior occurs under more than one condition. For example, the behavior may be observed both in the presence of a particular person and in a setting when that person is absent. Importantly, such observations should be consistent across the conditions in question; that is, the disruptive behavior should be exhibited consistently whenever the participant encounters that person and/or that setting.
5. Perspective categories may include subjective assessments. While open to interpretation, it is recommended that these items be carefully considered and scored to determine an accurate performance criterion based on behavior function.

(continued)

Table 4.2a (continued)

Measurement details
1. In terms of planned treatment intensity, 1 to 5 intervention sessions per week can be considered "low," 6 to 10 sessions "moderate," and 11 or more sessions "high."
2. As for the baseline stability of the targeted decreasing behavior, the guidelines proposed by Lane and Gast (2014) can be followed. They suggested that a stability envelope defined as ±20% of the baseline mean or median can be used to evaluate stability. Within this framework, if 80% or more of the baseline data points fall within this stability envelope, the baseline data can be considered "highly stable." If 50%–79% of the baseline data points fall within the stability envelope, the baseline data can be classified as "moderately stable." When 49% or fewer of the baseline data points fall within the stability envelope, the baseline data can be considered "highly variable."
3. There may be no limit at the top level of a problem behavior. In such cases, the highest data point obtained in the baseline phase can be considered the top level.
Other details
• Notes column: This column allows notes to be taken for unspecified or unforeseen circumstances of the scored items.
• If a percentage reduction from the baseline average is aimed, then the baseline average is accepted as 100%. For example, a study aims to decrease problem behaviors by 80% from the baseline average. In this case, the baseline average is accepted as 100% and supposes that the problem behavior is targeted to be reduced to 20%.
• If the study will set another type performance criterion (e.g., count, score, frequency, duration), that type can be considered as percentage. Minimum count (i.e., 0), score (e.g., 1), frequency (i.e., 0), or duration (i.e., 0) can be considered 0% and the targeted count, score, frequency, or duration can be converted to the targeted percentage.

identified in Chap. 3, the chapter first distinguished between two fundamentally different intervention targets: increasing and decreasing behaviors. And then systematically organized these targets into well-defined domains and functional categories. This distinction provided the conceptual foundation for the development of two separate, domain-sensitive rubrics designed to guide the selection of optimal performance-criterion levels and frequencies.

For behaviors targeted for increase, six main intervention domains were delineated: (a) academic tasks, (b) social communication/social skills, (c) verbal language, (d) daily living skills, (e) safety skills, and (f) health-related skills. Although these domains differ substantially in their instructional demands, functional significance, and risk profiles, the findings underscore that performance criteria operate as a dependent variable-sensitive design feature rather than an arbitrary form. The rubric for increasing behaviors reflects this sensitivity by integrating participant and skill characteristics, measurement details, and pairing the resulting scores with domain-specific interpretation tables. In doing so, the rubric moves beyond artificial mastery thresholds and provides a structured mechanism for aligning criterion stringency with the functional role of the skill, its expected variability, and its real-world consequences.

Similarly, the rubric developed for decreasing behaviors acknowledges that behavior-reduction goals require a fundamentally different logic than skill

Table 4.2b Interpretation of rubric scores for decreasing behaviors and recommended performance criteria

Total score range	Recommended PC level	Recommended PC frequency	Suggestive information
≤18	Lower-range (>20% remaining behavior)	1 or 2	A substantial reduction may be sufficient when problem behavior occurs in the presence of a single specific context, is low in severity, and poses minimal risk. Allowing residual behavior above 20% can be functionally acceptable when remaining responses are manageable for families and practitioners and do not meaningfully interfere with safety, participation, or quality of life. This level supports social validity and avoids excessive instructional demands. *The heavily favored performance criteria for behavior reduction studies in the autism literature, as shown in Chap. 3.*
19–24	Mid-range (11–20% remaining behavior)	2	Appropriate when problem behavior requires reliable reduction, but some residual responding is tolerable and does not pose a risk that could endanger a person's life. This range supports functional improvement while acknowledging contextual variability and natural fluctuation in behavior reduction outcomes. *The other heavily preferred performance criteria for behavior reduction studies in the autism literature, as shown in Chap. 3.*
25–30	Mid to high (1–10% remaining behavior)	2 or 3	This range promotes behavioral stability, maintenance, and generalization while minimizing meaningful disruption across conditions (see Chap. 3). Suitable when near-elimination is desirable but absolute suppression is not functionally required.
≥31	High/strict (0%)	3	Zero-tolerance criteria are warranted only when any residual occurrence of problem behavior is severe, high-risk, or consistently pervasive across diverse conditions and is functionally unacceptable due to safety, health, or quality-of-life concerns.

acquisition targets. Rather than assuming that zero occurrence is always desirable or feasible, the rubric explicitly incorporates functional considerations such as severity, risk, contextual pervasiveness, and the acceptability of residual behavior. This approach reflects prevailing practices in the autism intervention literature, in which partial but functionally meaningful reductions are often sufficient to improve engagement, safety, and quality of life. By linking rubric scores to graded performance-criterion ranges, the chapter provides a defensible framework for determining when lower, mid-range, or strict criteria are warranted, and when zero-tolerance criteria should be reserved for high-risk or life-threatening behaviors.

An important contribution of this chapter lies in its emphasis on transparency and social validity in performance-criteria selection. The inclusion of practitioner and family perspectives, along with explicit guidance on instructional intensity and baseline characteristics, acknowledges that performance criteria are not merely statistical endpoints but decision points with practical and ethical implications. The focus group validation process further strengthened the ecological validity of the rubrics, ensuring that they reflect both empirical evidence and expert judgment grounded in applied experience.

Overall, this chapter offers a systematic and empirically informed framework for setting performance criteria in autism interventions. By operationalizing performance-criterion decisions through structured rubrics and domain-specific interpretation tables, it provides researchers and practitioners with a practical tool for improving consistency, interpretability, and functional relevance in intervention design. In the broader context of this book, the proposed rubrics serve as a bridge between descriptive analyses of existing practices and actionable guidance for future research and applied studies.

References

Aydin, O., & Tanious, R. (2022). Performance criteria-based effect size (PCES) measurement of single-case experimental designs: A real-world data study. *Journal of Applied Behavior Analysis, 55*(3), 891–918. https://doi.org/10.1002/jaba.928

Baer, D. M., Wolf, M. M., & Risley, T. R. (1968). Some current dimensions of applied behavior analysis. *Journal of Applied Behavior Analysis, 1*(1), 91–97. https://doi.org/10.1901/jaba.1968.1-91

Koegel, R. L., & Frea, W. D. (1993). Treatment of social behavior in autism through the modification of pivotal social skills. *Journal of Applied Behavior Analysis, 26*(3), 369–377. https://doi.org/10.1901/jaba.1993.26-369

Lane, J. D., & Gast, D. L. (2014). Visual analysis in single case experimental design studies: Brief review and guidelines. *Neuropsychological Rehabilitation, 24*(3–4), 445–463. https://doi.org/10.1080/09602011.2013.815636

Mahoney, G., Kim, J. M., & Lin, C. (2007). Pivotal behavior model of developmental learning. *Infants & Young Children, 20*(4), 311–325. https://doi.org/10.1097/01.IYC.0000290354.39793.74

Rosales-Ruiz, J., & Baer, D. M. (1997). Behavioral cusps: A developmental and pragmatic concept for behavior analysis. *Journal of Applied Behavior Analysis, 30*(3), 533–544. https://doi.org/10.1901/jaba.1997.30-533

Stahmer, A. C. (1995). Teaching symbolic play skills to children with autism using pivotal response training. *Journal of Autism and Developmental Disorders, 25*(2), 123–141. https://doi.org/10.1007/BF02178500

Wolf, M. M. (1978). Social validity: The case for subjective measurement or how applied behavior analysis is finding its heart. *Journal of Applied Behavior Analysis, 11*(2), 203–214. https://doi.org/10.1901/jaba.1978.11-203

Correction to: Optimal Performance Criteria in Autism Studies

Correction to:
O. Aydin, *Optimal Performance Criteria in Autism Studies*, SpringerBriefs in Modern Perspectives on Disability Research, https://doi.org/10.1007/978-981-95-8542-7

In the original publication of the book, several figure captions were incorrectly printed. The affected captions and their correct versions are listed below by chapter:

Chapter 2: Impact of Performance Criteria on Behaviors

Figure 2.2 (page 33): The caption originally read (Fig. 2.2 Regression analysis of performance criteria levels on response maintenance (*Source*: Aydin, n.d.)).

The correct caption should read: (Fig. 2.3 Descriptive features of generalization data of the included studies from JABA issues between 2019 and 2023. PC: Performance Criteria).

Figure 2.3 (page 35): The caption originally read (Fig. 2.3 Descriptive features of generalization data of the included studies from JABA issues between 2019 and 2023. PC: Performance Criteria).

The correct caption should read: (Fig. 2.2. Regression analysis of performance criteria levels on response maintenance (Source: Aydin, n.d.)).

The updated versions of these chapters can be found at
https://doi.org/10.1007/978-981-95-8542-7_2
https://doi.org/10.1007/978-981-95-8542-7_3

© The Author(s), under exclusive license to Springer Nature Singapore Pte Ltd. 2026

O. Aydin, *Optimal Performance Criteria in Autism Studies*, SpringerBriefs in Modern Perspectives on Disability Research,
https://doi.org/10.1007/978-981-95-8542-7_5

Chapter 3 Optimal Performance Criteria in Autism Intervention Studies

Figure 3.1a (page 52): The caption originally read (Fig. 3.1a Distributions of performance criteria levels in autism studies).
The correct caption should read: (Fig. 3.4 Descriptive distributions of maintenance data collected in autism studies).

Figure 3.1b (page 52): The caption originally read (Fig. 3.1b Distributions of performance criteria frequencies in autism studies).
The correct caption should read: (Fig. 3.3 Descriptive distributions of participant characteristics in autism studies).

Figure 3.1c (page 53): The caption originally read (Fig. 3.1c Distributions of performance criteria types in autism studies).
The correct caption should read: (Fig. 3.2 Descriptive distributions of dependent and independent variable categories in autism studies).

Figure 3.2 (page 54): The caption originally read (Fig. 3.2 Descriptive distributions of participant characteristics in autism studies).
The correct caption should read: (Fig. 3.6 Descriptive distributions of generalization data collected in autism studies).

Figure 3.3 (page 58): The caption originally read (Fig. 3.3 Descriptive distributions of participant characteristics in autism studies).
The correct caption should read: (Fig. 3.8 Descriptive information on sessions collected while meeting performance criteria in autism studies).

Figure 3.4 (page 61): The caption originally read (Fig. 3.4 Descriptive distributions of maintenance data collected in autism studies).
The correct caption should read: (Fig. 3.9 Descriptive information for the number of trials conducted in a session in autism interventions that met performance criteria).

Figure 3.5 (page 64): The caption originally read (Fig. 3.5 Regression analysis of performance criteria levels on response maintenance rates in autism studies).
The correct caption should read: (Fig. 3.1a Distributions of performance criteria levels in autism studies).

Figure 3.6 (page 66): The caption originally read (Fig. 3.6 Descriptive distributions of generalization data collected in autism studies).
The correct caption should read: (Fig. 3.1b Distributions of performance criteria frequencies in autism studies).

Figure 3.7 (page 69): The caption originally read (Fig. 3.7 Regression analysis of performance criteria levels on generalization rates in autism studies).
The correct caption should read: (Fig. 3.1c Distributions of performance criteria types in autism studies).

Figure 3.8 (page 71): The caption originally read (Fig. 3.8 Descriptive information on sessions collected while meeting performance criteria in autism studies).

The correct caption should read: (Fig. 3.5 Regression analysis of performance criteria levels on response maintenance rates in autism studies).

Figure 3.9 (page 72): The caption originally read (Fig. 3.9 Descriptive information for the number of trials conducted in a session in autism inter-ventions that met performance criteria which has been updated as below:).

The correct caption should read: (Fig. 3.7 Regression analysis of performance criteria levels on generalization rates in autism studies).

MIX
Papier aus verantwortungsvollen Quellen
Paper from responsible sources
FSC® C105338

If you have any concerns about our products,
you can contact us on
ProductSafety@springernature.com

In case Publisher is established outside the EU,
the EU authorized representative is:
Springer Nature Customer Service Center GmbH
Europaplatz 3, 69115 Heidelberg, Germany

Printed by Libri Plureos GmbH
in Hamburg, Germany

SpringerBriefs in Business

AF794138

SpringerBriefs present concise summaries of cutting-edge research and practical applications across a wide spectrum of fields. Featuring compact volumes of 50 to 125 pages, the series covers a range of content from professional to academic. Typical topics might include:

- A timely report of state-of-the art analytical techniques
- A bridge between new research results, as published in journal articles, and a contextual literature review
- A snapshot of a hot or emerging topic
- An in-depth case study or clinical example
- A presentation of core concepts that students must understand in order to make independent contributions

SpringerBriefs in Business showcase emerging theory, empirical research, and practical application in management, finance, entrepreneurship, marketing, operations research, and related fields, from a global author community.

Briefs are characterized by fast, global electronic dissemination, standard publishing contracts, standardized manuscript preparation and formatting guidelines, and expedited production schedules.

Hiroshi Kawakami

Case Collection of the Benefits of Inconvenience

Springer

Hiroshi Kawakami
Graduate School of Engineering
Kyoto University of Advanced Science
Kyoto-shi, Kyoto, Japan

ISSN 2191-5482 ISSN 2191-5490 (electronic)
SpringerBriefs in Business
ISBN 978-981-92-3980-1 ISBN 978-981-92-3981-8 (eBook)
https://doi.org/10.1007/978-981-92-3981-8

© The Editor(s) (if applicable) and The Author(s), under exclusive license to Springer Nature Singapore Pte Ltd. 2026

This work is subject to copyright. All rights are solely and exclusively licensed by the Publisher, whether the whole or part of the material is concerned, specifically the rights of translation, reprinting, reuse of illustrations, recitation, broadcasting, reproduction on microfilms or in any other physical way, and transmission or information storage and retrieval, electronic adaptation, computer software, or by similar or dissimilar methodology now known or hereafter developed.
The use of general descriptive names, registered names, trademarks, service marks, etc. in this publication does not imply, even in the absence of a specific statement, that such names are exempt from the relevant protective laws and regulations and therefore free for general use.
The publisher, the authors and the editors are safe to assume that the advice and information in this book are believed to be true and accurate at the date of publication. Neither the publisher nor the authors or the editors give a warranty, expressed or implied, with respect to the material contained herein or for any errors or omissions that may have been made. The publisher remains neutral with regard to jurisdictional claims in published maps and institutional affiliations.

This Springer imprint is published by the registered company Springer Nature Singapore Pte Ltd.
The registered company address is: 152 Beach Road, #21-01/04 Gateway East, Singapore 189721, Singapore

If disposing of this product, please recycle the paper.

Preface

This book is the first to gather vivid, down-to-earth examples showing that inconvenience often brings real benefits. There is a common belief that faster, easier, and more efficient is always better, but this is not necessarily true. Unlike heavy, abstract philosophical works questioning that belief, this book takes a very different approach, presenting concrete, relatable stories from everyday life and a wide range of disciplines. The reader then sees how inconvenience can lead to sharper thinking, deeper understanding, and unexpected insights.

From small frictions that spark creativity to deliberate inefficiencies that produce richer experiences, the book makes a strong case for the fact that some of the most meaningful gains appear only when things are not perfectly smooth. Stretching the mind, creating something new, or seeing the world from a fresh angle thus offers the powerful insight that some benefits cannot be achieved without inconvenience.

The latter half of the book features a unique reverse index, organizing examples by academic field. Whether the reader's interests lean toward science, engineering, design, education, or the humanities, a quick look at the contents may reveal surprising connections to a particular discipline or answer a question that simply arises out of curiosity.

Kyoto, Japan Hiroshi Kawakami

Competing Interests The author has no competing interests to declare that are relevant to the content of this manuscript.

Contents

Chapter 1
What is the "Inconvenience" and How to Make "Benefit of Inconvenience (BoI)" a Good Reference for Effective Design

It is common for people to think that convenient tools and methods are beneficial, and they do not want to use inconvenient ones. Even when it is argued that certain benefits can only be attained through inconvenience, such a claim is not readily understood. Accordingly, this book presents several case studies to facilitate a clearer understanding of this perspective.

Definition of Convenience and Inconvenience

In this book, convenience and inconvenience are defined as follows:

Convenience: A situation in which the effort to complete a task is small.

Inconvenience: A situation that is not convenient.

The word "small" is used here to show that convenience and inconvenience are relative. In other words, they depend on comparison. We take the position that absolute convenience, absolute inconvenience, or a fixed degree of convenience cannot be defined.

In addition, "effort" includes the following two types:

Physical effort: Work that requires time and physical action.

Psychological effort: The use of cognitive resources, such as paying attention, remembering, and thinking, or the need for specific skills.

From this point of view, the rules that restrict each sport can also be seen as a form of inconvenience. In such cases, the benefits that can only be obtained through inconvenience are the enjoyment of sports that would not exist without rules. Of course, examples of the benefits of inconvenience (BoI) are not limited to sports, and the benefits are not limited to enjoyment. In this book, we introduce examples from many different fields where various kinds of benefits can be obtained.

Common Features of Examples of the Benefits of Inconvenience (BoI)

The following three points are common to examples of the benefits of inconvenience (BoI):

1. The same person experiences the inconvenience and also receives the benefit.

© The Author(s), under exclusive license to Springer Nature Singapore Pte Ltd. 2026

H. Kawakami, *Case Collection of the Benefits of Inconvenience*,
SpringerBriefs in Business, https://doi.org/10.1007/978-981-92-3981-8_1

2. The benefit can only be obtained through inconvenience.
3. The benefit is gained in addition to the main goal of the task

In contrast to point 1, if a person causes trouble (inconvenience) to others and gains benefits for oneself, this is not a benefit of inconvenience. In contrast to point 2, if the same benefit can be obtained by a convenient method, there is no need to choose an inconvenient one. In contrast to point 3, the statement "abdominal exercises were hard, but my abdominal muscles became stronger" simply means that the main goal was achieved and does not represent an additional benefit.

Design of Systems that Provide the Benefits of Inconvenience

Focusing on the benefits of inconvenience (BoI) is not simply a form of nostalgia, nor is it a movement that argues we should "return to the good old ways of the past." Rather, it is both a point of view for reexamining existing things and a guideline for designing new ones.

When reexamining existing things, the three points described above can be used as criteria for identifying whether a case represents the benefit of inconvenience (BoI). In addition, to serve as useful references, Chapter 2 of this book presents examples classified into the following four categories:

- Disappointing convenience (imaginary cases)
- Disappointing convenience (real cases)
- Experience of benefits of inconvenience (or beneficial inconvenience)
- Design incorporating intentional inconvenience

When used as guidelines for designing new things, the three points above serve as necessary conditions for a system that produces benefits through inconvenience. Because they are only necessary conditions, satisfying all three does not guarantee that the result will be an interesting or effective system. To provide helpful references, Chapter 3 of this book introduces some designs that were proposed in past design workshops, exercises, and design competitions.

Chapter 2
Collected Examples

2.1 Disappointing Convenience (Imaginary Case)

This section collects imaginary cases where convenience derives disappointment.

Fuji Mountain Escalator

Mount Fuji is the tallest mountain in Japan. Standing at just under 4000 meters, many people enjoy climbing it outside of the winter season. Some people even climb it every year. Many foreign tourists also climb Mount Fuji to create memories of their visit to Japan. Climbing Mount Fuji has become a very popular tourist activity.

But what if an escalator were installed from the base to the summit so that the round trip, normally taking about ten hours, could be done more easily? Figure 2.1 illustrates such a fictional escalator. It would certainly be convenient because it would save time and effort. However, at the same time, it would also be quite disappointing.

Although it is physically challenging, the process of climbing the highest mountain in Japan is itself enjoyable. Because it is challenging, reaching the summit provides a strong sense of achievement. It builds confidence in one's physical ability and becomes a lasting memory. A convenient escalator would destroy all these values. A place that can be reached simply by paying money has little appeal.

Model Kit Assembly Service

Many people enjoy building plastic models as a hobby. Subjects range widely, including cars, motorcycles, airplanes, ships, robots, and anime characters. Model kits contain many parts, which are painted and assembled. Some people paint the parts after assembly to make the seams less noticeable. Through their own ingenuity, they aim to create a finished product that is unique.

This process requires time, effort, and careful thought. So, what if there were a service that assembled the model on your behalf as shown in Fig. 2.2? Disappointing!

Although assembling and painting many small parts takes time and effort, it is enjoyable. Because of this investment, people can incorporate their own ideas into

© The Author(s), under exclusive license to Springer Nature Singapore Pte Ltd. 2026

H. Kawakami, *Case Collection of the Benefits of Inconvenience*,
SpringerBriefs in Business, https://doi.org/10.1007/978-981-92-3981-8_2

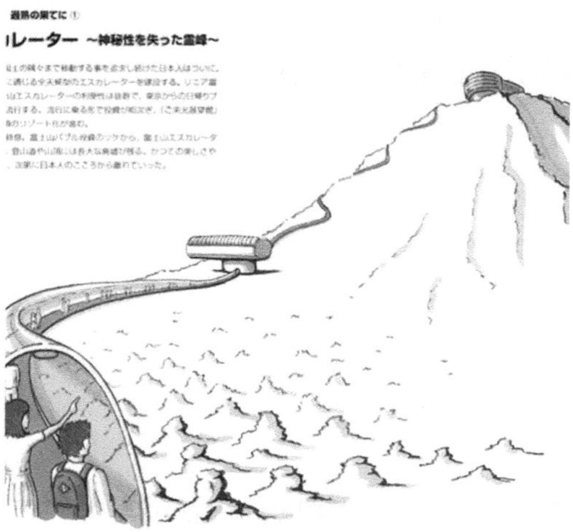

Fig. 2.1 Fuji Mountain escalator

Fig. 2.2 Pre-assembled model kit

the work, experience a strong sense of achievement, and develop an affection for the finished piece. When a new idea works well, they also feel that their skills have improved. An assembly service would take away all these experiences.

Pre-defeated Final Boss

Role-playing games (RPGs) are a long-established and popular genre of video games. Players defeat enemies, gain experience points, level up, and gradually become stronger. At the highest level, the most powerful enemy, "the final boss," awaits. Defeating this boss marks the completion of the game.

Advancing through levels takes time, and defeating the final boss often requires many hours in front of a screen. What if there were a service that defeated the final boss in advance, as shown in Fig. 2.3? It would certainly save time and effort and therefore be convenient, but it would also be disappointing.

Each level contains carefully designed characters and events, which are enjoyable. As players progress, they feel a sense of growth and anticipation for future developments. Defeating the final boss brings immense satisfaction. A service that completes this task in advance would take away all these rewarding aspects.

Fig. 2.3 Pre-defeated final boss of RPG

Fig. 2.4 A handheld device for raising games

Pre-nourished Tamagotchi

There is a genre known as "character-raising games" or "simulation games," in which players raise animals, monsters, idols, or athletes within an application. In the 1990s, a famous example of this type was a dedicated handheld device, as shown in Fig. 2.4, rather than an app. It had a built-in clock and involved raising a virtual pet.

Users fed it, cleaned up after it, turned off the lights when it slept, and played with it. If neglected, it would become unhappy or even die. Over time, depending on how it was cared for, it evolved into a more mature form.

Raising such a pet requires time and effort, and that is why the built-in clock was necessary. Now consider: what if the pet were already fully grown from the beginning? It would save your time and effort, but it would also be disappointing.

Because care requires effort, successfully raising it brings satisfaction. The individuality of each user's approach produces a unique final form that can be a source of pride. A pre-raised pet would take away all these meaningful experiences.

Pre-assembled Jigsaw Puzzle

A jigsaw puzzle is a puzzle in which a single picture or photograph is cut into many small pieces, and the pieces are reassembled to their original form by using the image on them and the shapes of the pieces as clues.

The greater the number of pieces, the more difficult the puzzle becomes, and a 1000-piece puzzle can take dozens of hours to complete. One enjoys spending this time and effort gradually bringing the puzzle closer to completion, piece by piece. Coming up with various strategies, such as starting from the edges, sorting the pieces by color or pattern, or classifying them by shape, can also be part of the enjoyment.

In the sense that it takes a long time, it can be seen as inconvenient. With that in mind, what would it be like to have a service where the puzzle is already assembled when you buy it and open the box? Figure 2.5 illustrates such a puzzle. It would save time and effort, but it would also be disappointing.

Fig. 2.5 Pre-assembled jigsaw puzzle, you need to just put the last piece

The value of a puzzle does not lie in the completed picture itself. Its value lies in allowing people to enjoy the process of assembling it. If it is already put together in advance, that value is completely lost.

Pre-found "Where's Wally?"

"Where's Wally?" (also known as "Where's Waldo?") is a series of books for children created by a British illustrator and first published in the 1980s. Each book contains illustrations spread across two pages, depicting hundreds of people engaged in a wide variety of amusing activities, drawn in meticulous detail. Among these hundreds of figures, one of them is Wally. Children patiently search for Wally by relying on his face, clothes, and hat. When they finally find him, they joyfully turn the page. On the next spread, there is another completely different scene filled once again with hundreds of illustrations, and the children, feeling slightly overwhelmed, nevertheless begin a new challenge.

It is inconvenient in the sense that it takes time, requires patience, and can be somewhat tiring. With that in mind, what would it be like to have a service that marks Wally in advance, as shown in Fig. 2.6, to save children's time? That would be disappointing.

Because it takes time and requires patience, the joy of finding him is great. The sense of satisfaction that comes from succeeding in the challenge is also significant. Such satisfaction would be spoiled by a marker.

Pre-cooked DIY Candy for Kids

Some candies are completed by cooking them yourself. Although it is called "cooking," the process is simple enough even for small children, for example, dissolving powder in water and kneading it into shape, or simply adding chocolate chips as toppings. Children enjoy making these treats "by themselves." A representative product of this type in Japan has continued to sell for around 40 years since its release in the 1980s, reaching a total of 900 million servings.

Fig. 2.6 Pre-found "Where's Wally?" A marker saves your time

Fig. 2.7 Pre-cooked DIY candy

However, while ordinary sweets can be eaten immediately after opening the package, this type of candy requires children to spend time and effort dissolving the powder in water and kneading it. If one considers this time and effort inconvenient, what about a service that provides them already dissolved and formed in advance, as shown in Fig. 2.7? That would be disappointing.

Because it requires time and effort, one can truly feel that they are making it themselves, take joy in completing the preparation, and look forward to seeing it finished. A pre-cooked version would take away all these experiences.

All-Inclusive Travel Agency: Agent Travels for you

Travel agencies are convenient. They plan various travel itineraries on your behalf and arrange the necessary tickets for you. In some cases, staff even accompany you on the trip. In such situations, you only need to go to the designated meeting place at the specified time. After that, you simply follow the guidance of the staff, without having to think through the details yourself.

However, from the moment you leave home to head to the meeting place until you return home after the trip, travel requires both time and effort from you. So, what about a service in which the staff travels entirely on your behalf, as shown in Fig. 2.8? It would place no burden on you and would not consume your time. You could even use that time to take care of other tasks. It would certainly be convenient. However, it would also be disappointing.

It is precisely because you invest time and effort and travel yourself that the journey becomes a real experience, creating memories and stories to share. A fully outsourced travel service would take away all of these.

Overseas Travel with Doraemon's "Anywhere Door"

Overseas travel is enjoyable. Visiting countries introduced on television or in magazines, exploring cities for the first time, taking part in unfamiliar events, encountering unknown cultures, and having experiences that one had never even imagined, all of

Fig. 2.8 An agent travels on your behalf

these are exciting. It is also a pleasure to discover that things you had imagined turn out to be exactly as expected, or sometimes completely different from what you had imagined.

However, the time required for travel is inconvenient. Sitting for many hours in the cramped space of economy class, waiting for hours at a transfer airport, and then sitting again for many more hours in a narrow seat on the connecting flight can be quite painful. So, what about using Doraemon's "Anywhere Door"? If you open the door while thinking of going to Paris, you would see the Arc de Triomphe right there, and once you step through, you will find yourself in Place Charles de Gaulle. It would certainly be convenient. However, it would also be disappointing.

It is precisely because one spends time and endures some discomfort during the journey that traveling abroad becomes a real experience, and memories of the journey itself are created. Because of the effort involved, arriving at Place Charles de Gaulle feels truly rewarding. The Anywhere Door would take away all these experiences.

Lure that Guarantees Catches, Requiring no Fishing Skill

Fishing is one of many hobbies. You can cast a line from the shore or a riverbank, or head out on a boat and fish offshore. Even if you do not catch a single fish, that is still part of the experience. Preparing your equipment, thinking about the best setup for the type of fish you are targeting, and experimenting with how to cast and retrieve the line are all enjoyable. And when you successfully catch the intended fish by your own skill, it is especially rewarding.

However, because it takes time and requires thought, this hobby can be considered inconvenient. So, what if there were a dream-like lure that would attract exactly the fish you want, as shown in Fig. 2.9, the moment you cast your line, without requiring any thought at all? It would be convenient. However, it would also be disappointing.

Because fish are not easily caught, catching one brings joy, and being able to devise your own setup gives you a sense of pride in your skill. You can truly feel that your abilities have improved. A lure that guarantees nonstop bites would take away all these experiences.

Ultimate Bat that Always Hits Home Runs

My son was a member of a baseball club from elementary school through university. Even now, he still enjoys playing casual weekend baseball games with his former teammates. As it is a sport, there are wins and losses, winning brings happiness, and

Fig. 2.9 Lure that guarantees catches

Fig. 2.10 Ultimate bat that always hits home runs

losing brings frustration. However, it seems that my son and his teammates enjoy playing the game itself with their friends even more than the outcome of winning or losing.

However, compared to their student days, their physical strength has declined. I have heard that some of his teammates now have batting averages that have dropped to levels unimaginable when they were students. So, what if there were an ultimate bat that would guarantee a hit every time you swing, as shown in Fig. 2.10? For those whose batting performance has declined, it would be convenient. However, it would be disappointing.

Because it is hard to get a hit, getting one brings joy, and it gives a sense of pride that one's batting ability has not yet faded. You can truly feel that you achieved the hit through your own strength. An ultimate bat would take away all these experiences.

AI-Proposed Date Plan that won't Go Wrong

One of the students in my laboratory was struggling because he could not settle on a date plan. He felt that every plan might have some flaw, and there was no guarantee that his date would fully enjoy it. Although he seemed to be struggling, he also appeared to be enjoying the process of thinking things through, recalling his date, and considering various possibilities.

However, of course, it would be reassuring if there were a guarantee that his date would definitely have a good time. So, what if there were an AI-proposed date plan that could never fail? It would be convenient, as the student could go on the date with complete peace of mind. However, it would also be disappointing.

Because there is a possibility of failure, success brings genuine joy, and it serves as proof that he truly understands his date. It is precisely because the plan was created by oneself that the date feels like a real experience. An infallible date plan would take away all these aspects.

Ability to Read People's Minds

When I was younger, I was sometimes consulted by friends about their romantic relationships. However, rather than offering clever advice, I mostly just listened as they spoke at length. My friend struggled with how to convey his feelings to the person he liked.

In such a situation, what if my friend had the ability to read other people's minds as shown in Fig. 2.11? They would already know whether the person had feelings for him, even before the person expressed their own feelings. There would be no need

Fig. 2.11 Ability to read human minds

to worry or agonize, so it would be a convenient ability for my friend. However, it would also be disappointing.

Because there is a possibility of rejection, my friend can make the effort, and the joy of success becomes greater. Their feelings of love would likely endure longer as well. The ability to read people's minds would take away all these experiences.

Life that can be Foreseen

There are many turning points in life, such as when choosing a university or selecting a job. At each of these moments, it is impossible to know which choice is the right one or at what timing one should choose one path over another. Looking back on past turning points, there are times when one regrets not having chosen a different path. Because of this uncertainty, one becomes cautious about the choices one makes in the present. Even immediately after deciding, one may feel uneasy and sometimes even turn back.

Then, what would it be like if one had the ability to foresee one's own life? If one could know, at a crossroads, what kind of life would result from each possible choice, it would certainly be convenient. One could make decisions with a sense of security. However, that would be disappointing.

It was precisely because we could not foresee it that we felt a thrill in making choices in life and excitement about the life that followed. Once one passes the point of no return, one resolves to move forward and becomes motivated to enjoy the life one has chosen. The ability to foresee one's life would undermine all these experiences.

Lucky Bag with Visible Contents

In Japan, there is a way of selling products known as a "lucky bag." Assorted items are packed into a bag whose contents cannot be seen, and the lucky bag is sold at a price much lower than the total value of the items inside. The goods contained are not simply unsold leftovers bundled together; rather, the shop selects items, taking pride in choosing products that anyone would be happy to receive. One can also sense the shop's good taste in the combination of items. In addition, they are often sold at the beginning of the new year, and lucky bags carry the meaning of a New Year's gift from the shop to its customers. At popular shops, long lines form early in the new year for the purpose of buying these bags.

However, it is still unsettling to pay money for something when one does not know what is inside. With that in mind, what would it be like to have a transparent lucky

Fig. 2.12 Lucky bag with visible contents

bag as shown in Fig. 2.12? Since one could confirm that the contents match one's preferences, it would certainly be convenient. However, that would be disappointing.

It was precisely because the contents were unknown that opening the bag was something to look forward to, and it brought excitement. Most of the time, the items inside are pleasing, but even so, there are occasions when one makes a poor choice. Precisely because of this, when one chooses a good bag the following year, the joy becomes even greater. A lucky bag with visible contents would ruin all these experiences. It would be nothing more than a simple bargain bundle.

Lucky Clover Finder

A clover is supposed to have three leaves. However, on rare occasions, a four-leaf clover appears. These are not easy to find. That is precisely why finding a four-leaf clover becomes proof that one is lucky. For this reason, people sometimes search for four-leaf clovers to make themselves feel fortunate.

If one finds one, it brings a feeling of luck, but it is difficult to come across one. With that in mind, what would it be like to have a drone equipped with a camera search over a wide area from above for four-leaf clovers, as shown in Fig. 2.13? AI can recognize four-leaf clovers in the images taken by the camera. Since it would find them on one's behalf, it would certainly be convenient. However, that would be disappointing.

It is precisely because they are hard to find that, when one finally discovers a four-leaf clover, one can truly feel a sense of fortune. One can also feel that luck belongs to oneself. A machine for finding four-leaf clovers would ruin all these experiences.

Fig. 2.13 A drone detects lucky clovers

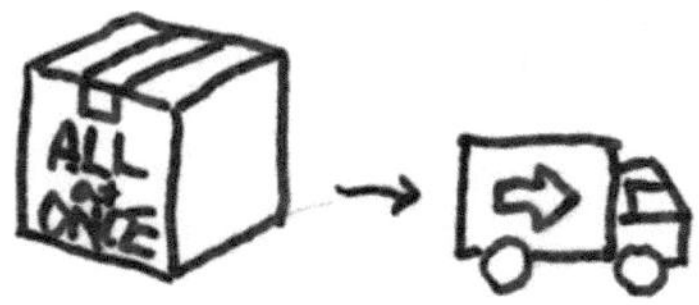

Fig. 2.14 Deliver all parts of DeAgostini at once

Deliver all Parts of DeAgostini at Once

Magazines published by DeAgostini come with model parts as supplements, and by subscribing regularly and gradually collecting the parts, one can complete a model over time. The range includes not only models (such as cars, aircraft, and robots) but also craft materials and DVDs.

However, a regular subscription takes time. Typically, it takes about two years to collect all the parts, but some series are said to take six or seven years. With that in mind, what would it be like to have a service that delivers all the issues at once, as shown in Fig. 2.14? In the sense that it saves time, it would certainly be convenient. However, that would be disappointing.

It is precisely because it takes time that one eagerly awaits the arrival of the parts each week. When all the parts have finally been successfully gathered, there is a sense of joy. It is like the happiness one feels when completing a collection of something. Receiving everything all at once would ruin all these experiences.

University where Credits can be Bought

In many countries, it takes four years to graduate from a university. During that time, students attend lectures, participate in exercises, and earn credits by passing examinations. Each department has fixed requirements for the number of credits necessary for graduation and for advancing to the next grade. Students accumulate credits year by year, and in the end, as proof that they themselves have grown through the investment of time and effort, they receive an academic transcript and a diploma.

However, there may be students who do not wish to spend either effort or time. With that in mind, what would it be like to have a university where credits can be exchanged for money? By paying an amount equivalent to the admission fee and four years of tuition, one would be issued a diploma immediately. It would certainly be convenient. However, that would be disappointing.

It is precisely because one has invested effort and time that one can truly feel one's own growth and be convinced that one's efforts have been rewarded. One also gains classmates and colleagues in the laboratory. An instantly issued diploma would ruin all these experiences.

Digital Gravestone

My grandchildren live about an hour away by car if I take the expressway. It is enjoyable to visit each other from time to time and spend time playing together. I often wish that this could continue forever. Even seeing their faces looking reluctant at the moment of parting is, in fact, something that makes me happy.

However, someday an eternal farewell will inevitably come. At that time, I will likely make my grandchildren wear such sorrowful expressions. With that in mind,

Fig. 2.15 My gravestone acts exactly like me

what would it be like to digitalize my gravestone? By having generative AI read the books I have written and articles of conversations I have taken part in, and by giving it the ability to engage in conversations as if it were me, it could display my avatar on a monitor embedded in the gravestone and converse with my grandchildren as shown in Fig. 2.15. With this, it would not matter if I died. It would be convenient. However, that would be disappointing.

It is precisely because there is an eternal farewell that my present existence has meaning. A substitute that is almost indistinguishable from my being alive would ruin all of this.

2.2 Disappointing Convenience (Real Case)

In the previous section, fictional things that do not exist in the real world were collected. In this section, cases that have actually existed are gathered. These are examples of disappointing convenience.

Swimsuits that Allow Swimmers to Swim Faster

At the Olympic Games held in 2008, world records were broken more than 20 times, and Olympic records were broken more than 60 times across 34 swimming events. Almost all the athletes who got those records were wearing swimsuits of the same brand. Figure 2.16 illustrates an image of such a swimsuit.

For competitive swimmers, these swimsuits are convenient. By wearing one, a swimmer can swim faster than with other swimsuits. However, this is disappointing.

Fig. 2.16 Swimsuits that make swimmers swim faster

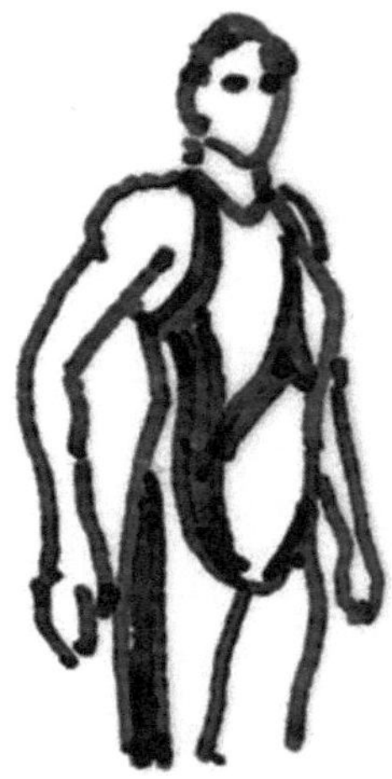

The swimsuit may have produced results beyond the swimmer's own ability. The credit for setting the record may lie not only with the swimmer.

Shoes that Allow Runners to Run Faster

There is a long-distance running event called Ekiden. Unlike a marathon, in which a single runner goes from start to finish, Ekiden is a relay-style long-distance race in which a team of several runners covers the distance and competes on total time. Some well-known races are broadcast on television, making it a popular sport in Japan. A university relay race held every January is also televised.

What drew attention in the 2020 race was that almost all the runners were wearing pink shoes. Figure 2.17 illustrates a scene of the race. At first, it seemed as if this might be part of the race regulations, but it was not. They were shoes of the same type.

In the early stages of the race, the runners who recorded the fastest times in each section were all wearing these shoes. For the runners, these shoes are convenient: by wearing them, they can run faster. However, this is disappointing. It may be that, thanks to these shoes, they were able to run faster than their own ability would allow. The credit for winning the sectional prize may lie with the shoes rather than with the runner.

Fig. 2.17 Shoes that make runners run faster

Fig. 2.18 New Year's gifts by QR code

New Year's Gifts or Christmas Presents by QR Code

In Japan, there is a custom called otoshidama. As a New Year's celebration, children receive cash wrapped in special envelopes from their parents, grandparents, uncles, and aunts. In my case, since my grandchildren are still young, I greet them when we meet for the first time in the New Year and give them otoshidama. It is like Christmas presents in the West. It is a once-a-year, heartwarming event.

There is a similar custom in Vietnam as well. During the Lunar New Year, people give newly issued cash wrapped in special envelopes, wishing for good fortune and health. An exchange student from Vietnam said that this year, she was surprised because her grandfather presented not a special envelope but a QR code, as shown in Fig. 2.18. By scanning the QR code, a certain amount of money would be transferred to the student's account instead of giving otoshidama. It is convenient because it eliminates the need to use cash. However, it is disappointing. It does not feel as if wishes for good fortune and health are being conveyed. It would also feel disappointing if, instead of a Christmas present, a QR code were handed over.

Remote Hatsumōde

In Japan, there is a custom called hatsumōde. When the New Year arrives, people visit a shrine or a temple to pray for happiness and good health in the coming year. It is common to go during the New Year holidays, but the best way is to visit a shrine or a temple on the last night of the previous year and offer prayers at the very moment the New Year begins. This is a once-a-year enjoyable event. Izumo Taisha, located in my hometown, is one of the shrines that records a large number of visitors, and many people travel for hours by car from outside the prefecture to visit, causing traffic congestion to become a problem. Kyoto, where I live, has shrines and temples of various sizes scattered throughout the city, and despite it being midnight, the entire city becomes crowded with worshippers.

A few years ago, a shrine started the service that allows people to perform hatsumōde remotely. By accessing the website of that shrine, it was considered that one had performed hatsumōde. Figure 2.19 illustrates an image of such hatsumōde. This is convenient, as there is no need to go out to a shrine or a temple in the cold winter. However, it is disappointing. In Christianity, this would correspond to Sunday worship. Without going to church, one could simply access the church's website from home, be considered to have attended the service, and even make offerings by cashless payment. That would be disappointing.

Fig. 2.19 An image of the remote hatsumōde

Digital Goshuin Available for Download

In Japan, there is a cultural practice called goshuin. As proof of having visited a shrine or temple, one can receive a stamp with a unique design specific to that place, along with the name and date written in Japanese calligraphy. It has become popular to collect many goshuin in a small notebook. Among foreign tourists as well, there are people who visit Japan and collect goshuin, which can only be obtained by going to shrines and temples, as mementos of their travels.

A few years ago, a service was introduced that allows people to download goshuin remotely. It is convenient because there is no need to go to the shrine or temple, and there is no need to stand in long lines to receive a goshuin. In just a few minutes, one can fill all the pages of a notebook with goshuin from various shrines and temples. However, it is disappointing. I have heard that in other religions, there are also customs of marking a pilgrimage notebook with stamps as proof of visits; if those marks could be downloaded as digital data, that too would surely be disappointing.

All Clovers Are Four-Leaf

Most clovers have three leaves. Four-leaf clovers are very rare, so finding one is considered lucky, and such a clover is called a lucky clover.

However, near a pond in front of Angkor Wat in Cambodia, there is an area where all clovers have four leaves, as shown in Fig. 2.20. It was unclear whether this was due to a mutation that had spread or because they had been selectively bred that way.

Even though the entire area was full of lucky clovers, it did not necessarily make one feel extraordinarily lucky. Since every clover there had four leaves, each individual plant had no rarity or special value. In that area, it had simply become the norm, which was somewhat disappointing in that sense.

However, upon realizing that the entire area was covered with four-leaf clovers, there was a feeling of excitement. It was a rare place unlike anything that had ever been seen before.

Movie Summary Videos

Watching movies in a theater is the best, if possible. One can enjoy the impact of a large screen and powerful sound. However, going to a theater requires the effort and time to travel, and one cannot always choose to watch whichever movie one wants at any time. Therefore, it is not bad to relax on a sofa at home and watch whatever movie one likes, whenever one likes, via a subscription service. In any case, watching movies is enjoyable.

Fig. 2.20 All clovers have four leaves (photographed at Angkor Wat)

However, movies are generally long. The movie that attracted the largest audience in Japan last year had a running time of three hours. It is difficult to remain tied to the screen for such a long time. One wants to know the moving ending as soon as possible. Therefore, there are people who create and publish summary videos of movies. It is certainly convenient to be able to understand the plot and the ending in a short time. However, it is disappointing. What one wants to experience is not simply knowing the ending, but the process by which every detail of the movie weaves together to produce that ending. In general, all spoiler-type services are convenient but disappointing.

Authentic Restaurants Everywhere

In my town, there is an Indian restaurant recommended by international students from India. There is also a Vietnamese restaurant recommended by international students from Vietnam. The students say that both places are delicious and taste just like the food in their home countries. I have been on a business trip to Vietnam, and indeed, the taste I experienced at restaurants there seemed the same as at the Vietnamese restaurant in my town.

From now on, it is possible to easily enjoy authentic Vietnamese cuisine without going to Vietnam. That is convenient. However, it is also a little disappointing. In fact, since I have not yet had the opportunity to go on a business trip to India, I had been looking forward to doing so someday and eating authentic Indian food there. And yet, I can eat something that international students assure me tastes the same, right in my neighborhood (Fig. 2.21). My motivation to go on a business trip to India has diminished.

Fast Food with Consistent Taste Anywhere

When I was an associate professor, I once took a professor with me to attend an academic conference held in Spain. Since it was a rare opportunity to be in Spain, I wanted to include not only work but also a bit of a travel experience. So, after the

Fig. 2.21 Authentic restaurants everywhere in the world

conference, for dinner we chose Spanish restaurants lined up along a nearby coast. Almost every day, I took the professor to restaurants along the coast. Since each restaurant had different dishes and flavors, we enjoyed Spanish cuisine by trying a different restaurant each day.

However, one day the professor said, "I want to eat fast food." Indeed, if we headed not toward the coast from our lodging but toward the city center, there were fast-food chain restaurants that are also common in Japan. We could probably have meals that tasted almost the same as what we eat in Japan. This was certainly convenient for the professor, who had begun to miss food in Japan. But it was disappointing. Even though we had come all the way to Spain, our dinner ended up being hamburgers.

Large Shopping Malls Everywhere
In the suburbs of moderately large cities, there is usually a large shopping mall. No matter which city I travel to, I can obtain the same goods at the same prices as those sold in the mall in my own town. In other words, almost anything is available. It is convenient.

However, it is somewhat disappointing that all cities seem to be becoming uniform. Certainly, efforts are made to create a sense of uniqueness by displaying items specific to each city in a small section of a large mall. Nevertheless, overall, the same stores line up in malls in every city, selling the same products.

Hokkaido Product Fairs Everywhere
Japan is a country that stretches from north to south, and Hokkaido, located at the northernmost end, has its own distinctive products. These are very popular throughout Japan. Department stores across the country host traveling Hokkaido product fairs; people in each city are pleased that they can obtain Hokkaido products in their own town, and the department stores are pleased to attract large numbers of customers.

It is convenient to be able to obtain Hokkaido specialties in one's own town without going to Hokkaido. However, for me, it is also somewhat disappointing. In the past, when I went on business trips to Hokkaido, if I found items that were available only there, I would buy them as souvenirs for my family and present them with stories from the trip. Now, there is nothing that can be obtained only in Hokkaido. If I go to a product fair, I can get them in my own town, and if I use online shopping, I do not even need to go to the product fair.

Level 5 Autonomous Driving
Car autonomous driving is divided into levels from 0 to 5. Level 0 is completely manual, and Level 5 is completely automatic. Compared with Level 4, which works

only under certain conditions, and Level 3, which still needs the driver to respond properly, Level 5 is more convenient. People such as elderly drivers who cannot drive anymore, and bus or taxi companies that have fewer services because of a lack of drivers, are waiting for Level 5 to become available.

However, for people who love driving, this may be a sad situation. Driving by oneself is not easy, but it is enjoyable. Being able to control a big machine as one wishes is fun and also builds self-confidence. But in Japan, convenient automatic transmissions have replaced manual transmissions, and now one must choose from a limited number of so-called sports cars to get a manual transmission. If convenient Level 5 driving replaces manual driving in the same way, and people can drive manually only if they choose very expensive and special cars, that would be disappointing.

Markets Stocking Specialties from around the World

Markets stocking specialties from around the world have appeared here and there. They are somewhat being overtaken by online shopping, but in any case, it is now possible to obtain goods from all over the world while staying in one's own town. It is convenient.

However, this has become something of a disappointment for my aunt, who married and moved to Germany. Since she returns to Japan only once every few years, she carefully selects souvenirs to distribute to acquaintances when she comes back. As there are many children among the relatives, she must choose items that can be carried in large quantities, are appreciated by children, and can be obtained only in Germany. When I was a child, she would choose things such as Staedtler stationery, German-brand multi-purpose knives, a pencil case whose brand I have forgotten but which was thin and yet did not tear even after decades of use, and German board games.

However, nowadays it is a disappointing time for her. Items such as Staedtler stationery are now commonly sold in stationery stores in Japan.

2.3 Experience of Benefits of Inconvenience (or Beneficial Inconvenience)

This section collects experiences in which people felt that benefits were gained from the inconvenience.

Commuting on Foot

A student said, "Last week, my moped broke down, so I had no choice but to walk back and forth between my home and the laboratory. It took a long time, and I strongly felt how convenient the moped is." The student said that commuting on foot was inconvenient.

However, the student also said that a cafeteria, which the student had never paid attention to when commuting by moped, caught the student's eye. After the student

Fig. 2.22 Single television in the lobby of a budget hotel

stopped by casually and went in, the cafeteria has now become the student's favorite place.

Let's think about this situation a little more abstractly. Having to follow a continuous path step by step, even though it is inconvenient and takes effort, has the benefit of increasing opportunities to notice things ("Oh, there is a cafeteria") and encourages trying something (stopping by casually).

In general, being able to skip intermediate steps is convenient. Commuting is also convenient if one can skip the way (ultimately, if one could use Doraemon's "Anywhere Door"). However, in that case, there would be no chance at all to find a favorite cafeteria.

Single Television in the Lobby of Budget Hotels

If you want to travel abroad for a long time without spending a lot of money, you must stay in cheap hotels. Such budget hotels usually use an inconvenient system in which all the guests share just one television in the lobby, as shown in Fig. 2.22. If each room had its own TV, it would be convenient because you could lie on your bed and watch whatever channel you want whenever you like. On the other hand, with a lobby TV, you must compete with others for the channel if there is a program you want to watch.

One student traveled for a month through several countries in Europe, and during that time, a FIFA World Cup soccer match between Japan and another country was broadcast on TV. The student really wanted to watch it, so the student did their best to use unfamiliar English and managed to win the channel competition. Then, the student noticed that the person sitting next to the student and watching together had a completely opposite level of excitement. The student wondered about this and tried talking to that person, and just as expected, that person was from the country playing against Japan. After that, the two became very excited together, and they later became friends who still exchange emails.

Let's think about this situation a little more abstractly. The inconvenience of having limited freedom (you must be in the lobby to watch TV) also has benefits: it gives opportunities to notice things (people who can become friends) and encourages trying something (starting a conversation). Normally, having less freedom seems like losing opportunities. In fact, however, it can give you different opportunities instead.

Fig. 2.23 Newspapers at a convenience store

Newspapers Bought at a Convenience Store

One student in my laboratory stopped subscribing to a newspaper. It was for job hunting. The student gave up the convenient system in which the newspaper was delivered to the student's boarding house, and the fee was automatically withdrawn from a bank account. Instead, the student chose an inconvenient system of going to a convenience store every day and buying the newspaper with cash.

After switching to this method, the student began to read the newspaper, because it felt wasteful not to read something that had been deliberately bought, even though it cost only a little over 100 yen. As a result, the student became more knowledgeable about current events. This helped with job hunting, and the student succeeded in finding a job.

The inconvenient method, which requires time and effort, motivated the student to read the newspaper. When the student used the convenient system, there were many days when the delivered newspaper was not read (Fig. 2.23).

Snacks for the School Trip Are Limited to 300 Yen

In Japan, when children are in elementary school, they go on a school trip every year. They take a one-day trip together with their classmates. This is a very enjoyable event for the students. For the trip, they bring a lunchbox and snacks.

When I was a child, the snacks for the trip were limited to 300 yen. At that time, I thought it was very unfair. However, looking back now, if we had been allowed to buy as much as we wanted, we would not have cared so much about the snacks. On the day before the trip, it was fun to spend hours in a supermarket thinking about how to combine different sweets so that the total would not exceed 300 yen.

We were motivated to act in this way because of the inconvenience of having a restriction. Inconvenience motivates people. And the original combination of snacks that each person chose in this way was something valuable.

Film Camera Vs Digital Camera

There are several types of cameras, such as digital cameras and film cameras.

Among film cameras that can take only a limited number of photos, there is a type called a disposable camera. Figure 2.24 illustrates an image of a disposable camera. With this camera, you cannot see the results until you send the film for development later, and you cannot use zoom or take close-up shots. It is less convenient than taking pictures with a digital camera or a smartphone.

Fig. 2.24 An image of a disposable camera

However, this kind of film camera is popular among younger people who have had digital cameras or smartphones since they were born.

With digital cameras or smartphones, you can take as many pictures as you want, so you just press the shutter button. Since you can see the picture immediately after taking it, you just press the shutter for now. As a result, you end up with many similar photos. Later, you do not feel like organizing them, and your memory of when you took them becomes vague.

On the other hand, when using a single-use film camera, each shot is taken with great care. You think about whether the subject is worth using one of the 27 limited shots on the film. The viewfinder is just a hole in the box, so unlike a digital camera, where what you see on the monitor is exactly what will be recorded as an image file, there is no such guarantee with a film camera. Therefore, you think carefully about the shooting conditions, such as the light.

Because of this, you remember when, where, and with what feelings you took the picture. In this way, the value of each photograph becomes higher.

Mechanical Key Lock Door

Car keys today are mostly convenient remote-control types, but in the past, they were the kind you insert and turn. Putting a key into a narrow slot takes a little effort, and you also need some force to turn it. This is somewhat inconvenient.

However, when you turn the key, you feel a reaction force in your wrist, so you can tell that something is actually working (the lock is operating). Also, because you must approach the car to insert and turn the key, you can hear the mechanical sound of the locks moving in each door. This makes you confident that the car is locked.

A remote-control car key is more convenient than the type you insert and turn. However, when you lock a car with a remote control, even if the hazard lights flash, there is no guarantee that the car is actually locked. There is no physical cause-and-effect relationship between the lock and the flashing lights. It is simply a rule decided by people.

By the way, not many people know that one flash means lock and two flashes mean unlock. This is also just a human convention. There is no natural mapping between locking or unlocking and the number of flashes.

On the other hand, the reaction force felt in your wrist when you turn the key and the mechanical sounds from each door are supported by the laws of physics, and they assure you that the car is locked or unlocked. This brings a sense of safety and trust.

Manual Transmission

In Japan, automatic transmission (AT) cars are considered more convenient than manual transmission (MT) cars, so most cars are AT. However, in Europe, there is a common joke: "The reason I was dumped by my girlfriend was that my car was an AT." Because of such a culture, the rate of AT cars there is much lower than in Japan. In recent years, even in Japan, the number of people who choose MT cars instead of automatically choosing AT has been gradually increasing.

MT cars are less convenient than AT cars in the sense that they require more operation and the use of more mental resources. Most of the people around me are engineers, including myself; the rate of MT users is unusually high. Engineers usually try to pursue convenience in their work, yet when they are away from work, they choose the less convenient option. When I think about this, the reason seems to be that MT cars allow drivers to control the car as they like and to develop their own driving style.

For example, you may notice something like, "Oh, the car does not slow down as much as I expected even if I keep the clutch disengaged." This kind of experience encourages you to try something, such as keeping the clutch disengaged a little longer than usual. By doing so, you can improve your skills and learn to drive smoothly without sudden acceleration or sudden braking. MT cars give drivers room to adjust and improve their own skills in this way.

For this to happen, it is essential that the driver is allowed to act (through operation) and can imagine the state of the car. An inconvenient system increases opportunities for noticing things, leaves room for active creativity, and, through feedback based on physical principles, makes it easier to understand the system you are dealing with.

Printed Dictionary

There are two types of dictionaries: printed dictionaries and electronic dictionaries (including online dictionaries). For looking up the meaning of a word, electronic dictionaries are more convenient because you can jump directly to the word you want. However, quite a number of people still prefer printed dictionaries. When asked why they use the less convenient option, most of them give reasons like the following.

They say it is good that, while searching for the target word, they can see other words before reaching it, and also words around it. When they notice another word and think, "Oh," their attention may shift away from the original purpose. There is also a kind of enjoyment that comes from this kind of detour, for example, discovering that words with similar spellings but different meanings share the same origin.

When I was a high school student, a competition to look up words quickly in a dictionary became popular. At that point, the purpose of using a dictionary had completely changed. It is quite different from looking things up quickly with an electronic dictionary. With an electronic dictionary, it would only be a competition of how fast you can type. Such a competition would not work without printed dictionaries.

However, when the rules were changed so that everyone had to use the same dictionary to keep the competition fair, the popularity suddenly declined. The reason

Fig. 2.25 Printed dictionary

is that physical objects, through interaction with their users, gain unique marks of use and wear, becoming a unique object in the world. Because of this, users feel that the object fits them. Owners have the sense that they have "grown" their own belongings and have mastered using them (Fig. 2.25).

Brick-and-Mortar Bookstore

When I buy books for work, I use online bookstores. They are convenient when I already know which book I want to buy. If I know the title or the ISBN, I only need to enter it in the search box on the bookstore's website. Among the huge amount of data, the book I want is almost certainly included, it is almost certainly in stock, and if I pay online, it will be delivered to my workplace within a few days.

In contrast, traditional brick-and-mortar bookstores are inconvenient. It takes time and effort to go to the store and to look for the book I want inside the store. Even if I make the effort to go there, the book I want may be out of stock. In that case, I need to ask when it will arrive and then go to the store again on that day.

However, this inconvenience applies only when the purpose is simply to buy a specific book. While searching for the book I want, I may become interested in other books. If I pick one up and look at it, I may decide to buy that one instead. Or, even when the book I want is not there, I may look at the spines of books to see if there is anything interesting and discover an unexpected book. This kind of experience is one of the pleasures of a physical bookstore. It is different from being recommended books by an online bookstore.

Primary School Students Walk on the White Parts

In Japan, children can go to and come home from school by themselves without adult supervision. Parents tell their children to go straight to and from school so that they will not be late and will not come home too late. In other words, they are taught not to make detours.

However, children do not seem to like such efficiency-focused ways of traveling. They come up with many different, inefficient ways of going home.

For example, they challenge themselves to get from school to home without stepping on the black asphalt, walking only on lighter-colored areas such as lane markings or concrete (Fig. 2.26). Almost everyone seems to have come up with and tried this challenge when they were in primary school. Although it takes more time and effort than going home in a normal way, children enjoy this kind of challenge.

Fig. 2.26 Primary school students tend to walk only on white areas

Fig. 2.27 Carving a pencil into a spiral shape

Sharpen a Pencil with a Knife

Almost no one uses pencils as writing tools anymore. When students take notes during lectures, they seem to write on pads, take photos, or use a PC keyboard. Writing instruments themselves are not often seen.

On the other hand, when I take notes, I use a pencil. And when I sharpen the pencil, I use a knife instead of a convenient pencil sharpener. A knife is less convenient in the sense that it requires practice to sharpen well and takes a little more time.

However, inconvenient tools allow for learning and give opportunities for discovery. They also leave room for active creativity and personal ingenuity. One day, I noticed that if I rotate the hand holding the pencil at a constant speed while sharpening it, the shaving marks become interesting. By experimenting, I developed the skill to carve a pencil into a spiral shape as shown in Fig. 2.27.

The Cherry Blossom Season Is Short

When I ask international students who are studying in Japan, they say that one of their enjoyments here is seeing the cherry blossoms (Fig. 2.28) in spring. Many foreign tourists also visit Japan in spring to see the cherry blossoms. Japanese people, even if beautiful cherry blossoms bloom in their own towns, travel a little farther to gather at places known as famous viewing spots, and the crowds at these places are shown on television news.

One reason why everyone becomes so enthusiastic in this way is that each cherry blossom starts to fall about three days after it blooms, so the period when many flowers are blooming all at once is very short. If there were always many flowers in bloom, it would be more convenient because people would not all go at the same time. However, it is precisely because of this inconvenience, the short blooming period, that people love to see and appreciate cherry blossoms.

Fig. 2.28 An image of cherry blossom

Outdoor Camping

Outdoor camping is also something that people enjoy the inconvenience. People cook, eat, and sleep. These activities can be done easily at home where convenient facilities that support these activities are available. Even so, people deliberately go outside their homes to camp because they want to enjoy something different from everyday life, and for that, it needs to be inconvenient. It is precisely because it is inconvenient that people can feel that they are having an experience different from their daily life.

It is also pleasing to feel that one's skills improve each time one goes camping, such as the skills of making a fire, cooking delicious barbecue, and setting up a tent as shown in Fig. 2.29. Even during the COVID-19 pandemic, when people were asked to avoid going out, some people camped in their own gardens. Even though convenient facilities were very close by just inside the front door, they slept in tents in the garden.

DIY

DIY, in which people make or repair things in their homes or prepare food by themselves instead of paying companies to do it, is enjoyable. DIY often helps save money, but even when the cost of buying tools and materials is higher than the cost of buying a finished product, people still choose to do DIY. The purpose is not to save money, but to enjoy the act of creating something by spending one's own time and effort.

People take pleasure in how well the finished item turns out and in realizing the level of their own skills. In general, tasks that require time and effort are inconvenient. Therefore, DIY is an activity in which people gain benefits from the inconvenience.

Fig. 2.29 An image of outdoor camping

Cash against Cashless Payment

Paying with cash is less convenient than cashless payment. As a physical object, cash is bulkier than a cashless card and is not easy to carry. It also takes time to count coins when making a payment, and sometimes you may not have enough money with you.

Although cash is inconvenient, I carry not only a cashless card but also cash. One reason is that in Japan, there are still stores that accept only cash. Another reason is that I find some benefits in the inconvenience of cash. First, the physical entity of cash makes the flow of value visible. The increase and decrease of money in my wallet make it clear that an exchange of value has taken place. In the case of cashless payment, the remaining balance on a prepaid card or in a bank account is shown only as numbers. Compared with this, cash has a stronger ability to show the decrease and make me feel anxious.

Also, organizing the coins in my wallet through payment is a small pleasure. For example, if I buy something that costs 97 yen and pay with only a 100-yen coin, I receive 3 yen in change, and the number of coins in my wallet increases by two. In my case, I give one 100-yen coin and two 1-yen coins and receive one 5-yen coin in change. The number of coins in my wallet decreases by two, and I feel satisfied.

Pilgrimage Stamp Book, Goshuin-Cho

In Japan, there is something called a Goshuin-cho, a book for collecting temple and shrine stamps. There is nothing exactly like a Goshuin-cho in other countries, but there are similar ideas. For example, in Europe, pilgrims use a "pilgrim's passport" to collect stamps from churches they visit. This is like a Goshuin-cho because it records visits to religious places. However, a Goshuin-cho is unique because it combines handwritten calligraphy, stamps, and religious meaning, which is special to Japanese culture.

Collecting Goshuin requires time and effort. Even if you can receive a stamp at temples and shrines near your home, you still need to visit many temples and shrines far from home to fill all the pages of a Goshuin-cho. In general, things that require time and effort are inconvenient. It is easier to just stay at home without collecting Goshuin. There are even convenient services that allow people to download Goshuin online.

However, many people still carry a Goshuin-cho and visit temples and shrines. The pleasure of collecting Goshuin comes from this inconvenience.

2.4 Design Incorporating Intentional Inconvenience

2.4.1 Artifacts/Products Designed with BoI

This section collects artifacts and products that are intentionally designed to be inconvenient. The designer assumes from the outset that such inconvenience will provide benefits to the user.

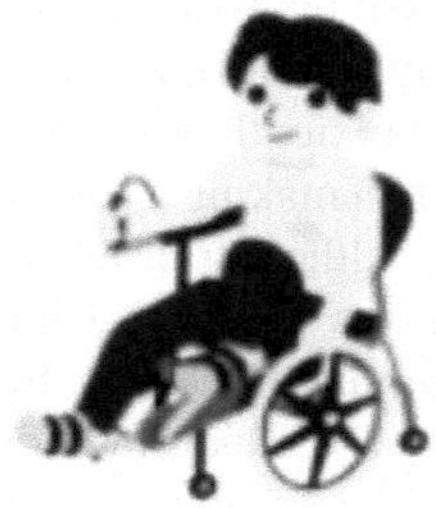

Fig. 2.30 Pedal-powered wheel chair

Pedal-Powered Wheelchair

When I first heard about a pedal-powered wheelchair, I thought, "Wheelchairs are for people who cannot use their legs, so a wheelchair that you have to pedal with your legs must be inconvenient." However, after watching a demonstration in which it moved smoothly through a slalom course, I understood.

Many wheelchair users are people who cannot move one leg or cannot keep their balance well enough to stand because their muscles are weak. These users may find it difficult to walk, but they can sit and pedal. For this reason, a wheelchair was developed that is moved not by turning the wheels with the hands and not by using electricity, but by pedaling with the legs like a bicycle, as shown in Fig. 2.30.

Originally, this wheelchair was developed for rehabilitation purposes. As an option, sockets can be attached to the pedals. By placing both feet into the sockets and pedaling with the leg that can move, the paralyzed leg also moves along as it is pulled. This condition is said to be useful for rehabilitation.

However, I feel that its benefits are not limited to rehabilitation; it also helps mentally. For the original purpose of a wheelchair, transportation, there are other more convenient methods. Nevertheless, by intentionally choosing a system that requires effort from the user, the benefits are not limited to rehabilitation alone.

Because I have a background in engineering, if I were asked to design a mobility aid based on a conventional wheelchair, I would probably try to make it more convenient, for example, by adding power assistance or installing an automatic braking system like those in cars that applies the brakes when a collision is likely. However, the pedal-powered wheelchair takes the opposite approach. It says, "Move yourself by pedaling." Compared with electric wheelchairs, it is more physically demanding and less convenient. However, being able to move by one's own leg is said to bring great satisfaction to the user. By intentionally making it less convenient, it improves the quality of life.

Bumpy Playground Kindergarten

Playgrounds at nursery schools and kindergartens are usually flat. However, some principals intentionally make the playground bumpy so that children may trip and fall. For adults, a flat playground is more convenient because it is easier to supervise children and to ensure their safety. For the children as well, flat ground makes it easier to move around and to play games such as tag. If the ground is bumpy, it

Fig. 2.31 Bumpy playground

becomes harder to move, and there is a greater risk of falling and getting hurt, so it may seem inconvenient. However, this inconvenience makes the children livelier and more active, as shown in Fig. 2.31.

On the website of one kindergarten, it says, "When children encounter inconvenience, they think for themselves, and through this thinking, they grow." If children are forced into inconvenience and have no choice but to think of solutions reluctantly, that would be unfortunate. However, this concern turns out to be unnecessary. Looking at the photos on the website, the children look lively and energetic.

Because there are uneven surfaces and steps that make movement difficult, even in running races, it is not always the fastest kid who wins. Instead, children who think carefully about how to run can win. In addition to running, this kind of environment creates opportunities for children to think actively and come up with their own ideas in many kinds of play. Having more chances to think independently seems to be the key to making children lively and engaged.

Furthermore, it is also important that children can experience how they might fall and what happens when they fall.

Barrier-Aree Versus Barrier-Free

There is an idea called "barrier-aree." This is the opposite way of thinking from "barrier-free." The word "aree" is a Japanese term meaning the opposite of "free," in the sense of "exist." This idea started at a day service center in Yamaguchi, Japan.

In this facility, barriers such as stairs and long corridors are intentionally placed inside the building. Barriers are inconvenient for daily activities such as moving around. However, by intentionally adding them and turning everyday life into a kind of training (Fig. 2.32), the speed at which physical ability declines can be reduced. In fact, it may even help people recover their physical ability as a form of rehabilitation.

These barriers are designed by a person with several decades of experience as an occupational therapist. The idea is based on the understanding that too much assistance in care facilities can take away users' independence and make them more dependent. In this way, barrier-aree affects not only physical ability but also people's attitudes.

This idea does not mean going back to the "good old days." Instead, it means intentionally introducing barriers at a level that makes everyday life a form of training, using modern facilities. The staff, who have learned the skill of judging the exact point at which they should not help, so that barrier-aree works effectively, are a new kind of person that did not exist in the past.

Fig. 2.32 Appropriate barrier turns everyday life into a training

"How's That Project Going?" Button on a Core Information System

At a large comprehensive manufacturer in Kyoto, a "How's that project going?" button was added to the core information system. Until then, the company's system had a convenient feature that automatically generated reports, allowing managers to grasp the overall business situation simply by looking at those reports.

However, when the system was renewed, the company president had this convenient feature removed. In the new system, unless a manager takes action, information such as budgets and performance results cannot be viewed. It is as if the organization has gone back to the pre-system era, when reports would not come up from subordinates unless the manager explicitly asked, "How's that going?" In that sense, compared with the previous system, it requires an extra step and has become less convenient.

Nevertheless, this change naturally drew out a more proactive attitude from managers, improving their capabilities. This is because the reports from subordinates, which used to be push-type information, became pull-type information in the new system. Furthermore, if a function were added to notify subordinates when a manager accesses the reports they have entered into the system, it might create a sense that "I am entrusted with important work that my manager is paying attention to," which could lead to even better outcomes.

A Resort Hotel in Arashiyama, Kyoto

In western Kyoto in Japan, there is a tourist destination called Arashiyama, which attracts not only Japanese visitors but also many tourists from overseas. The Katsura River flows alongside Arashiyama mountain, with old, large, and solemn temples and shrines on the opposite side of Katsura River to the mountain, and charming bamboo groves attract visitors. It is also enjoyable to cross the bridge over the Katsura River, walk along a street lined continuously with souvenir shops, and then make one's way to a slightly rustic and atmospheric area.

Within this Arashiyama area, on the site where the Arashiyama hot springs once stood, there is now a highly popular (and also very expensive) resort hotel. This hotel is situated between the cliffs of Arashiyama mountain to the west, and the Katsura River to the east, as shown in Fig. 2.33, and the only way to reach it on foot is by using a narrow path along the cliff. It is an inconvenient location. However, this inconvenience of access enhances its popularity. Precisely because it is difficult to

Fig. 2.33 A resort hotel is located between a mountain cliff and a big river

get to, people become more eager to visit. Guests must find a ferry boat and take it to reach the hotel.

In contrast to the way inconvenience can motivate people to go somewhere, convenience can sometimes fail to create any motivation to go. When I was a student, I lived in a boarding house near Ginkakuji known as the "silver temple", located in eastern Kyoto. It was a very convenient location, and I could go there anytime I wished. However, before I realized it, I had moved out without ever once visiting the temple. Because I could go anytime, there was nothing that motivated me to think, "I'll go today."

2.4.2 User Experiences Designed around BoI

This section collects services or methods that are intentionally designed to be inconvenient. The designer assumes from the outset that such inconvenience will provide beneficial experiences to the user.

Cell-Production System

As a method of manufacturing in factories, the process in which products under assembly move along a conveyor belt is called the line production system. In this method, each worker's task is finely divided into specific roles such as "tightening screws," "fitting parts," or "checking quantities." Workers wait for products to arrive on the line and repeatedly perform the same task. This approach is convenient for mass production. Workers are required to have the ability to carry out routine tasks accurately, but they are not required to possess artisan-level skills; with a certain amount of training, they can reach a level at which they can work on the line.

On the other hand, around the time when I began to collect examples of "benefit of inconvenience", many manufacturers introduced the cell production system. In the cell production system, one worker or a small group gathers and assembles a product in one place called a cell. Figure 2.34 illustrates an image of the cell production system. The products involved are complex systems such as information devices, home appliances, and automobiles. As a result, the range of tasks handled by each

Fig. 2.34 An image of the cell production system

worker becomes extensive, higher skills are required, and there is more that must be learned. In other words, it is an inconvenient method for the workers.

Despite this inconvenience, many manufacturers adopted the cell production system. The reason given is that it can accommodate high-mix, low-volume production and enables timely product supply. Indeed, these advantages can be evaluated in terms of numerical measures such as production volume and manufacturing cost.

On the other hand, I would like to focus on the "benefits" that cannot be evaluated by numbers. Each worker, if they choose to, can assemble a complex product such as a compact car on their own. Then, every time they see such a car running on the road, they may feel, "That might be one I assembled myself; it's running well." This increases motivation and a sense of responsibility toward the work. These, in turn, lead to improved skills, and as skills improve, motivation increases even further. In other words, between "a job where one can assemble an entire car" and "a job of accurately repeating screw-tightening," the difference lies not in which job is better or worse, but in the level of sense of achievement and motivation. In this way, when work becomes enjoyable, people become more willing to put in effort. As a result, improvements in skill and motivation reinforce each other in a virtuous cycle.

Shared Space Experiment

There was an experiment called "shared space." This was conducted from 2004 to 2008 in various European countries, including the Netherlands, Belgium, Germany, Denmark, and the United Kingdom. On roads designated as experimental spaces, traffic lights, signs, and road markings were all removed. Figure 2.35 shows an image view of the shared space. Before the experiment began, responsibility for road safety lay with the authorities and with the road infrastructure itself. However, this responsibility was entirely entrusted to the users of the road, both drivers and pedestrians.

Fig. 2.35 A view of shared space

Having to be careful oneself is generally considered an inconvenience. However, taking responsibility for safety became a personal matter. As a result, vehicle speeds decreased, and accidents involving injuries were the same as on normal roads. Even today, in the city center of Nantes in France, there are areas without traffic signals or similar safety devices, and both accidents and traffic congestion have been reduced there.

U-Shaped International Support

One group engaged in international aid refers to its method of support as a "U-shaped" model. In conventional international aid, the supporting side takes on all costs and responsibilities. Since everything is neatly contained, this can be called an "O-shaped" model. In contrast, the support provided by this group is designed in such a way that matters cannot be resolved unless something is done locally. This is referred to as a "U-shaped" model, in the sense that one end remains half-open.

For those receiving aid, the O-shaped model is more convenient. They do not have to do anything themselves, since the supporting side takes care of everything. For the supporting side as well, the O-shaped model is more convenient, because they can simply handle everything on their own. In the U-shaped model, however, the design of the support process becomes more complex, for example, by introducing interactions with local people.

Nevertheless, the inconvenient U-shaped model has the advantage that, through the process of resolving issues locally, local partners and users are identified, and a deep relationship is established between the supporting side and the local community. For the local people as well, the supported project becomes something their own matter.

Not Judging by the Cover (Not Jacket-Based Renting)

In an era when rental shops that lent DVDs containing music or movies were the norm, quite a few people engaged in "jacket-based renting." Without checking the contents of the music or film, they would choose which DVD to rent just by looking at the cover in the rental shop. This was an act akin to gambling: whether the selection turned out to be interesting depended on luck, and encountering an enjoyable work was a matter of good fortune. In search of that lucky encounter with an interesting movie they had never known before, people engaged in jacket-based renting. In general, having less information is inconvenient. However, this inconvenience brings the benefit of expanding opportunities for new encounters.

There was even a rental shop that offered a method of borrowing with even less information. In this case, customers were not even allowed to see the jacket. The DVDs were hidden inside paper bags so that the covers were not visible, and only a single intriguing phrase was written on each bag as shown in Fig. 2.36. Examples included phrases such as: "If you packed all the rotten aspects of humanity together, this is what you'd get," "Ranked number one as a movie couples should never watch together," and "Would you like to have your face collapse from crying?" This approach seemed entertaining, and it made people feel irresistibly inclined to rent one.

Fig. 2.36 Not judging by the cover

JAL's "Somewhere Miles"

The service that exchanges accumulated miles for airline tickets is offered by most airlines. Japan Airlines (JAL) started an interesting service in 2015 called "Somewhere Miles." Because the pronunciation of mile is the same as the Japanese word mailu ("to go"), one can immediately get an intuitive sense of what this service entails. For a smaller number of miles than usual, customers can exchange them for a ticket that presents four possible destinations. At the time of applying for this service, the traveler does not know where they will go; the destination is revealed later. This service has been popular and has won several design awards since around 2017.

In general, having less information is inconvenient. However, this inconvenience introduces a light element of gambling and brings the benefit of creating a sense of excitement.

Peach's Travel Gacha

Peach, one of Japan's low-cost carriers (LCCs), offers a service that goes beyond JAL's "Anywhere Miles" program. In this service, you can purchase an airline ticket through a "gacha" (capsule toy machine). Figure 2.37 shows the gacha machine. In the case of "Anywhere Miles," since fewer miles than usual are required, some people may have applied for the service simply because it is cheaper, rather than for the excitement of not knowing the destination. In addition, for the airline, there is the advantage of being able to control passenger numbers.

On the other hand, with Peach's Travel Gacha, if you pay 5000 yen, you receive a ticket worth about 6000 yen from the machine. This is hardly a significant discount. Customers purely enjoy the thrill of not knowing where they will go. Because it is a gacha system, the airline cannot control passenger numbers.

This service is also popular. When a pair ticket could be obtained from the gacha by paying 10,000 yen, a long line would form in front of the gacha machine. Setting off on a trip without knowing the destination together with one's girlfriend sounds very exciting.

Environmental Enrichment

Environmental enrichment refers to efforts to improve the living conditions of animals kept in places such as zoos to reduce their stress and elicit their natural behaviors. When categorized into five types, one of them is feeding enrichment. In

Fig. 2.37 Gacha machine for airline ticket

this category, a commonly adopted approach is to make feeding "inconvenient," for example, by hiding food or making it difficult to access. Known methods include burying food in the ground, hiding it in grass, hanging it from high trees, suspending it in places that can only be reached by jumping from the water's surface, providing food at irregular times, and requiring problem-solving to obtain it. For example, in one zoo, the food for elephants was placed inside the enclosure in such a way that the elephants had to skillfully use their trunks to eat it.

Such inconveniences bring the benefit of enjoyment to the animals. Searching for food and trying different ways to obtain it resemble life in the wild, so the animals become livelier. Even if it takes time, they can feel as though they have obtained their food by themselves.

Chapter 3
New Products or Services that Provide Users with Benefits of Inconvenience (BoI)

The product or service that brings "benefits of inconvenience (BoI)" to users is called BoI system. There are four methods for designing new BoI systems. This chapter introduces ideas designed using each of these methods.

3.1 Problem-Solving Method

The first method is the problem-solving type. In the field of engineering, it is often said that "engineering is problem solving." In the field of design as well, it is said that "design is problem solving." Both engineering and design share the common aspect of creating something new that has not existed before. As a student, I belonged to a faculty of engineering, and as a university faculty member, I have been affiliated with engineering, information science, and design studies, so I am familiar with the idea that these fields are about problem-solving. The problem-solving type is useful as one of the methods for designing a BoI system.

In this type, the process is as follows:

* Identify cases in which convenience causes harm to users and define these as problems to be solved.
* Solve those problems by "making things inconvenient."

This process shifts the design target, as shown in the four-quadrant diagram (Fig. 3.1), from Harm of Convenience to Benefit of Inconvenience.

Barrier-aree, introduced in Sect. 2.4, is a design by a person not directly related to the concept of the benefit of inconvenience; however, if we interpret it according to the problem-solving type, it can be described as follows:

* Barrier-free design is convenient in daily life, but it has the problem of promoting a decline in physical abilities over the long term.

© The Author(s), under exclusive license to Springer Nature Singapore Pte Ltd. 2026
H. Kawakami, *Case Collection of the Benefits of Inconvenience*,
SpringerBriefs in Business, https://doi.org/10.1007/978-981-92-3981-8_3

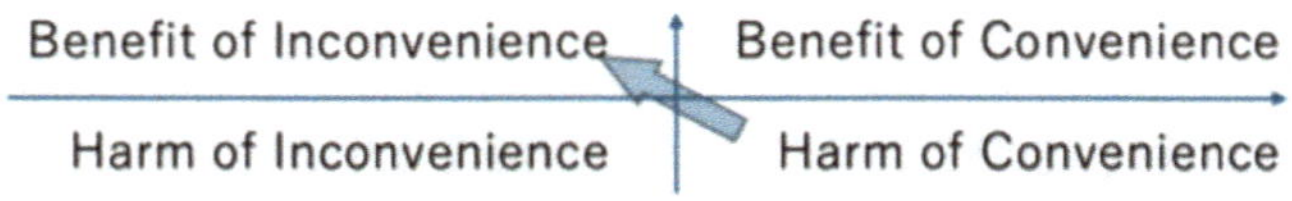

Fig. 3.1 Problem-Solving method is interpreted as a shift from the lower right to BoI

* To solve this problem, slight barriers are installed in facilities. Although this creates inconvenience in daily life, it helps suppress the decline in physical abilities over the long term.

Below, several designs conceived through the problem-solving type are introduced.

3.1.1 PathFade Navigation

It is a navigation system in which the route you have already traveled gradually fades and wears away on the screen. Figure 3.2 shows its user interface and a promotional illustration.

The essence of convenience in ordinary navigation systems lies in the reliable provision of accurate and detailed information. Therefore, by deliberately removing this essence, we designed an inconvenient navigation system. Roads that have been passed once, along with their surroundings, gradually fade out, and if the same place is passed three times, it becomes completely blank and can no longer be seen. Even if one thinks, "When I came here before, I am sure I turned at a corner around here, but where exactly was it?" and looks at the navigation system, the display has slightly faded, making it impossible to see the exact corner.

We implemented this fading function as an experimental device in a pedestrian navigation system for tourism. We created two types of navigation systems that were identical in every aspect except for whether they faded or not. We asked several participants to walk around the streets of Kyoto using them. Afterwards, we showed

Fig. 3.2 Interface of PathFade navigation and its promotional illustration

the participants photos taken along the routes they had walked, along with photos of different routes as dummies, and asked, "Have you seen this scene?" The proportion of correct answers was significantly higher in the group that used the fading navigation system.

We propose the following hypothesis. When using ordinary navigation systems, people subconsciously assume that because information is always available on the device and can be retrieved at any time, there is no need to store it in their own memory. The fact that many people feel that "using a car navigation system makes it difficult for me to remember the routes" also supports this hypothesis.

3.1.2 WordFade Dictionary

It is a dictionary in which the display of a word fades and becomes harder to read each time it is looked up, and after being looked up three times, it becomes completely unreadable.

When learning a foreign language, a dictionary that maps one's native language to the target language is indispensable. Nowadays, it is convenient because online dictionaries can be easily accessed from smartphones and PCs. However, when people want to acquire a language, many seem to prefer paper dictionaries over convenient online ones. In my case, I find that I remember things more easily when I look them up in a paper dictionary than when I use an online dictionary. When I look something up in an online dictionary, I sometimes cannot recall what I just looked up, and I even continue working with the page left open in the browser. It may be that we instinctively feel there is no need to store in memory information that can always be obtained easily and reliably.

If that is the case, how about making an online dictionary that fades and becomes harder to read each time it is used? Since the information gradually disappears, one would instinctively try to retain it in one's own memory.

3.1.3 2D-Curve Microwave Oven

It is a microwave oven that has an interface requiring effort for input. On its front, there is only a two-dimensional touch panel and a start button. The start button cannot be pressed unless a curve resembling a function graph, with time on the horizontal axis and power on the vertical axis, is drawn on the two-dimensional panel. Figure 3.3 shows its promotional illustration.

The "one-minute heating button" found on ordinary microwave ovens is convenient. By simply pressing that button without much thought, it heats for about one minute at a constant power. My father likes to have hot liquor for dinner, and every evening he pressed the "one-minute hot liquor button." This button consistently produces the same output for anyone at any time. However, it leaves no room for

Fig. 3.3 2D-Curve microwave oven

ingenuity. There do not seem to be any hidden commands, such as changing the output by pressing the button at a slight angle.

On the other hand, when using the 2D-curve microwave oven, even if one simply wants to prepare hot liquor as usual, one must draw a graph each time. Compared with the one-minute heating button, it requires more effort and is cumbersome.

However, with this interface, one might accidentally draw a different curve than usual due to a slip of the hand, and think, "Well, why not," and start it as is, perhaps leading to the discovery of a personal best curve for hot liquor. It would also be a good idea to create a website where the discovered curves can be published as recipes. There is even a possibility that they could spread with names such as "the best hot liquor curve discovered by the father of Mr. K."

3.1.4 LagMail

It is an email client that introduces a time lag between pressing the send button and the actual transmission of the email. Figure 3.4 shows its user interface. It features icons of the planets in the solar system: the Mercury button sends immediately, the Venus button sends within one hour, and the Earth button sends within the same day. With the delay gradually increasing, pressing the Pluto button sends the email within ten years.

Email is a convenient tool for work. It allows information to be transmitted instantly. Unlike the telephone, the recipient does not need to be available to receive it at that moment; it is sufficient if the recipient can read it at some later time. Nevertheless, there are people who feel offended if they do not receive a reply immediately after sending an email. Even though the recipient may be in a situation where they cannot read the email at that moment, such people assume that the recipient has read the message and is deliberately leaving it unanswered. They seem to believe that one has an obligation to reply immediately upon receiving an email.

LagMail is helpful for such people. If you inform the recipient in advance that you are using LagMail, they will understand that any delay in your reply is not due to neglect but is caused by the functionality of the email client. Although taking time is inherently inconvenient, LagMail derives benefit from this inconvenience.

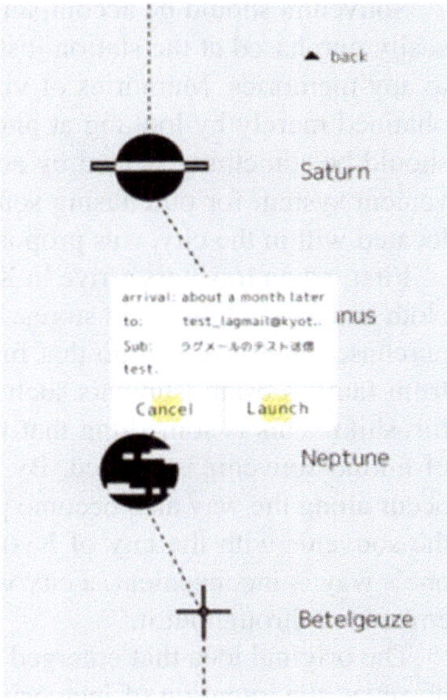

Fig. 3.4 User interface of LagMail

3.1.5 Authentic Kyoto Souvenirs

It is a system for purchasing souvenirs by visiting the main shops of long-established stores. The left part of Fig. 3.5 shows such a shop in Kyoto.

Nowadays, it is easy to buy well-known Kyoto souvenirs at Kyoto Station on the way home from sightseeing. This is a global and standardized system seen all over Japan, not just in Kyoto. Moreover, it is even possible to buy specialties from other regions at Kyoto Station. This is simply too convenient.

Fig. 3.5 Main shop of a long-established shop in Kyoto and the booklet for authentic Kyoto souvenirs

Souvenirs should be accompanied by memories. However, souvenirs that can be easily purchased at the station just before boarding a Shinkansen home are not tied to any memories. Memories of visiting the city of Kyoto should not be something obtained merely by looking at photos or videos that overflow on the Internet; they should be something gained by actually being present in that city. Thus, an inconvenient system for purchasing souvenirs, one that requires visiting the main stores located within the city, was proposed.

First, when travelers arrive in Kyoto, they purchase a special furoshiki wrapping cloth and a list of the main stores. Then, when they go to a main store, they have the purchased item placed into that furoshiki. After visiting several such stores, sweets from famous establishments such as Tsuruya and Kameya are gathered in a single furoshiki. This is something that would not normally occur. In other words, a one-of-a-kind souvenir is created. By going all the way to the main stores, events that occur along the way also become part of the memories, various aspects that connect the souvenir with the city of Kyoto remain in one's mind. Although going out of one's way is inconvenient, a city with a long history returns small surprises that are embedded throughout it.

The original idea that emerged from the design work could not be implemented; however, the intention of increasing travelers' memories of the city through inconvenient souvenirs took shape in a booklet titled "Authentic Kyoto Souvenirs." This booklet introduces 18 main stores of long-established Kyoto businesses, each with an average history of about 280 years. By bringing this booklet to the main stores and purchasing souvenirs, visitors can receive a kaō (stylized signature) or shop seal, making it a booklet like a goshuin stamp book. The left part of Fig. 3.5 shows the booklet.

3.1.6 Trip Guided by the First Issue of a Travel Guide Magazine

It is a tour where participants travel guided by a guidebook from about 40 years ago. In Japan, there are travel guide magazines published by Japanese travel agencies that cover destinations throughout the country. In 2010, this series was listed in the Guinness Book of World Records as the travel guide series with the largest number of issues published in the world. Its first issue was Kyoto, published in 1984. Figure 3.6 shows a fictional image of such a magazine.

Kyoto remains a popular tourist destination even today, attracting many visitors from both Japan and abroad. Throughout the city, there are countless places where one can feel Japan's history and culture. Even if you walk around all day, you can only see a small part of them.

Today, for enjoying a walk through Kyoto, the latest guidebooks from various publishers are readily available and convenient. It is also convenient to obtain travel information from the web. However, in this tour, one deliberately walks through the

Fig. 3.6 An image of the travel guide magazine published in 1884

city with a guidebook from about 40 years ago in hand. Just imagining it sounds enjoyable. Some places have changed dramatically since then, while others have changed only subtly. Of course, there are also many places that remain completely unchanged, retaining the atmosphere of that time. In Kyoto, which served as the capital of Japan for a long time from the eighth century, historical elements have been carefully preserved and maintained. The subtle differences between a guidebook from nearly half a century ago and the present-day city allow one to sense the passage of history.

In general, having incorrect or missing information is inconvenient. However, this project transforms that inconvenience into something enjoyable.

3.1.7 Recipe Website with "a Pinch of Salt"

It is a recipe website in which exact quantities are not specified. Figure 3.7 shows its promotional copy and logo. Messo is a Nagoya dialect in Japan meaning 'roughly.' When posting a recipe, the use of precise measurements (for example, 3 g) is prohibited, and contributors are required to use expressions that allow for broad interpretation (for example, "a pinch"). If a submission contains numerical values, an AI automatically converts them into appropriate alternative expressions before the recipe is displayed on the site.

Numerical information is convenient. Contributors can publish their recipes accurately, and those who follow the recipes can faithfully reproduce dishes. However, such convenience eliminates room for ingenuity. It takes away the enjoyment of adjusting quantities to create one's own unique flavor, as well as the pleasure of inventing dishes whose identity is unclear and serving them to friends while saying, "This is a dish that doesn't have a name yet."

Fig. 3.7 The promotional copy and logo for the rough recipe website

In general, having less information is considered inconvenient. Expressions that allow for broad interpretation are often disliked in professional settings. However, in cooking, this inconvenience expands the scope for creativity and increases the chances of making discoveries.

3.1.8 Tourist Photos you cannot Take by Yourself

It is a service that prevents tourists from taking selfies at sightseeing spots.

Security cameras installed at various tourist locations are equipped with a function that can read IDs transmitted from smartphones. Tourists who register for this service provide their contact information (such as an email address) and install an application on their smartphones that transmits their ID. This application also disables the smartphone's camera function.

While enjoying sightseeing with the app running, if they happen to pass near a security camera equipped with an ID-reading function, the camera takes a photo, as shown in Fig. 3.8, and uploads it to a server. When the day's sightseeing is over, and they are relaxing at their accommodation, they receive a URL to the server where the photos have been stored. The tourists are surprised to realize that there was a camera in such a place, feel satisfied with the quality of the photo, and admire the good taste of the shop that installed the camera. For the shop as well, the scenery in front of the shop spreads through these photos, increasing its recognition, so they devise camera angles that reflect a refined sense of style.

This service is inconvenient for tourists. They are not told where they need to go to have their photos taken. If they are unlucky, the day may end without passing any location where cameras are installed, and they may not receive even a single photo. However, if they do obtain photos, those images become treasured memories of the trip, recalling the scenery and the events that occurred around it.

Normally, smartphones and digital cameras are essential items for travel. They are convenient tools that allow one to take an almost unlimited number of record photos. However, as it's so handy, they tend to just snap a photo for the time being.

Fig. 3.8 A photo of a user of the service

As a result, even when reviewing photos later, many similar images may be stored on a server, and one may not remember what the subject was or where the photo was taken. Originally, travel photos should serve as meaningful keepsakes, but they don't.

3.2 Value Mining Method

The second method is the value-mining type. This method follows the process below:

* Forcefully make a convenient product or service inconvenient.
* Discover value in that inconvenience.

This process shifts the design target, as shown in the four-quadrant diagram (Fig. 3.9), from Benefit of Convenience to Benefit of Inconvenience.

When this method is used in workshops for designing BoI systems, participants seem to enjoy it very much. Making existing things inconvenient results in designs that seem like jokes, and coming up with such ideas is an enjoyable activity.

Below, several designs conceived through the value-mining type are introduced.

3.2.1 Prime Number Ruler

It is a ruler that shows marks only at prime numbers as shown in Fig. 3.10. Universities often have some original goods. The "prime number ruler" is one of

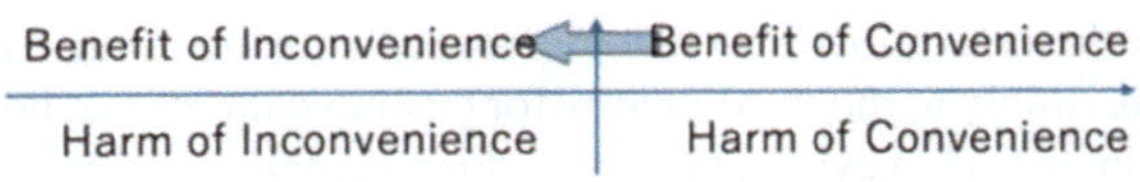

Fig. 3.9 Value mining method is interpreted as a shift from the upper right to BoI

Fig. 3.10 Prime number ruler

Kyoto University's original items. This ruler is also designed to be intentionally inconvenient.

Normally, a ruler has marks at every number, and we are satisfied with that. However, the prime number ruler has missing marks and shows marks only at prime numbers. At first, it may seem that you can measure only prime numbers with it. But, for example, 4 can be expressed as $7 - 3$, so it can be measured as the difference of two primes. Since $1 = 3 - 2$, $2 = 5 - 3$, and $3 = 5 - 2$, one might think of a hypothesis that perhaps every integer can be expressed as the difference of two prime numbers.

In fact, it is not about differences, but in the eighteenth century, Goldbach conjectured that "every even number greater than or equal to 4 can be expressed as the sum of two prime numbers (that is, every odd number greater than or equal to 5 can be expressed as the sum of three prime numbers)." The fact that no one has yet proved this conjecture adds interest to the idea above.

Furthermore, when you look at the marks on the prime number ruler, you can see that even the same length can be measured in more than one way, as in $4 = 7 - 3 = 11 - 7 = 17 - 13$. Every time you measure a length, you need to do a simple subtraction, so it might even be good for brain training.

The prime number ruler may look like just a novelty item, but it is a simple demonstration of the benefits of inconvenience. Now it has become a standard souvenir from Kyoto University.

3.2.2 Navigation System that Shows Only Direction and Distance

It is a navigation system that does not display detailed maps but shows only the direction and distance to the destination, as shown in Fig. 3.11.

When traveling using a normal navigation system, it is easy because one can simply follow the system's instructions. This system is convenient. However, because a person only needs to match the system's instructions with the situation in front of them, there is little motivation to form a macroscopic image of the city. In situations where the goal is simply to move efficiently for business, there is no need to have such a macroscopic image. However, let us try adding a small element of trip for leisure to this simple act of movement. In that case, inconvenience becomes useful. Since

Fig. 3.11 An image of the user interface of the rough navigation system

only the direction and distance to the destination are displayed, decisions such as the detailed route or whether to turn at the next corner are left to the interaction between the individual and the surrounding urban environment. As a result, a macroscopic mental image of the city is formed within the person. This immediately creates a sense of being on a trip for leisure. However, care must be taken not to be late for an appointment of business.

3.2.3 Gesture-Based Unlocking

It is a smartphone unlocking method that uses gestures.

When unlocking a smartphone, user authentication is required, and common methods include image-based authentication (such as facial recognition or fingerprint recognition), as well as methods using previously registered passwords, passcodes, or sequences that trace a pattern among nine points. In the latter case, the number of patterns that can be registered is finite. Under the restriction that all nine points must be used at least once, there are 9 factorial possible sequences. Even without this restriction, the number of possible patterns remains finite.

A student, saying "Memorizing a single point in a finite solution space is too easy, I'll make it infinite!", developed gesture-based unlocking. To unlock a smartphone, one must perform the same gesture that has been registered in advance (Fig. 3.12).

This application is inconvenient. As one quickly realizes when using it, if a gesture that comes to mind at random is registered, it is almost impossible to reproduce it accurately. I tried registering the transformation pose of a Japanese live-action super-hero, Kamen Rider, which I liked in childhood, but unlocking was nearly impossible. On the other hand, the student who developed this application was a member of a table tennis club and registered the motion of their smash, enabling them to unlock the device with high reliability. The gesture to be registered must already be embodied in the user.

Fig. 3.12 Gesture-based unlocking for a smartphone

It feels satisfying that only oneself can succeed every time, while others can hardly unlock it, even when the gesture is shown right in front of them.

3.2.4 Cleaner Calendar

It is a tear-off daily calendar in which you cannot know the date unless you clean rooms. Figure 3.13 shows the poster for explaining the calendar. It uses a white adhesive roller (lint roller) for cleaning, with certain areas deliberately left without adhesive. When you clean, dirt does not stick to those parts, causing the number for that day to appear.

You use it once each day, and on the following day, you clean using a new surface. It is an inconvenient calendar because the date cannot be seen unless you clean something. Even if one checks "what day is it today?" on a smartphone, one tends to forget it quickly. On the other hand, the idea here is that the number that finally becomes visible after moving your hands will remain in your memory.

It is also inconvenient as a cleaning tool. Since the date must not become misaligned, this tool can be used for cleaning only once per day.

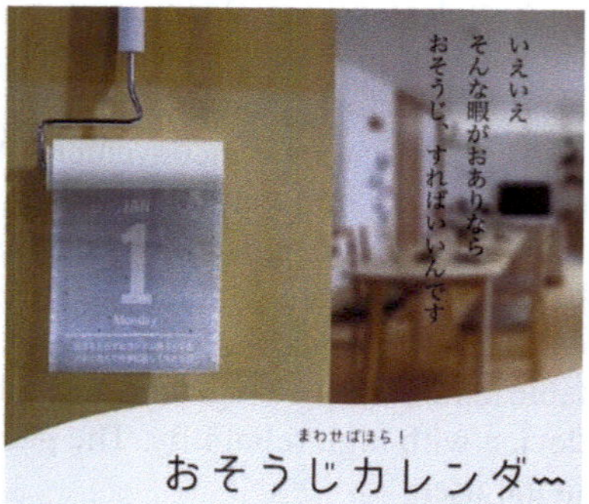

Fig. 3.13 Cleaning calendar

3.2.5 ReminDoor

This door is equipped with two keyholes. One is real, and the other is a dummy. The real and dummy keyholes are randomly swapped. What is inconvenient for the user is that the real keyhole and the dummy keyhole look identical and cannot be distinguished. Figure 3.14 shows the poster for explaining this door.

One day, when trying to lock the door, you insert the key into a hole and turn it, only for it to spin freely without engaging. At that point, thinking, "Oh, so this one is the dummy today," you need to reinsert the key into another hole and lock it. This is a door with a lock that requires more effort than a normal key. In other words, it is inconvenient. From this inconvenience, the following "benefit" is obtained.

When I go out, even though I am sure that I have locked the front door, after walking about ten meters, I often become uneasy and return to check again that it is indeed locked. As people pass the age of fifty, they tend to lose confidence in their memory, so many people have probably had the same experience as I have. However, if I had a ReminDoor, I believe I would clearly remember that I had locked the door.

With ReminDoor, there are days when you feel a slight "ugh." On another day, when you insert the key into the first hole and turn it, the lock clicks immediately. At that moment, you feel a small sense of "luck." With a normal door that has only one keyhole, there is neither "ugh" nor "luck." ReminDoor, through this small extra effort (inconvenience), gives you confidence in your memory of which keyhole was correct today, and at the same time, confidence that you have locked the door.

Fig. 3.14 ReminDoor

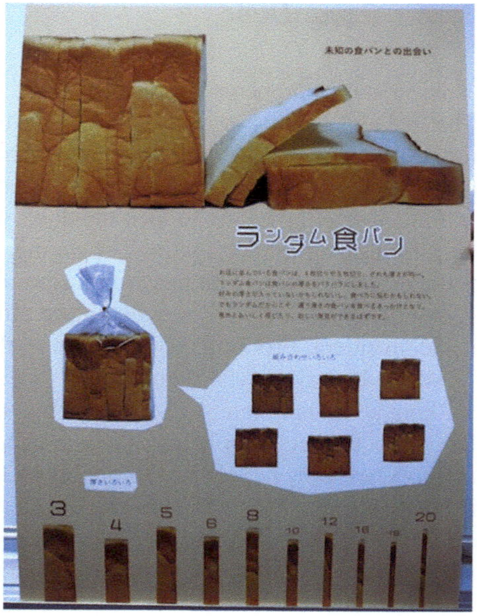

Fig. 3.15 Randomly sliced loaf of bread

3.2.6 Randomly Sliced Loaf of Bread

It is a loaf of bread in which the slices are cut to random thicknesses as shown in Fig. 3.15.

In general, it is more convenient for sliced bread to be cut to a uniform thickness. If one knows their preferred thickness, then by buying a loaf sliced to that thickness, every slice will be to their liking. If one decides to make sandwiches and buys a loaf sliced thinner than usual, all the slices can be used for that purpose.

In this sense, a loaf cut into slices of random thickness is inconvenient. However, it also offers opportunities for discovery. A thickness different from what one thought to be ideal might turn out to be more delicious. One might even be impressed that bread can be sliced so thinly, and upon toasting it, something resembling a cookie may quickly emerge.

3.2.7 Hard-To-Operate Hair Dryer

It is a hair dryer that continuously controls airflow and temperature based on the position and strength of the user's grip on the handle. Figure 3.16 shows the poster for explaining the dryer.

Increasing the pressure of the index finger gripping the upper part raises the temperature, while increasing the pressure of the little finger gripping the lower part

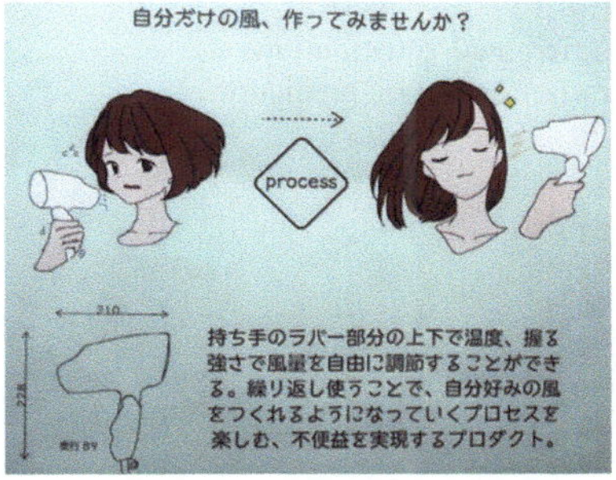

Fig. 3.16 Continuum dryer

lowers the temperature. These can both be adjusted continuously. In addition, the greater the total strength of the grip, the stronger the airflow becomes. This can also be varied continuously.

In general, it is more convenient if airflow can be controlled in discrete levels such as "strong," "medium," and "weak," and temperature can be controlled in stages such as "high," "medium," and "low." However, there is no guarantee that preset temperature and airflow settings will suit one's own hair.

On the other hand, although a continuous control method is difficult to operate and inconvenient, it allows users to find the combination of airflow and temperature that best suits their own hair. Furthermore, this combination changes continuously over time from the beginning of drying to the end. The inconvenient continuous control method can accommodate these changes as well.

3.2.8 Differential-Equation-Type Traffic Congestion Prediction

It is a system of congestion prediction in which the horizontal axis represents time, the vertical axis represents the route from the current location to the destination, and the predicted vehicle speed is plotted at each coordinate in color. Figure 3.17 illustrates an image of this system.

In regions with high population density, traffic congestion frequently occurs. If it were possible to predict where, when, and to what extent congestion will arise, it would be convenient because one could consider ways to avoid it. In Japan, on days when congestion is expected, predictions are published on the web indicating where and how much congestion will occur on expressways. The information is presented as sets of road sections, time periods, and required travel times.

This method of presentation is simple and easy to understand, and therefore convenient. However, it merely displays the prediction results, so it does not reveal the process by which the predictions were derived, nor does it allow users to consider how to avoid congestion. For this reason, the differential-equation-type congestion prediction was proposed.

Fig. 3.17 Differential-equation-type traffic congestion prediction

In differential equations, small differences in initial conditions can lead to large differences in results. Similarly, in the differential-equation-type congestion prediction, even a slight difference in the departure time from the current location can lead to a significant difference in arrival time at the destination. This can be confirmed by drawing one's own function graph on the congestion prediction chart. By doing so, one may be able to find an appropriate combination of departure time and intermediate rest stops that minimizes the time spent caught in congestion.

3.3 Emergence Method

The third method is the emergence type.

The problem-solving type and the value-mining type described above follow a fixed process in which two of the four quadrants are shifted and are therefore somewhat systematic. In contrast, the emergence type follows the process shown below:

* Accumulate many examples of BoI system design from various fields.
* Extract the essence from those examples.
* Apply that essence to the design target.

This process starts from the "Benefit of Inconvenience" quadrant in the four-quadrant diagram shown in Fig. 3.18 and returns to the "Benefit of Inconvenience" quadrant. It is also a process commonly adopted by professional designers, and it requires a high level of creativity and the ability to think analogically.

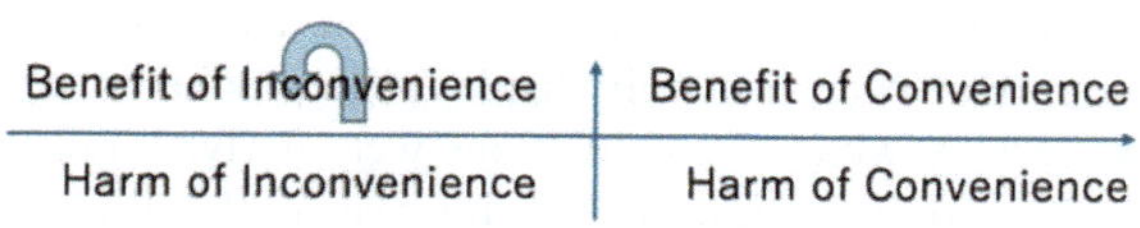

Fig. 3.18 Emergence method is interpreted as a shift within BoI quadrant

In the following, several designs proposed through the emergence type are introduced.

3.3.1 Left-Turn-Only Tour

It is a tour in the Left Ward of Kyoto City. We designed a "Left-Turn-Only Tour" inspired by the idea of "left." Fig. 3.19 is the call for participants of this tour. In this tour, participants walk through the city from a meeting point to a destination, with the rule that they are not allowed to make any right turns. Kyoto's streets are laid out in a grid pattern, and although being limited to left turns is inconvenient, the equivalent of a right turn can be achieved by going past one block and then making three consecutive left turns.

When repeating these three left turns, people tend, by habit, to want to turn at the nearest corner. Instinctively, they seem to prefer taking the shortest possible route and eliminating unnecessary detours. Even at the moment of signing up for the Left-Turn-Only Tour, participants presumably accept that the route will be inefficient if their purpose is to reach the sightseeing destination, yet this tendency still emerges, it is rather curious.

Fig. 3.19 Call for participants of left-turn-only tour

However, this leads participants into narrow alleys. Here is where the character of an old city comes into play. Such narrow alleys almost always offer discoveries. This tour combines Kyoto's geographical characteristics with the concept of the "benefit of inconvenience." Rather than prioritizing efficient arrival at the destination, it emphasizes wandering through the city and creating memorable experiences.

3.3.2 One Stroke No-Cross City Walk

It is a tour in which participants walk around a city under the rule that they must not walk along any road they have already taken, nor are they allowed to cross it. Participants in this tour install a dedicated map application on their smartphones. This application records the routes they have taken and emits a loud "Eeek!" sound if they step onto a road they have already used. There is also a website where participants can upload the routes they have taken that day, and their points increase if others imitate their routes.

Originally, wandering around an unfamiliar city is itself an enjoyable activity. It offers new discoveries and allows one to appreciate the atmosphere of the city. An idea was proposed to further enhance its entertainment value by introducing inconvenience into the experience. In general, having constraints that reduce freedom is considered inconvenient. However, as in the rules of sports, when constraints are skillfully applied, they can increase the level of entertainment.

3.3.3 Self-Cook Conveyor-Belt Sushi

It is a conveyor-belt sushi system in which sushi rice, toppings, seaweed, and other ingredients travel along a conveyor belt, as shown in Fig. 3.20. Customers take them and assemble the sushi by themselves.

In general, conveyor-belt sushi is a system in which fully prepared sushi moves along on a conveyor belt, and customers take what they want and eat it. In the past, if one hesitated to take a plate, it would pass by, so it encouraged customers to act quickly. Recently, many systems allow customers to place an order using a tablet at the table, after which the sushi arrives on a conveyor belt and stops at their table.

This system is convenient. However, by making it slightly inconvenient, an idea was proposed to turn the dining experience at a conveyor-belt sushi restaurant into entertainment: a system in which customers make the sushi themselves. When sushi ingredients are ordered using the tablet, they are delivered to the table, and customers assemble the sushi themselves and serve it to family members or friends at the same table. It becomes an opportunity to show off one's skills a little, and to feel like a sushi chef. It also seems to be enjoyable for visitors from overseas.

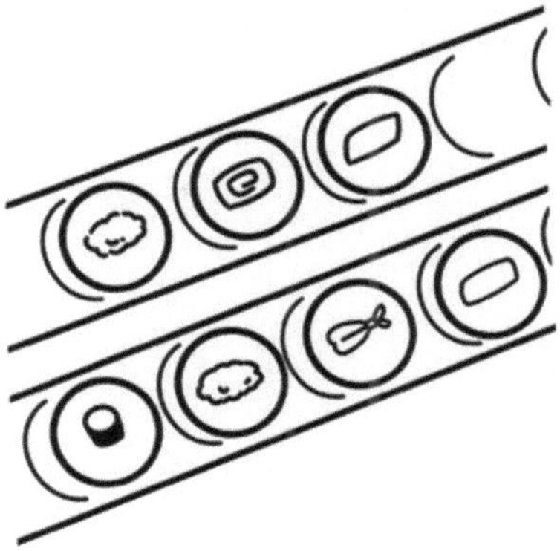

Fig. 3.20 Self-Cook conveyor-belt sushi

Fig. 3.21 A mouth with a well-worn look

3.3.4 Wooden Mouse, Keyboard, and Pad with a Well-Worn Look

They are a mouse, keyboard, and pad whose surfaces that people touch are made of wood. As they are used over time, grime from the hands accumulates, and through repeated cleaning, they gradually develop a unique texture and appearance (Fig. 3.21). This texture is proof of the interaction between the user and the tools, and it becomes a one-of-a-kind quality in the world. In addition, since wooden materials undergo plastic deformation, they gradually adapt to the shape of the user's hands, which also satisfies the user and brings joy in having tools that feel uniquely their own.

In general, getting dirty is inconvenient because it necessitates the effort of cleaning or washing. However, dirt that results from interaction with the user becomes something pleasing, as it reflects the relationship between the user and the object.

3.3.5 Vegetable Gacha at Supermarket

It is a gacha-style machine in which one cannot know what kind of vegetable will come out. It is placed in supermarkets, and when 500 yen is inserted, a vegetable worth about 500 yen is dispensed. Figure 3.22 shows an image of this machine.

Fig. 3.22 An image of a vegetable gacha machine

Normally, various vegetables are displayed in supermarkets with price tags, and we choose the vegetables we want while considering their price and freshness. Except for people who enjoy shopping, buying vegetables is generally not a particularly exciting activity.

An idea was proposed to introduce inconvenience into this activity and enhance its entertainment value. In general, having less information is inconvenient. While customers are informed only that the vegetable is worth 500 yen, they are not told what kind of vegetable it is. However, this inconvenience adds a sense of gamble to purchasing vegetables, making it enjoyable. Encountering a vegetable one has never eaten before becomes a new experience, and thinking about how to cook an unfamiliar vegetable also becomes part of the fun.

3.3.6 Alarm App that won't Stop Unless Both Partners Wake up

3It is an alarm app that keeps ringing until both users press the stop button. The app is installed on the smartphones of two people who wake up at the same time. At the set wake-up time, the app sounds an alarm on both smartphones. Even if one person wakes up and presses the stop button, the alarm will continue to ring, as shown in Fig. 3.23, until the other person also presses the stop button. Since it cannot be stopped by one person alone, it is inconvenient.

However, thanks to this inconvenience, one can understand the condition of the partner who is sleeping elsewhere. If the alarm stops immediately after one presses the stop button, it means that the partner responded to the alarm earlier and is therefore likely to have woken up alertly. If the alarm continues to ring even after pressing the button, it raises concern about the partner's condition.

Fig. 3.23 Buddy alarm

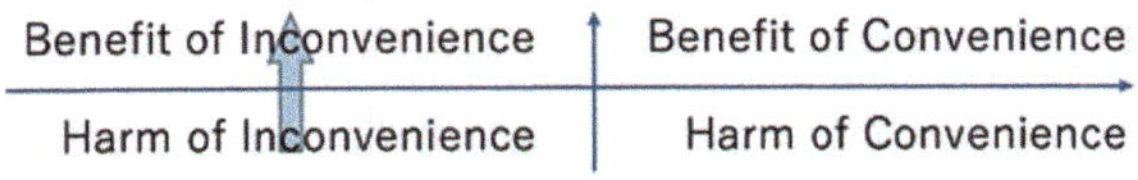

Fig. 3.24 Innovation of meaning method is interpreted as a shift from the lower left to BoI

3.4 Innovation of Meaning Method

Up to the previous section, three types that start from three of the four quadrants have been introduced. There remains one more type that starts from the "Harm of Inconvenience" quadrant, as shown in Fig. 3.24. This is called the meaning-of-innovation type. It is a type in which the interpretation of inconvenience is changed so that it provides not a harm but a benefit.

The resort hotel in Arashiyama introduced in Sect. 2.4 was designed by people unrelated to BoI design, but it can be regarded as an example of the meaning-of-innovation type. According to a map I used as a student 40 years ago, the resort hotel now stands on the site where "Arashiyama Onsen" once stood. When I was a student, I had never seen nor heard of Arashiyama Onsen. It was probably an obscure hot spring inn. With mountains to the west and a river to the east, it was an inn that could only be accessed by walking for a long way along a narrow path running along a cliff. The inconvenience of access brought about the harm of deterring visitors. In contrast, the resort hotel that stands there today has skillfully made use of the inconvenience of access and has succeeded in giving the hotel an image of a secluded area or a hidden gem. The current hotel is highly popular.

It is not known how the manager of this hotel changed the interpretation of inconvenience. As a well-known manager, that person must have led the hotel to success by employing strategies beyond our imagination. In this way, although there are existing examples of the meaning-of-innovation type, no generally applicable process that can be used by anyone is known.

Chapter 4
Reverse Case Search from Related Research Fields

4.1 Human–Machine System

The Apollo Program

The term "fuben-eki" (benefits of inconvenience) was created in the research field of human–machine systems. It is said that the term "human–machine system" began to be used around the time of the Apollo lunar landing program. Although the truth of this claim is uncertain, I will imagine the situation from the perspective of an astronaut on a lunar landing mission and consider it in terms of fuben-eki.

What would have happened if the rocket and its crew had not been regarded as a single human–machine system? In that case, we would only need to pursue higher functionality of the machine itself. Beyond that, there would be fully automated machines that achieve their goals without any need for human involvement.

If we apply this idea to a lunar landing mission, the rocket and the lunar module would land on the Moon and return to Earth automatically, without any involvement of the crew. The crew would be told, "Do nothing. Just sit still," because they must not interfere with the automated system. Even if an accident occurred, they would not be able to handle it manually. This situation would be extremely frightening. It would be as if they were guinea pigs.

On the other hand, when we view the system as a human–machine system, human intervention in the machine is designed as an essential element. In general, such intervention requires more effort than dealing with a fully automated system, and effort is often avoided because it is seen as inconvenient. However, for those on board the rocket for a lunar landing, this effort allows them to become active operators of the rocket rather than passive subjects like guinea pigs. The sense of not being a guinea pig comes from the fact that the effort gives the user a sense of agency.

Related examples:

2.2 Level 5 Autonomous Driving.
2.3 Mechanical Key Lock Door.

© The Author(s), under exclusive license to Springer Nature Singapore Pte Ltd. 2026
H. Kawakami, *Case Collection of the Benefits of Inconvenience*,
SpringerBriefs in Business, https://doi.org/10.1007/978-981-92-3981-8_4

Black Box Creates Trouble

We can find many things around us that have been turned into black boxes for the sake of a little convenience. A small example is the power window in a car. Compared with the old rack-and-pinion type, where you turn a knob to raise and lower the glass window, power windows require almost no physical effort. They are convenient devices that work by simply pushing or pulling a switch.

However, how many people understand the relationship between operating that switch and the movement of the glass window? Here, there is a small black box.

We have no choice but to trust black boxes, but sometimes that trust is betrayed. For example, there are cases where pressing the power window switch does not move the window. In my case, I used to drive my family back to my hometown during the summer vacation. One year, the power window stopped working while it was open. If it had been the old rack-and-pinion type, I could have removed the door panel and repaired it by myself. But a power window is a black box, and I had no way to fix it on my own.

I had no choice but to take the car to a dealer for repair. However, at that time (the end of the twentieth century), most dealers were closed in mid-August. Other repair shops were also closed during this period. I had a meeting in Kyoto the next day (in those days, it was not easy to participate remotely), so I had to travel 350 km that day. Driving on the highway with the window open would be very unstable and dangerous. If I drove slowly on local roads, I would have to attend the meeting the next day looking exhausted from staying up all night. This small black box created a troublesome situation.

While the adults, thinking rigidly, were struggling with the problem, my son, who was an elementary school student at the time and had a more flexible way of thinking, solved it. He opened the door, held the window glass between both palms from the inside and outside, and forcefully pulled it up to close it. The adults were impressed by this flexible thinking, saying, "We didn't think of that."

At that moment, we admired the solution. However, later, when I took the car in for repair, I found that the parts damaged by forcibly pulling up the window were quite expensive. This small black box created even more trouble.

Related examples:

2.2 Level 5 Autonomous Driving.
2.3 Mechanical Key Lock Door.

4.2 Human Factor

Risk Homeostasis

The concept of Shared Space introduced in Sect. 2.4.2 can be seen as a device that shifts responsibility for safety from "the government and the road ensure safety in this space" to "you yourself ensure safety." In other words, everyone who uses the space becomes responsible for maintaining safety.

In the sense that it requires effort and careful thinking, Shared Space can be considered more inconvenient for users than ordinary roads. However, because of this inconvenience, people can take an active role in ensuring safety. This is also related to the idea that "when external safety devices are removed, people tend to shift internally toward safer behavior." This tendency was called risk homeostasis by G. J. S. Wilde (Wilde 1982).

Through the combined effect of the "sense of agency" given to users as a benefit of inconvenience and risk homeostasis, experimental results showed that the accident rate did not increase compared to ordinary roads. In fact, the average speed of cars decreased.

Risk homeostasis is more often discussed in the opposite way. That is, when safety devices for avoiding danger are provided externally, people tend to behave more dangerously to the extent that they feel safer. The Japanese title of the book that proposed risk homeostasis is "Why do Traffic Accidents not Disappear?" which questions whether it is appropriate to install safety devices too easily.

Related examples:

2.2 Level 5 Autonomous Driving.

2.4.2 Cell-Production System, Shared Space Experiment.

Disadvantages of Partial Automation

In the field of human factors, the problems of partial automation have been examined in detail. First, because the automation is only partial, the operator loses a view of the whole system. In addition, only those operations that cannot be automated are left to the operator. These two factors make the operation even more difficult.

Moreover, automation creates a negative feedforward loop in which a decrease in the operator's motivation and a decline in skills promote each other. Furthermore, there are two additional causes that make accurate and rapid situation awareness difficult: automatic compensation for failures delays the appearance of those failures, and opportunities for on-the-job training are reduced.

If we organize these terms in causal relations, we can see that the root causes are "partiality" and "automation," and that these two terms are independent of each other. One possible way to solve this problem is to regard "partiality" as the main cause and aim for complete and error-free automation. However, unexpected events generally occur, and complete automation is not easy to achieve.

On the other hand, from the perspective of the benefits of inconvenience (BoI), another approach is to regard easy or excessive "automation" itself as the main cause and to address the problem in that way. The benefits obtained from inconvenience include "a wide scope for active ingenuity," "promotion of understanding of the target system," and "development of a sense of self-efficacy." These correspond to the key issues of the problem described above.

Related examples:

2.2 Level 5 Autonomous Driving.
2.3 Mechanical Key Lock Door, Manual Transmission.
2.4.2 Cell-Production System, Shared Space Experiment.

Dog Co-Pilot

Back in 1982, there was an accident off the coast near Haneda Airport in Japan. An aircraft was on its approach for landing when the captain suddenly switched off the autopilot, manually reversed the engine thrust, and crashed the plane into the sea just before reaching the runway. The accident itself was shocking, but at the same time, it was also surprising to realize that aircraft at that time were already capable of landing automatically using autopilot.

The following joke, which recalls this reverse-thrust accident, was said to have been told among pilots:

Co-pilot: "If autopilot is safer, then humans don't really have anything to do. I'm getting off the plane. Instead, I'll put a dog on board."

Captain: "Do we really need a dog?"

Co-pilot: "Yes. Its job is to bite you if you try to turn off the autopilot."

Captain: "If I'm trusted that little, maybe I don't need to be on board either."

Co-pilot: "Your job is to feed the dog."

Related examples:

2.2 Level 5 Autonomous Driving.
2.4.2 Cell-Production System.

4.3 Human Interface

Reassurance Provided by Twist-Lock Keys

"Mechanical Key Lock Door" in Sect. 2.3 is derived from the following story.

At the end of the twentieth century, a fair number of students owned their own cars. One student told me that he experienced the benefits of inconvenience through his old used car.

One day, he borrowed his father's new car to take his girlfriend for a drive. Around that time, remote-control car keys were becoming the standard. He wanted to show off to his girlfriend that the car had a new-type remote key instead of the old-type key that he need to insert and twist. So, he deliberately stepped a little away from the car and pressed the button on the remote.

The hazard lights flashed, which indicated that the car was locked. However, this student was studying mechanical engineering. He realized that there was no physical basis directly connecting the car being locked and the hazard lights flashing. As a person who can design machines, he understood that, depending on how the control system is designed, the lights could flash even if the car was not actually locked. So, even though he had gone out of his way to press the remote button from a distance, he ended up going back to the car and repeatedly pulling the door handle to confirm that it was locked.

On the other hand, the old-style key for his own car required the action of inserting and twisting it, which was slightly less convenient than simply pressing a remote button. However, when he twisted the key, the reaction force felt in his hand indicated that force was being transmitted somewhere. Because he was close to the car, he could also hear the clicking sound of the locks from four doors. These reliable physical laws and physical phenomena told him that the car was indeed locked, and this gave him a sense of reassurance.

This is an example where a small amount of effort (inconvenience) provides the benefit of reassurance.

Related example:

2.3 Mechanical Key Lock Door.

4.4 Design Theory

Human-Centered Design & User Experience

D. A. Norman proposed an approach called user-centered design in The Psychology of Everyday Things (Norman 1988), and he was a key figure who created an important turning point in usability design. Later, the computer company where he worked as a fellow and was involved in developing human-interface guidelines quickly became well known, and his approach became widely recognized around the world.

However, in 2004, Norman published a paper titled Human-Centered Design Considered Harmful. In that paper, he proposed activity-centered design as an alternative to human-centered design. In the same year, he also published Emotional Design (Basic Books, 2004). The cover of this book featured a lemon squeezer with a surface that is weak to acid, which satirized an excessive focus on usability alone.

Those who strongly believed in human-centered design were probably greatly shocked, feeling as if they had been betrayed by the very person who originally proposed it. However, when reading the paper carefully, one can see that he did not reject human-centered design itself. Instead, he warned against a shallow understanding of human-centered design that leads to a trend of seeking machines that adapt to users (adaptive or adaptable systems). Rather, he suggested aiming for designs that make use of human ability to adapt and change.

Convenient systems that adapt to users can take away opportunities for users to demonstrate their ability to change. One of the benefits of inconvenience is that the effort required and the need to think can help change the user.

IKEA Effect

One of the design principles is called the "IKEA effect." People tend to place a higher value on products that they have helped to create in some way. This is why it is called the "IKEA effect." The name comes from the Swedish furniture retailer that is famous for selling products that customers must assemble by themselves.

This idea applies not only to products but also to services. People feel greater value in things that cannot be completed without their own involvement. Therefore, designers must take the user's involvement into account when designing products and services. This requires more thinking than a method in which the designer completes everything alone.

Related examples:

2.3 Outdoor Camping, DIY.

2.4.1 Pedal-powered Wheelchair.

2.4.2 Cell-Production System, Shared Space Experiment, U-shaped International Support, Environmental Enrichment.

3.1 Authentic Kyoto Souvenirs.

3.2 Differential-Equation-Type Traffic Congestion Prediction.

4.5 Production Engineering

The Cell Production System introduced in Sect. 2.4.2 is a method in which one or a few workers assemble complex products in a place called a "cell." Compared with the Line Production System, which is based on division of labor, this method is less convenient. However, this inconvenience brings a benefit: motivation and skill improve each other through mutual interaction. This is exactly a subject of study in production engineering.

Related example:

2.4.2 Cell-Production System.

4.6 Tourism Studies

The difficulty of visiting a place makes people want to go there, and when they finally arrive, it gives them a sense of gratitude and accomplishment. In addition, skillfully hiding information can also make a trip more enjoyable. Tourism fits well with the idea of "benefits of inconvenience," and there are many examples of this.

Related examples:

2.1 Fuji Mountain Escalator, All-inclusive Travel Service, Overseas Travel with Doraemon's "Anywhere Door".

2.2 Hokkaido Product Fairs Everywhere, Markets Stocking Specialties from Around World.

2.4.1 A Resort Hotel in Arashiyama.

2.4.2 JAL's "Somewhere Miles", Peach's Travel Gacha.

3.1 PathFade Navigation, Authentic Kyoto Souvenirs, Tourist Photos You cannot Take by Yourself.

3.2 Navigation System that shows only Direction and Distance.

3.3 Left-Turn-Only Tour, One Stroke No-Cross City Walk.

4.7 Information Science

The concepts of pull-type and push-type are used in many fields, but they are especially often applied to information. In this context, when a sender forces information onto a receiver, it is called a push type. When a receiver voluntarily goes to get information from a sender, it is called a pull type.

If the extra effort required of the receiver in the pull type is regarded as an inconvenience, this inconvenience can play a positive role: it leads the receiver to treat the information more carefully.

Related example:

2.4.1 "How's That Project Going?" Button on a Core Information System.

4.8 Artificial Intelligence

How can we use generative AI in a human-centered way?

There are many situations in which AI performs better than humans, such as finding security holes more effectively than humans. If AI is more capable than humans, then in the business world, there will likely be more cases where companies introduce AI instead of hiring humans.

However, AI is used not only in business but also in many kinds of activities, and it is often used to "replace" oneself. Life may become easier, but it may also become less enjoyable. Losing one's identity and sense of self-worth is a sad outcome.

We would like to give meaning to the process in which people spend effort and think for themselves. In other words, we want to obtain benefits from inconvenience. We want to have a relationship with AI that is not simply one of "replacement."

To achieve this, it is helpful to keep in mind the idea that inconvenience can bring benefits.

Related examples:

2.1 Digital Gravestone.
2.2 Level 5 Autonomous Driving.

Generative but not Creative

I facilitate design workshops. In these workshops, I ask participants to brainstorm in groups, encouraging them to come up with as many ideas as possible, even if they seem a bit outlandish. However, since the time is limited, they usually come up with at most about ten ideas.

I have been running this workshop every year, and the situation had always been the same. However, in 2022, one group produced about 100 ideas in large quantities. This must have been done using generative AI.

When I read reports from groups that came up with only about ten ideas using their own brain, I found that they included ideas that I would not have come up with. They were creative. On the other hand, when I read the report with 100 ideas, all of them were ideas that I had "heard somewhere before." They were not creative, but merely generative.

4.9 Robotics

Robots can also work by replacing humans. However, from the perspective of "benefits of inconvenience," which aims to give meaning to human actions, we want to create a relationship between robots and humans that is not simply one of "replacement."

One example to focus on is the Weak Robot series. In this series, there is a trash can robot. A typical cleaning robot cleans in place of a human. Using a cleaning robot requires less human effort than cleaning by oneself. In contrast, the trash can robot has a high-level image processing ability to find trash. However, when it finds trash, it only approaches the trash and makes a gesture similar to a bow as shown in Fig. 4.1. This gesture encourages nearby people to pick up the trash and put it into the trash can robot.

In this way, the trash can robot forms a relationship with humans that is not based on "replacement."

4.10 Pedagogy

As part of creativity education, practical exercises are conducted using the design of systems based on "benefits of inconvenience" as the main theme. In general, people are not aware that benefits can come from inconvenience. Gaining this awareness broadens one's perspective and enhances creativity.

Fig. 4.1 Trash can robot

In addition to convenient tools and services, another option is introduced: tools and services in which inconvenience provides benefits to the user.

4.11 Value Engineering

Value engineering provides many methods for improving the value of products and services by balancing function and cost. They have been used in many different fields, from manufacturing to service industries, to reduce costs and improve quality.

Traditionally, value engineering has focused on two types of value: "Use Value" and "Esteem Value." Use Value is created by the functions that allow users to achieve the purpose of using a product. Esteem Value is the value that makes users want to obtain a product for reasons other than practical use. This includes rarity value, where people find value in things that are difficult to obtain, and aesthetic value, such as decorative beauty.

The "benefits of inconvenience," that is, the value created by inconvenience, are neither Use Value nor Esteem Value. For example, in the Cell Production System introduced in Sect. 2.4.2, the benefit was mutual enhancement of motivation and skill in work. This value does not come from a function that achieves a purpose, nor from a desire to obtain the product. However, it is clearly a form of value that the Cell Production System provides.

Related example:

2.4.2 Cell-Production System.

References

Wilde GJS (1982) The theory of risk homeostasis. Wiley
Norman DA (1988) The psychology of everyday things. Basic Books

MIX
Papier aus verantwortungsvollen Quellen
Paper from responsible sources
FSC® C105338

If you have any concerns about our products,
you can contact us on
ProductSafety@springernature.com

In case Publisher is established outside the EU,
the EU authorized representative is:
Springer Nature Customer Service Center GmbH
Europaplatz 3, 69115 Heidelberg, Germany

Printed by Libri Plureos GmbH
in Hamburg, Germany